THE RAMMED EARTH HOUSE

THE RAMMED EARTH HOUSE

DAVID EASTON

Photographs by Cynthia Wright

CHELSEA GREEN PUBLISHING COMPANY   White River Junction, Vermont   Totnes, England

Designed by Ann Aspell

Text illustrations by Jeff Reed. Additional illustrations by Mike Baushke and Don Callahan.

Printed in the United States of America
00 01 02 03   4 5 6 7

The information contained in this book is true and complete to the best of our knowledge. Due to the variability of local conditions, materials, skills, site, and other factors, Chelsea Green Publishing Company and the authors disclaim all liability for personal injury, property damage, or loss from actions inspired by information from this book.

Library of Congress Cataloging-in-Publication Data
Easton, David.
    The rammed earth house / David Easton ; photographs by Cynthia Wright.
        p. cm. -- (The real goods independent living books)
    Includes bibliographical references and index.
    ISBN 0-930031-79-2
    1. Earth houses--Design and construction. 2. Pisé. I. Title.
II. Series : Real goods independent living book.
TH4818.A3E27   1996
693'.2--dc20   96-11453

Chelsea Green Publishing Company
Post Office Box 428
White River Junction, VT 05001

Rammed earth has been written about many times before—by architects, historians, writers, and ordinary people. This version has been conscientiously assembled by one who has for two decades walked, tripped, and walked again…along the path of rammed earth.

I would not be able to tell the story without the help of two important friends. The drawings and the inspiration to make art out of earth belong to Jeff Reed. The hand that held mine each time I tripped belongs to Cynthia.

THE REAL GOODS SOLAR LIVING BOOKS

Wind Power for Home & Business: Renewable Energy for the 1990s and Beyond by Paul Gipe

Real Goods Solar Living Sourcebook: The Complete Guide to Renewable Energy Technologies and Sustainable Living, 10th Edition, edited by Doug Pratt and John Schaeffer

The Straw Bale House by Athena Swentzell Steen, Bill Steen, and David Bainbridge, with David Eisenberg

The Rammed Earth House by David Easton

The Real Goods Independent Builder: Designing & Building a House Your Own Way by Sam Clark

The Passive Solar House: Using Solar Design to Heat and Cool Your Home by James Kachadorian

A Place in the Sun: The Evolution of the Real Goods Solar Living Center by John Schaeffer and the Collaborative Design/Construction Team

Hemp Horizons: The Comeback of the World's Most Promising Plant by John W. Roulac

Mortgage-Free! Radical Strategies for Home Ownership by Rob Roy

The Earth-Sheltered House: An Architect's Sketchbook by Malcolm Wells

Y2K and Y-O-U: The Sane Person's Home-Preparation Guide by Dermot McGuigan and Beverly Jacobson

Wind Energy Basics: A Guide to Small and Micro Wind Systems by Paul Gipe

The New Independent Home: People and Houses that Harvest the Sun, Wind, and Water by Michael Potts

Real Goods Trading Company in Ukiah, California, was founded in 1978 to make available new tools to help people live self-sufficiently and sustainably. Through seasonal catalogs, a periodical (*The Real Goods News*), a bi-annual *Solar Living Sourcebook*, as well as retail outlets, Real Goods provides a broad range of tools for independent living.

"Knowledge is our most important product" is the Real Goods motto. To further its mission, Real Goods has joined with Chelsea Green Publishing Company to co-create and co-publish the Real Goods Solar Living Book series. The titles in this series are written by pioneering individuals who have firsthand experience in using innovative technology to live lightly on the planet. Chelsea Green books are both practical and inspirational, and they enlarge our view of what is possible as we enter the next millenium.

Stephen Morris
President, Chelsea Green

John Schaeffer
President, Real Goods

Contents

Preface

THE TIME IS RIGHT for the renaissance of earth architecture. In 1993 the American Institute of Architects (AIA) sponsored an international competition in search of "Sustainable Solutions." Books on the greening of American architecture abound. And people everywhere are celebrating the rustic, organic, and natural in all aspects of life—from food and cooking, to manufactured goods, to the houses we build and live in. In short, in these days of ecological concern as we seek simpler, more appropriate solutions to the environmental challenges that face ourselves and our children, the word "earth"—and all that connotes—has become once more a central concept for ourselves and for our civilization.

From our little earthwalled office on a side street in Napa, we can see it happening, out our windows and on the Internet. What began as a niche market for would-be provincials seeking Old World ambience in the wine country north of San Francisco has developed quickly into much more—a growing movement of people who value the tradition, the beauty, and the energy efficiency of rammed earth construction. Where just a few years ago, everything connected with rammed earth building anywhere in the entire state of California passed under our watchful eyes and felt the weight of our own rammers, now we hear only incidentally of the many other projects that are underway. Where last year our company, Rammed Earth Works (REW), built two small international projects, one in Nicaragua and one in Brazil, this year we're proposing major projects for rammed earth around the world. In ten previous years we constructed two small wineries and one microwinery for relatively unknown vintners. This year we'll be building three large wineries for some of the best-known names in the industry.

Given all this interest and the growing market for rammed earth structures, there is the potential for stablized earth, as a building material, to become the darling of the construction industry. "Old as the hills and twice as strong," the ad people might say, or possibly, "million dollar mud." Yet there is also a danger in earth becoming "big," if its popularity rises from the wrong source, from mere hype and trendiness rather than from its many environmental and aesthetic virtues. It would truly be a shame if rammed earth enjoyed a wild ride for a decade or so, only to be supplanted by another "new" material that emerges on the scene. After all, fashions do change.

There will be a difference, though. You see, unlike other types of building, earth architecture can never really die. It's part of the planet, and it touches something deep inside us, something perhaps that reminds us of our origins and reconnects us to the living earth.

Introduction

THERE IS A CERTAIN MAGIC to living in buildings with thick earth walls. It's hard to describe, but easy to notice. Just take a step inside one on some warm summer day and you'll feel it immediately. It's cool, of course—everyone knows adobe houses are "warm in winter and cool in summer"—but there's something else, too, a little harder to put your finger on. "It's quiet, feels somehow incredibly solid and sturdy, very different from other houses, timeless even. I feel secure in here…instantly comfortable…it's almost as if I'm in some ancient building with centuries of its own secret stories to tell…" I once had a happy homeowner tell me walking into her rammed earth house was like walking into her lover's outstretched arms.

All these words of praise for the ambience of earthwalls and very few detractors: It has to be related in large part to the durability and feeling of permanence created by solid buildings. Most Americans today have grown up with the idea that a house is a lightweight box with walls built of thin sticks covered on both sides with even thinner skins. The floors and roofs are also built of sticks with equally thin skins. In the past two decades, as our awareness of the value of energy conservation has increased, builders have begun to fill the spaces between the sticks with expanded petroleum-based fibers, but that insulation hasn't done much to eliminate the flimsy nature of the building. Step inside one of these houses and your deeper senses will instantly perceive the "transparency" of the walls. The signals from your human "sonar" somehow aren't bouncing back to give you the sense of security that is so necessary in a home.

Solid earth walls feel like home. After all, not that long ago, houses used to be built to last for generations. People actually lived in a house long enough to think of it as home. People died in the same house they were born in. Times have changed of course, and in our fast-paced world few of us expect to die in the same city we were born in, let alone the same house. That doesn't mean, however, that we can't still appreciate the special qualities of a house built solidly enough to last for several hundred years.

Think of the savings in natural resources that would result if today's houses were to last that long. A stick building with a thin skin needs replacing at least once every century. When its time is up, it has to be demolished, hauled away in trucks, and buried in some landfill. Then it has to be rebuilt with all new materials hauled to the job site from some mine, warehouse, or factory. A building constructed of solid materials, whether stone, brick, concrete, or earth, may use slightly more resources at first, but as the generations roll by, and the stick houses roll into the landfill, enormous savings begin to accrue.

Perhaps just as important as savings in resources, is the way an old house can grow into its landscape. Over time, a building "settles" into the site to create a sense of attachment and belonging. Trees and shrubs grow to maturity. Successive occupants make their individual contributions to the personality of the house—a grape arbor near the western wall, a rose garden by the lily pond, olive trees along the drive, new cabinets and appliances in the old summer kitchen. Before long, the house and its gardens have stories to tell. If you listen, you will hear them.

This book is about building a house that can grow to maturity. It's about a shift in attitude that takes into consideration the effects our choices have on future generations. Even though you may one day move out, the house you have built, in the garden you nurtured, will provide comfort and prosperity to scores of future occupants. If you build it right, your house, too, will have stories to tell.

Let's hope they are good stories. The ones told by the hundred-some-odd houses I have built are, admittedly, not all good. There was that time when the footpath from the garage to the back steps became a river and flooded the house because I hadn't paid close enough attention to site drainage; or the time I attempted a Santa Fe-style building in a high rainfall area, then watched the water migrate through 24 inches of solid earthwall during a ten-day deluge. Fortunately, the good stories outnumber the bad ones. But, good or bad, I'm willing to share them all.

The lessons in this book are compiled from twenty years of experimenting with houses that grow out of their landscape. The past two decades have been a quest of sorts—to learn how to build houses that connect people with the earth.

Logically, the point of beginning in such an undertaking is to use the earth itself as the primary component of the building. For that reason, a major portion of this text deals with one of the most widely used, historic earth construction techniques—rammed earth. I discovered the technique almost by accident while searching for information on adobe construction.

In the mid 1970s, I was making plans to build my own house, and since I had far more time and energy than I had money, using earth for building the walls seemed like my only alternative. I had come across the concept of soil-cement mixtures during my work in the civil engineering department at Stanford University, and had even poured a small stamped soil-cement floor as part of a remodel project earlier in the decade. In terms of structural walls, however, I had no knowledge of any earthwall building system other than the sundried straw and adobe bricks I had become familiar with during our family visits to the California missions. We made it a goal to visit as many of them as we could, enjoying our link with California's past. Even as a young child, I felt the power and the calm of those massive-walled buildings. Perhaps it was those early impressions that led inevitability to my life's work.

While searching the *Readers' Guide to Periodical Literature* for more technical information on adobe construction, I came across a few current references to an alternate earthbuilding method known as "rammed earth." Further research led to the discovery of a multitude of thirty- and forty-year-old references. As it turned out, the rammed earth technique had enjoyed widespread popularity during the first half of the 20th century. I obtained copies of the current information—Ken Kern's *The Owner-Built House,* and Australian George Middleton's *Build Your House of Earth*—and as many of the old publications as I could find. What I read—that moist soil compacted directly into movable formwork yielded immediately load-supporting walls—seemed almost too simple to be true. No sticky mud, no waiting for the bricks to dry, no mortar to mix, and no bricks to lay—it was an industrial engineer's dream. One-fifth the water, one-quarter the mixing time, one-sixtieth the drying time. Could this possibly be? If this technique had all these things going for it, why wasn't it in widespread use?

Twenty years and 500,000 cubic yards of moist soil later, I'm still asking myself the same question: Why isn't rammed earth in more widespread use? Without doubt it is a lot of work, as are most things of value in life, but the beautiful simplicity of converting raw, natural earth into human habitat involves a sort of sweaty alchemy. If you attempt to build your own rammed earth house, and if the process works as well for you as it has for me, you won't regret the effort.

The connection between house and earth is much more involved than just a set of walls. To create shelter that keeps out the weather and at the same time nourishes the soul is the real challenge. Building a house is in itself an enormous undertaking. Creating an environment that can yield emotional prosperity is even more of a commitment. It will require scrupulous research and planning, and meticulous follow-through.

For these reasons, I've felt compelled in this book to write about more than just how to build rammed earth walls. The chapters on construction are bracketed between sections on design and planning, and a chapter on garden elements.

We've learned a great deal over the years, Cynthia and I and the clients who have become our friends. How sensitively the house is positioned, how correctly it is designed for the resources on the site, and how thoroughly it is reintegrated into the landscape are far more important decisions than what it looks like to your neighbors or whether the kitchen counters are formica or black granite.

In no time at all, you'll discover that months can go by without your neighbors commenting on the way your house looks; but trust me, not one day will pass without you appreciating how good it feels.

THE RAMMED EARTH HOUSE

CHAPTER ONE

The Evolution
of Earthbuilding

*(Facing page) A pisé de
terre house on the Rhone
River, France.*

EARTH HOUSING IS PREHISTORIC. It even predates the development of the opposable thumb. The quest for shelter is in fact instinctive, and to the vast majority of the planet's species, shelter *is* earth. When the early hominids first crept from the security of their caves, they built with earth—*Homo erectus architectus.*

Five million years after the evolution of the opposable thumb and 130,000 years after the appearance of the first *Homo sapiens*, most of the planet's species and 50 percent of the planet's humans still live in shelters made of earth. The exciting fact is, unlike the primitive earth shelters of our evolutionary forebears and the simple earth houses of our prehistoric ancestors, today's earth buildings can be as refined as we care to make them—as different from a mud hut as the opposable thumb is different from a claw, as different as a Rembrandt is different from a petroglyph.

In the millennia between the simple shelter of the archeological past and the sophisticated earth housing of the late 20th century lies a fascinating story. We can make suppositions about the Neanderthals creeping from their caves to plaster mud onto a woven framework of willow branches, but we lack artifacts for documentation. We do, however, have archeological evidence nearly 10,000 years old of entire cities built of raw earth: Jericho, history's earliest city; Catal Huyuk in Turkey; Harappa and Johenjo-Daro in Pakistan; Akhlet-Aton in Egypt; Chan-Chan in Peru; Babylon in Iraq; Duheros near Cordoba in Spain; and Khirokitia in Cyprus. All the great civilizations of the ancient Middle East— the Assyrians, the Babylonians, the Persians, and the Sumerians—built with mud brick and rammed earth. Not merely primitive, simple housing either, but vast and imposing monuments, temples, ziggurats, churches, and mosques.

In the deserts of Yemen, where sun is intense and wood for construction nonexistent, thick earthwalls rise up several stories to create shade and deflect hot winds.

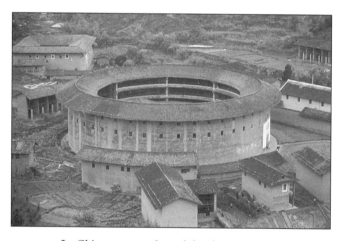

In China, rammed earth has been practiced for millennia. Wood is an available resource, but so too is a high-quality soil for wall building. Architecture conforms to the lifestyle of the residents of this circular, three-story, multi-family housing complex.

The Tower of Babel, seven stories tall, was built of sundried mud bricks in the 7th century B.C. In the book of Exodus, we are told that the Children of Israel made bricks of earth.

Excavations in China have uncovered rammed earth construction dating from the 7th century B.C. The Great Wall of China, begun more than 5,000 years ago, was built of stone and rammed earth. To this day, it remains one of the largest construction projects ever undertaken. Architectural history can trace 6,000 years of continuous earth construction in the Far East, and people still build with rammed earth in China today.

An unbroken tradition of earthbuilding survives in many other parts of the world as well, especially in Africa and the Middle East. In these regions, the scarcity of trees, the low annual rainfall, and an abundance of labor combine to favor earth as the only logical building material. In North Africa, from the time the Pharaohs ruled Egypt into the present, the peoples of the desert have constructed their villages of adobe and rammed earth. High in the Atlas Mountains, in Morocco east of Marrakech, Berber tribesmen today build rammed earth dwellings exactly as their forebears have done for generations. Massive walls and small windows protect the inhabitants from the heat. Cities enclosed by tall walls, and intentionally narrow streets create shade and protection from the winds that blow off the desert.

Earth building is not, however, restricted to arid climates. Rammed earth construction was brought to the temperate regions of Europe by the Romans and Phoenicians. The Roman historian, Pliny the Elder, in the 1st century A.D., writes in his *Natural History,*

> Moreover, are there not in Africa and
> Spain walls made of earth that are called

framed walls, because they are made by packing in a frame enclosed between two boards, one on each side, and so are stuffed in rather than built, and do they not last for ages, undamaged by rain, wind, and fire, and stronger than any quarry-stone? Spain still sees the watchtowers of Hannibal and turrets of earth placed on the mountain ridges.

Throughout the Rhone River valley, in the regions around Lyon, France, the tradition of "stuffed earth" dates to the era when Phoenician ships plied the Mediterranean. Up the Rhone River to Lugdunum, the capital of Roman Gaul, traders brought not just goods, but new construction techniques as well. *Pisé de terre*, as it was later called, was a dominant wall-building method for 2,000 years. Those soils that washed down from the Alps had an ideal composition for rammed earth construction. Even today, some 15 percent of rural buildings are still made of pisé.

When the Moors invaded Spain they brought with them the technique of mud brick construction. *Adobe*, an Arabic and Berber word, describes bricks that are molded wet and cast small enough to shrink without cracking. Adobe construction is better suited to heavy clay soils than is pisé de terre. When the Spaniards began their conquest of the New World, primarily in search of gold and other new wealth, they carried with them the knowledge of building with adobe.

From South America, particularly Peru, the adobe method migrated northward through Mexico and eventually into the southwestern United States. In what is now New Mexico, it replaced earlier earthbuilding techniques utilized by cultures that had flourished in the region since 700 A.D. Prior to the arrival of the Spanish, these Pueblo

Egyptian builders favor mud bricks made from Nile river silts, which are susceptible to erosion during the occasional heavy rains.

CHRISTIAN LIGNON/CENTRE GEORGES POMPIDOU

High in the Atlas Mountains, east of Marrakech, Berber tribesmen build with rammed earth just as their parents and grandparents did before them.

6

Where rainfall is scarce, earthwalls can survive for centuries, even after the civilizations that built them have collapsed.

In France, the tradition of pisé de terre continues from the early days of the Roman occupation, interrupted only briefly by the "modernization" of the postwar decades.

When the Portuguese and the Spaniards invaded the New World in the 16th century, their principal settlements mirrored the architecture of their homeland. Here, in Grenada, Nicaragua, sun-dried mud bricks have been covered with plaster and embellished with classical details.

people either laid roughly dressed stone in mud mortar or tamped the mud directly into formwork in a manner similar to pisé and to modern concrete.

In California, prior to the arrival of the Spaniards, the native people were more nomadic, living primarily in simple bark-covered shelters. When the Jesuit priests arrived to start the mission system and to Christianize the natives, they taught the people how to make adobe bricks. Confusing as these enormous buildings and a new religion must have been to the natives, the California missions are today an inspiring example of the beauty and success of a simple, "permanent" material.

While the adobe technique prospered on one side of the North American continent, pisé took a foothold on the other. In St. Augustine, Spaniards constructed the first permanent structures in their Florida colony using a mixture of soil and ground seashells rammed into heavy wooden formwork. This *tapial* mixture (known as "taipa" in Portuguese and "tabby" in English) was used significantly in the region and may in fact have been the inspiration for the construction of the beautiful Alcazar Hotel by Bernard Maybeck in 1906. Very recent archeological excavations on the Island of San Cristobal indicate that Columbus may have built his first fortifications there of tapial.

In South America, the use of tapial gained a more permanent hold on the architecture than it did in North America. In fact, until very recently, the technique of packing moist earth into wooden forms was used widely there. Century-old buildings of taipa construction are still in use in Brazil, Peru, and Chile.

In Australia, the first use of pisé appears to have been made during the goldrush period of the 1850s, when the technique was introduced to the remote continent by European gold hunters. Not surprisingly, the greatest concentration of still-existing old pisé structures are to be found in the goldfield areas. Mud brick construction also migrated to Australia during the

(Above left) In what is now the southwestern U. S., Native American peoples evolved their own methods and styles from earlier "apartment buildings" on the cliffs and mesas of the canyonlands. Taos Pueblo is the oldest continually occupied structure on the continent.

(Above right) Jesuit priests trekked into California during the 18th century. The Mission San Diego is one of many such mission buildings dating from this period.

8

Spaniards introduced a type of rammed earth called tabby to Florida, where several examples still survive. The Hotel Alcazar in St. Augustine was constructed in the early part of the 20th century of packed sand, cement, and seashells.

same period, most likely brought by gold miners abandoning the played-out California diggings. Just as earth has always been the predominant construction material in the arid Middle East and North Africa, it was the most practical material for construction in the dry and timberless regions of Australia. Today rammed earth is experiencing a renaissance in Australia that is unparalleled anywhere else in the world.

So it is that earthbuilding, like civilization, migrated in all directions until it eventually encircled the globe. In much the same way that the human race gradually evolved over the millennia in response to variations in climate and topography, earthbuilding techniques have evolved in response to different climate and soil types. Pisé predominates where soils are sandy, adobe where they are clayey. To build with adobes the climate must have an annual period of drought in order for the mud bricks to dry out enough to be mortared into a wall. Pisé, on the other hand, can be built nearly year-round. What's more, if the soil is dug and rammed early in the year when the ground is still moist from winter rains, no water need be added.

Other earthbuilding technologies can be found in various regions of the world, although they are less widely distributed than pisé or adobe. *Cob*, or *clay lump,* is a technique in which clayey soils are mixed into a sticky mud, then laid up directly into a free-standing wall. Lumps of earth are piled up along the building line to the maximum height at which they will support their wet weight, then shaved straight once the wet earth begins to firm up. Subsequent layers are piled one on top of another until the desired finished height of the wall is reached. Many examples of clay lump buildings survive to this day in the British Isles and other parts of Northern Europe.

The oldest of the earthbuilding techniques must certainly be "wattle and daub," very likely originating when early humans emerged from their caves. *Wattle* is a woven framework of twigs. *Daub* is a mud covering applied over the framework. Not as thick as the other three techniques, wattle and daub lacks thermal mass, but for simplicity and speed it excels. It also falls short in terms of longevity, and for this reason few examples have survived the passage of centuries.

In Central America, the word tapial is also used to describe a technique that is actually a hybrid of rammed earth and wattle and daub. A gridwork of vertical wood posts and horizontal lathing is nailed together and then packed full of mud. Typically covered with earth and lime plaster on both sides, it is not uncommon for tapial structures to last a hundred years or more. Both tapial and wattle and daub structures, relying as they do on the framework rather than the mass for their structural support, do not possess the same thermal characteristics as do pisé, adobe, and cob buildings. They are neither as warm in the winter nor as cool in the summer as the more massive wall systems.

Over time, earthbuilding techniques undergo gradual adaptation through a process analogous to the well-known evolutionary principle of survival of the fittest among plants and animals. In much

A modern rammed earth house in Eagle Bay, Western Australia.

Wattle and daub, in which mud is plastered onto a woven framework of sticks, is perhaps the oldest of all earthwalling techniques and is still used in many parts of the world.

the same way, the most appropriate wall-building variation will outperform and outlive its less-successful siblings. The building method best suited to a particular region evenutally comes to predominate, as structures using inferior techniques fall to the rigors of earthquakes or wet winters.

Rammed Earth and the Industrial Revolution

As public awareness grows regarding the importance of environmentally responsible building methods, rammed earth in the United States is experiencing a modest revival. The current level of interest is not new to the method. In fact, this late 20th century fascination is actually the third wave of popularity that has embraced the rammed earth technique in the past 200 years. The first wave reached its high point during the 1840s, and the second during the Great Depression of the 1930s. Both surges were stimulated by the quest for a low-cost, owner-capable method of construction. And both were brought to an end by the availability of mass-produced manufactured materials, capable of being assembled in less time than cumbersome earth walls.

As we've seen, the technique of pounding moist earth into movable formwork to create monolithic walls has been used worldwide for thousands of years. The requisite knowledge needed to build with solid earth has always been slowly and painstakingly transferred from one generation to another. This slow, methodical rate of technology transfer ended abruptly during the latter part of the 18th century. During this period a French builder, Francois Cointeraux, "discovered" pisé de terre in use in the region around Lyon and began his own experiments with the method. Although he was not the first to scientifically document the technology, Cointeraux's enthusiasm was enormous. He saw pisé as a means by which the common man could vastly improve the quality of his own life. Free earth and "honorable labor" were philosophically consistent with the ideals of the French Revolution, underway at that time, and Cointeraux adopted as his personal mission the dissemination of the knowledge of pisé. With help from the Royal Agricultural Society, he founded a school in Paris in 1788 for the "study of rural achitecture," specifically to promote the use of pisé in construction. For Cointeraux, pisé represented:

> a gift of Providence…a present which God has made to all people.
> If agriculture is the basis for all science, pisé is also the first of all the
> arts…Factories will multiply with pisé and commerce will flourish
> …One should employ this kind of building throughout the realm,
> for the decency of villages and the honor of the nation, to save

A technique that surely evolved from wattle and daub, tapial utilizes a framework of vertical posts and horizontal nailers to support an infill wall of packed mud. Once plastered, tapial walls look no different than any other masonry wall.

wood, which is used in such great abundance in constructions, to avoid fires, to protect laborers from cold or excessive heat, at the same time to conserve and protect their health, and for so many other objectives, too long to list....

In 1790 and 1791, Cointeraux published four separate short texts on tools, soil, formwork, and methodology for building with pisé. These notebooks were translated into English and circulated in Great Britain, where, along with the work of some of the students trained in his school, they contributed to a significant increase in the use of rammed earth as a replacement for the more commonly used technique of clay-lump construction. Foremost among the new converts in Great Britain were architect Henry Holland and surveyor Robert Salmon, each conducting experiments with rammed earth and publishing writings on their work. Although basically following techniques described by Cointeraux, they did both propose minor variations to formwork and construction details. Their work, especially that of Holland, who was a writer for the Board of Agriculture's publication *Communications*, gave new credibility to pisé. The first decade of the 19th century in England bore witness to numerous other experiments in rammed earth and subsequent published books and articles.

Throughout the Rhone River valley in central France, the vast majority of buildings in the villages and the countryside are built of pisé de terre. In a combination of civic pride with fiscal common sense, it is typically only the street side of the residence that receives the plaster finish. The barn and off-street sides remain raw earth.

Word of the suitability of rammed earth also spread to the United States. The first experiments of record were conducted by Stephen W. Johnson, a lawyer and builder in New Brunswick, New Jersey. Johnson constructed a pisé building near Trenton using Holland's writings as his guide, and upon completion published his own book on rammed earth entitled *Rural Economy: Containing a Treatise on Pisé Building, etc.* As is frequently the case, new converts beginning their experiments with earth find that disbelievers vastly outnumber proponents. This passage from Johnson's book shows some of the frustrations he felt with his project's detractors:

> The completion of the work and the proof of a whole winter upon it, giving it additional credit, did not prevent this humble and disinterested attempt from meeting with enemies, amongst a class of people found more or less in all countries, who never did a single act in their lives that might promote the public good, without remaining the slaves of avarice, and being hired to it by such motives as avaricious men are haunted with; ever standing ready to trample a laudable effort underfoot, although at another's expense it might have been the foundation of their own prosperity. Such characters circulated a report of the building having fallen by reason of frost having burst the walls, and induced the author to have this one examined in every particular, and a certificate of its then present state signed by the examinants.

(Facing page) The Church of the Holy Cross, in South Carolina, is the best intact example of rammed earth from the 19th century.

As a result of Johnson's book, numerous other experiments with pisé were undertaken. John Stuart Skinner, editor of *The American Farmer* from 1819 to 1830, published reports of actual projects undertaken by American builders and farmers, along with a complete version of Holland's translation of Cointeraux. Two of the more significant experiments reported on by Skinner were the work of John Hartwell Cocke in building slave quarters and outbuildings at Bremo plantation near New Canton, Virginia, and the work of William Anderson on his plantation in South Carolina. Anderson constructed five pisé buildings on his land, and, most noteworthy of all, a large church in nearby Statesboro. Built in 1850, the Church of the Holy Cross measures 105 feet long by 27 feet wide with gable end walls 43 feet high at their peak. The church, built of pure earth, still survives after hurricanes, the massive Charleston Earthquake of 1886, and over 140 years of southeastern rainfall and high humidity.

Information about these and many other 19th century experiments with pisé comes to us more through published reports than from the historical

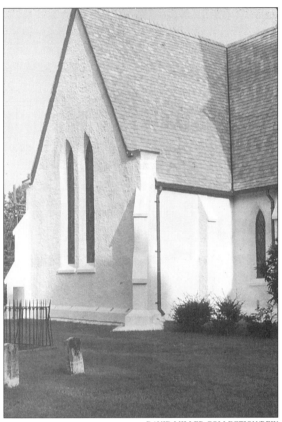

DAVID MILLER COLLECTION/REW

with the work of Cointeraux began to die out in the 1850s as other building materials, such as sawn lumber and fired brick, replaced earth. Improved methods of harvesting and production, along with efficient railroads and canals for transporting goods, made manufactured materials more readily available and affordable. Although not as economical as raw earth, these other materials were easy to work with and, more importantly, resulted in structures consistent with the self-image of a prosperous America. Earth walls, unfortunately thought of as housing for the "dirt poor," were certainly nothing to brag about. Although still very likely in use on the farms, experimentation and construction with earth was no longer in the press. Interest in earthbuilding lay dormant for over half a century, awakened at last by the shortages following World War I and the Great Depression, and by a new generation of enthusiasts.

structures themselves. In addition to the work of Johnson and Skinner, Henry L. Ellsworth, America's first patent commissioner, conducted experiments of his own and wrote about his findings in a series of annual reports from the Patent office. His writings in turn encouraged other publishers of agricultural journals to solicit articles from their readers. Between the years of 1843 and 1855, John Stephen Wright, editor of Chicago's *Prairie Farmer*, published over forty separate articles and references to rammed earth. The *Prairie Farmer* became a sort of information highway of its time, where farmers from all over the Midwest could share the results of their experiments.

The first wave of popularity that began in 1780

The first of these new practitioners was the English architect and writer, Clough William-Ellis. Searching for solutions to the wartime housing shortage, William-Ellis "discovered," beneath the plaster veneer of countless English country cottages, solid, enduring walls of earth. He shared his surprising discoveries with his father-in-law, editor J. St. Loe Starchey, who immediately began an information-gathering campaign in his magazine, the London *Spectator*. Reader response must have been encouraging. In 1920 William-Ellis wrote and published a survey of English earth housing titled *Cottage Building in Cob, Pisé, Chalk and Clay*.

Perhaps in some way stimulated by William-Ellis's findings, the Division of Agricultural Engineering of the U.S. Department of Agriculture sent T. A. H. Miller to investigate and report on the condition of the rammed earth church in Statesboro, South Carolina, built in 1850 by William

14

Anderson. Miller's positive report on a structure over seventy years old, built with walls of raw earth and still completely serviceable, apparently generated a great deal of interest within the Department.

Harry Baker Humphrey, chief plant pathologist of the Department of Agriculture, was inspired enough to undertake the construction of his new residence in Washington, D.C., using rammed earth. Credited as the first modern earth home in this country, the Humphrey house, built circa 1926, was far from a simple cottage. Eighteen-inch-thick walls support a second floor and large tile-covered roof. Photos taken in 1950 show a well-designed, well-constructed, and well-maintained residence.

Both Dr. Humphrey and the Department of Agriculture fielded numerous inquiries about the house and its construction process. Coupled with a great deal of interest resulting from the republication of several of the *Spectator* articles in *The American Literary Digest*, the USDA authorized T. A. H. Miller, the agricultural engineer who inspected the Statesboro church, and architect M. C. Betts to draft a manual for rammed earth construction. Published in

Harry Baker Humphrey's house near Washington, D.C., contributed to an exciting reemergence of rammed earth into the national spotlight.

1926, *Farmer's Bulletin No. 1500: Rammed Earth Walls for Buildings*, provided enough technical information and construction expertise to allow builders and novices to construct their own low-cost earthwalled houses. Several hundred, perhaps thousands, of people did just that, and for two decades rammed earth construction experienced another renaissance. Although earth walls are just as hard to detect beneath their stucco or clapboard veneers in this country now as they were in William-Ellis's England of the 1910s, without a doubt many of those economical, self-built houses are still in use today, as completely serviceable as William Anderson's church was when Miller visited it in 1926.

The level of interest in rammed earth during this second great wave of construction exceeded that of the previous century. Not only did the Department of Agriculture promote building with rammed earth through the distribution of *Farmer's Bulletin No. 1500*, but research projects were undertaken and numerous papers published by engineers, scientists, and other professionals at colleges and universities across the country. These academic reports led in turn to further experimentation and implementation on the part of the general public, each person searching in one form or another for affordable housing. A review of the *Reader's Guide to Periodical Literature* reveals more than 100 articles printed in both trade journals and popular magazines during the period from 1926 to 1950.

The most prolific of the academics was Professor Ralph Patty of the Agricultural Experiment Station at South Dakota State College. Over a span of twenty years, Dr. Patty and his students built test walls, farm buildings, and garden walls to study soil types, weathering characteristics, stabilization admixtures, floors, and wall coatings. Students and professors at other colleges and universities conducted additional tests, with Texas A & M, University of California–Berkeley, and Clemson University being three of the more active. The technical papers published by the academic community, and the many articles appearing in popular home and architecture magazines, written by builders and occupants of rammed earth houses, fueled the resurgence of earthbuilding. The principle reasons behind this renewed interest in earth as a building material were the Depression-induced shortages of money and building materials, and an abundance of cheap, available labor.

It was precisely this combination of labor surplus and material shortage that inspired architectural engineer Thomas Hibben of the Resettlement Administration to argue for the use of rammed earth in a subsistence homestead project being planned near Birmingham, Alabama. Since one of the guiding principles of Franklin Roosevelt's New Deal was to put as many people as possible to work and to devote as little money as possible to "other than labor" costs, rammed earth seemed a natural solution.

As part of the National Industrial Recovery Act of 1933, rural properties were to be developed as homestead communities where "stranded agricultural and industrial population groups" could be relocated from crowded cities to small farms. The people could work part-time in the city, yet still raise crops on their own land to feed their families when work was scarce. Roosevelt's belief was that homestead farming would encourage basic "American values" and restore dignity to the common people.

Homestead projects were constructed in North Carolina, Wisconsin, Georgia, West Virginia, Pennsylvania, Ohio, and Alabama. Of the $25 million allocated to the program and the several hundred houses planned at the various locations, Thomas Hibben with his enthusiasm for rammed earth was able to secure funds and approval for a total of seven "experimental" houses to be built on the back side of the Gardendale, Alabama, project. The experimental "dirt" houses were to be kept secret, at least during the early stages, so that if the walls failed, as few people as possible would know about it.

Tom Hibben began construction with only the information he had been able to gather from reading the books, papers, and articles written on the subject and some sample experimentation conducted on his own. The designs for the houses were his own, and he planned to train the crew, comprised of unskilled labor, as he went. The earth was dug from the site and the 17-inch-thick walls were all rammed by hand. The wooden formwork was similar to that used by Cointeraux, Johnson, Patty, and others. As testimony to Hibben's belief that he could teach unskilled laborers a useful and self-respecting trade, the first house took fourteen men five weeks to build and the last took the same fourteen men five days. Each house cost between $2,000 and $2,700 in 1937, and they are all still occupied today. In fact, residents of the rammed earth houses maintain that they are cooler in the summer and warmer in the winter than the frame and brick houses that were built "out front."

Frank Lloyd Wright also designed with rammed earth. Like Hibben, Wright was interested in architecture as a way of improving the welfare and self-esteem of ordinary people. He saw subsistence homesteading and rammed earth, with its "sweat equity" investment, as a way for people to improve their circumstances. Wright proposed to use rammed earth to build houses for a group of Michigan auto workers who were attempting to create a community along the lines of the Gardendale concept. For reasons not related to construction, the Michigan community never developed. Nor, unfortunately, did Wright's far grander plan to provide humanity with a better way of life.

Simple and affordable, the rammed earth houses in Gardendale, Alabama, proved to yet another generation of disbelievers that earth could indeed be rammed into durable walls. Even today, the homeowners praise the performance of their "experimental" houses.

Broadacre City was Frank Lloyd Wright's vision of a model community, with green space and fresh air in abundance, and where every family would own a house and enough land to grow much of their own food. Conceptually, Broadacre City was an idealization of what decades later became the suburbs.

Shortly after Hibben's Gardendale project, and during the time that Dr. Patty was conducting his experiments at South Dakota State College, another Dakotan undertook the construction of what was at the time the largest rammed earth building in the country. Elbert Hubbell, a vocational instructor at the Turtle Mountain Indian School in Belcourt, North Dakota, realized that rammed earth could be adapted to suit the needs of the Indian reservation. Over a period of a few years, he and his workers built barns, Indian houses, and a school building 108 feet long by 63 feet wide. In 1941, Hubbell was brought to the Washington office of the Bureau of Indian Affairs to write a report on his work in all forms of earth construction.

The success of Hibben's houses in Alabama and Hubbell's work in North Dakota, along with the continued research by the academic community, stimulated persistent inquiries and experimentation on the part of the general public. Interest was strong enough, in fact, to motivate the United States Bureau of Standards to include various earthen materials in a major testing program, the "Building Materials and Structures Reports," then underway in Washington. Assisting the scientists and engineers at the Bureau, who admittedly knew little about earth construction techniques, were Thomas Hibben,

Elbert Hubbell, and T. A. H. Miller. Five kinds of material were tested: adobe block, asphalt-stabilized adobe block, monolithic soil-cement, monolithic plain rammed earth, and soil-cement block. Built in wall-panel–sized blocks, each of these materials was tested for strength, resistance to water, and heat transfer properties. The results, published as *BMS 78*, confirm that all of the earthen wall systems tested were suitable for the construction of ordinary one- or two-story houses. Compressive and shear tests demonstrated that monolithic soil-cement (cement-stabilized rammed earth) walls were stronger than walls of either hollow-core concrete block or wood frame construction.

As this testing was underway, interest in rammed earth persisted in many parts of the United States. I've had the privilege of visiting several of these older houses and hearing the stories of how they were built. Artist and architect Millard Sheets constructed an impressive rammed earth house in Claremont, California. A skeptical official at the local building department insisted that Mr. Sheets reinforce the earth walls with a structural concrete jacket, adding significantly to the cost of the project. Years later this supplemental coating proved completely unnecessary, as the contractor in charge of a remodeling project learned. While attempting to cut a doorway through the wall from the original structure into the new addition, he found the earth every bit as durable as the concrete that encased it.

Orange rancher Millard Beemer's rammed earth story has a fun twist to it. The house he and his wife built during the first year of their marriage still stands, surrounded by orange and eucalyptus trees in the Pauma Valley near San Diego. The grain marks from the rough boards used for the formwork are still visible through the white paint that covers the walls. In answer to why he built with

The Miller house in Greeley, Colorado, an early demonstration of the potential for energy efficiency in rammed earth.

rammed earth, Mr. Beemer replied it was a matter of money. In fact, he had so little of it at the time, as he jokingly told me, he married his wife for her money, "all hundred dollars of it."

David and Lydia Miller have perhaps the best rammed earth story. Over the span of a decade, David, a lawyer specializing in water rights, and Lydia, a high school English teacher, built several rammed earth houses on land their family owned in Greeley, Colorado. The last one, designed by architect J. Palmer Boggs, included not only 16-inch-thick rammed earth walls, but a radiant slab floor as well. The visit I had with the Millers on one cold winter day in 1982 was my first experience with the indescribable feeling of comfort inside a radiant-heated thermal mass house. The Millers lived a quiet life in their house for thirty years, raising children and vegetables, following their separate careers, and taking the occasional trip to Europe (David was of Russian descent), where they photographed old rammed earth buildings just as matter of interest. In the early 1980s, *Mother Earth News* magazine discovered the Millers, their rammed earth house, and Lydia's pantry full of garden produce. The story the magazine printed generated such enormous interest that the Millers became overnight folk heros for thousands of young people in the back-to-the-land movement. David and Lydia were recruited to lecture and teach workshops, and finally the demand for information grew so great that they founded Rammed Earth Institute International, a nonprofit outreach and resource center.

Despite the successful utilization by hundreds of owner-builders of rammed earth building techniques, along with the official "certification of suitability" by the Bureau of Standards, earthbuilding once again faded from the public eye. Just as the improved manufacturing processes of the 1850s brought a temporary halt to earthbuilding, the mass-production capabilities developed during the Second World War sounded taps for rammed earth. When the troops who won the war returned home in need of quick and inexpensive housing, clever industrialists converted the assembly lines that had built war material into building-supply factories. Lightweight and quick to assemble, wood-frame houses sprang up across America practically overnight. A system as slow as rammed earth, albeit solid as a rock and bound to last for centuries, just couldn't compete. Once again, earth was put out to pasture for a few decades, to be revived by yet another set of circumstances and another group of enthusiasts.

Rammed Earth Redux

In the mid 1970s, growing awareness of dwindling natural resources and a degrading environment prompted a reconsideration of the advantages of building with earth. The Arab oil embargo of 1973 shocked the American public into the realization that current rates of energy consumption were unsustainable. Amory Lovins, the country's unofficial czar of energy conservation, conceived of the "negawatt" as a means of demonstrating how the conservation of electricity could actually increase profits for power companies and other businesses. California governor Jerry Brown initiated solar tax credits, providing direct financial rewards for firms and consumers willing to invest in the mechanisms of conservation. Stewart Brand published the *Whole Earth Catalogue* in response to a rapidly growing interest in "appropriate technology." Environmentalists, entrepreneurs, inventors, and renegade builders began an exploration for alternatives to the high-consumption practices of "business as usual."

In the spirit of this ecological reawakening, a handful of architects, contractors, and owner-builders rediscovered rammed earth. Among them were Tom Schmidt in Arizona, Giles Hohnen in Western Australia, Patrice Doat and Hugo Houben in France, and myself in California. Each

RICHARD DAY

The Beemer house near San Diego was built during the Depression, when unemployment was high and money for materials was scarce.

"discovered" the existence of rammed earth through a different source. Tom Schmidt's father had built rammed earth in the Ohio River Valley before the war. Giles Hohnen read a book entitled *Build Your House of Earth*, published in 1953 by Australian architect and low-cost housing expert George Middleton. Patrice Doat and Hugo Houben were graduate students at the University of Grenoble researching a paper on historical vernacular architecture in central France. I first heard of rammed earth while reading Ken Kern's 1972 bible for the back-to-the-land movement, *The Owner-Built Home.*

Each of us was inspired by the apparent simplicity of the system and the inherent logic of building with such a basic material. Here to be sure was the answer to ecologically correct construction practices. We were to be the Cointeraux, Johnson, Anderson, Patty, Hibben, and Hubbell of the late 20th century. Surely this time rammed earth was here to stay.

Twenty years have passed since our group "rediscovery" in the mid- seventies. Since that time, the environment has degraded further, population and energy consumption have increased, serious concerns have been raised about the long-term effects on human health of synthetic building materials, and manufacturing processes have threatened the health of the planet's air, water, and soil. Yet earthwall construction, which holds such promise for affordable, durable, efficient, healthy housing, still struggles for respectability.

Patrice Doat and Hugo Houben founded CRATerre, the Center for the Research and Application of Earth. The group offers the world's only Master of Architecture degree through their two-year study program at the School of Architecture in Grenoble. In conjunction with Belgian architect Jean Dethier, Doat and Houben organized a magnificent exhibition of earth architecture which travelled around the world in the 1980s, and they initiated the construction of a demonstration earthhousing project, Domaine de la Terre, in the Rhone River region, which has gained worldwide attention.

CRATerre assists housing ministries and nongovernmental organizations on three continents in the design and implementation of earth construction strategies. Their resource library, program of education, and commitment to promoting the use of earth worldwide are unequalled. They regularly sponsor international conferences on preservation of the earth architectural heritage and on low-cost housing for developing nations.

Ironically, despite the success and importance of CRATerre on the international scene, earth construction both within France and throughout the rest of Europe struggles for a niche. In very recent years, the growing interest in "green" architecture is offering some hope for a revival of earthbuilding, with

TH. JOFFREY/CRATERRE

P.E. VERNEY/CRATERRE

explorations currently underway by architects in Germany, Denmark, Holland, and Great Britain.

In the southwestern United States, Tom Schmidt and a handful of other architects and builders continue to use rammed earth construction methods. Quentin Branch and Tom Whuelprin operate Rammed Earth Development in Tucson, Arizona, building eight to ten homes per year. Michael Frerking, architect and owner-builder consultant, designs and assists in constructing rammed earth homes in northern Arizona. Stan Huston and Mario Bellestri build rammed earth in the area around Santa Fe, New Mexico. Despite the proven performance records of thermal mass in hot dry climates and the widely recognized association of the "adobe" style with the American Southwest, neither rammed earth nor adobe brick construction holds any significant share of the new home market at this time. The simple fact is that both methods are competing against the less-expensive thick-wall look-alike: plaster and stucco on double framing.

The situation is very different in Western Australia. Beginning in 1976 with the construction of a small rammed earth shed at the Cape Mentelle Winery in Margaret River, Giles Hohnen and Stephen Dobson (once partners, now competitors) have created a level of confidence in and appreciation for rammed earth that has allowed it to capture up to 20 percent of the new home construction market in some regions. Their organizations—Hohnen's Stabilised Earth Structures and Dobson's Ramtec—as well as several other wall-building companies started by former employees, have constructed over 1,000 homes, schools, shops, museums, tourist retreats, and other public buildings across the continent. Construction by SES and its affiliates of the Muja Mine Office, which incorporates nearly 2,500 cubic yards of earth wall, ranks as possibly the largest single rammed earth project since the Great Wall of China. And in Queensland, on the east coast near the Great Barrier Reef, architect David Oliver has designed and constructed the $26 million, 100-room, three- and four-story Kooralbyn Hotel-Resort.

Why has rammed earth been accepted by the Australian population, achieving mainstream status in less than twenty years, while in the United States it still suffers an identity crisis? Giles Hohnen cites three reasons, all unique to the Australian continent and people. First, because framing lumber is scarce and termites are abundant, most construction in Australia is brick. Rammed earth, as just another masonry wall system, fit easily into the established building practices. Second, because fast and flimsy wood frame construction isn't an option, rammed earth is actually a less expensive wall system than the other common masonry materials, limestone and double-brick. Third, the "earthy"

(Facing page, top) The Cape Mentelle Winery in Western Australia takes advantage of its solid earthwalls, not just for protection from insects but for temperature stability as well.

(Facing page, middle) Parishioners of the St. Thomas More Church in Margaret River, Western Australia, used congregation labor to capitalize on another of the great advantages to building with earth—affordability.

(Facing page, bottom) Australians continue to race ahead of the world's other earth rammers, as seen here in the three-story Kooralbyn Hotel-Resort on the Queensland Gold Coast, designed by architect David Oliver.

CRATERRE

and "rugged" character of rammed earth walls are somehow in keeping with the Australian self-image, much more so than with that of the American home-buyer who is far more familiar with painted sheetrock walls.

It is exactly this only-in-America perception that a "proper house" should be built with wood frame walls covered in sheetrock that has hindered the growth of the rammed earth industry in Northern California, where I work. For the past ten years, our firm has been involved in the construction of an average of six to ten earthwalled structures per year, a fraction of the number now being built annually in Australia. We receive a surprising amount of free publicity each year in both trade journals and the popular press, and yet earth walls are still considered "fringe" architecture. For the most part, our clients are people already familiar with the benefits of Old World architecture, who have a deep appreciation for the ambience of thick-walled buildings. We believe this appreciation will grow in the years ahead, and that someday soon the benefits of living in earth will trigger a new housing revolution.

The growing concern worldwide over the future of the planet's air, water, soil, and natural resources is fostering a critical exploration of alternatives to "building as usual." One direction this exploration leads is toward more highly processed building components such as steel studs, recycled plastics, and engineered wood products. The other direction, and the focus of this book, is toward the use of earth—a solid, simple, and proven building solution for 10,000 years. Perhaps as the 21st century dawns, we can re-echo the enthusiasm and appreciation which Francois Cointeraux held for pisé: "a gift of Providence...a present which God has made to all people."

CHAPTER TWO

The Point of Beginning

(Facing page)
Traditional-style earth
home in the Napa
Valley.

SHOPPING FOR HOUSE PLANS at the supermarket magazine racks is like planning the honeymoon before picking the groom. Both floor plans and formalwear might look good on the rack or in a catalog, then later turn out to be completely inappropriate for the people or the place.

Design criteria for an integrated project must grow out of the site. It goes without saying that architecture should be responsive to the climate of its region—the Cape Cod saltbox and the Texas dog run evolved to suit very different sets of climatic conditions—but working with specific site conditions is equally important to successful design. Where does the sunlight enter the house? When and from where do the winter storms come and the prevailing breezes blow? Does the topography or a great view dictate a preferred spot for the garden, the kitchen, or the living room? How about privacy, road noise, or potential future development? These factors and many others come into play during the development of a site-appropriate design.

Let's assume we've only been browsing the magazine racks and the travel brochures for our house plans and honeymoon spot. We haven't committed to anything yet. Likewise, let's assume we don't own any real estate and are just now starting the search. What do we look for in an "ideal" house site?

Above all, we want to look for property with good "character traits." These include: abundant solar access, good drainage, a deep and fertile soil, a reasonable (for you) distance from work and shops, and the right "aspect." This last trait is the most difficult to define, but possibly the most important. It has to do with you and how well the site conforms with your sense of place. For some people, this means a neighborhood defined by old trees and city parks. For others, it may mean two acres of bottomland located ten minutes

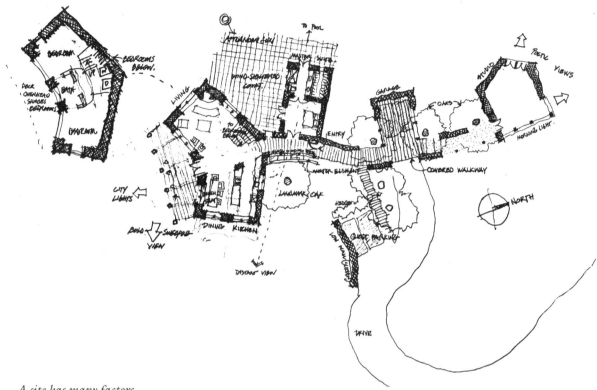

26

A site has many factors that come into play: sun, breezes, exisiting tree cover, views, and a less-definable trait deemed "character."

from town, or forty acres of woodland out beyond the end of the county road.

Wherever you choose to live, close in or far from town, on a quarter acre or a quarter section of land, each building site will offer unique situations for the enhancement of a building's performance. Resources that are available on site—sunlight, water, natural shading, prevailing winds, topography, soil—must be catalogued and evaluated. They become key factors in the decision of what kind of property to buy and, later, what kind of house to design.

Sunlight

The single most effective contributor to the comfort and livability of a home is solar energy. The health benefits of abundant winter sunlight, both for combating cold and damp and for supplying needed vitamin D, are significant. Perhaps even more important in today's economy is the financial savings possible through utilization of free energy from the sun. It's hard to believe that for the past thirty or forty years, since the beginning of the tract house heyday, builders have been plopping down identical floor plans on opposite sides of the street. This approach, totally disregarding the way in which sunlight falls onto and into a home, is not only unnecessarily expensive for the occupants who pay the utility bills, but wasteful of the nonrenewable resources that fuel furnaces and power plants.

The concept of solar heating is simple. Sunlight warms through *radiation*, allowing us to feel comfortable at lower air temperatures, while the cooler air in turn contributes to improved respiration and circulation. Profuse sunlight pouring into a well-designed structure creates a healthier indoor environment than a forced-air furnace. Forced-air furnaces and heat pumps heat through *conduction*, that is, by filling the space and enveloping our bodies with warm, typically "stuffy," air. Fans, the force behind the system, are audible if not downright noisy. Air from the ductwork is hot and dry, which is not healthy for skin and mucous membranes, and it's frequently laden with household dust, outside dirt, pollens, molds, and other irritants. The next time you have an opportunity, notice how dirty the wall looks next to a furnace register in a house that has been heated by a forced-air furnace for a few years. What you are seeing is a "litmus test" of the air that is coming up into the house from the heater and the ducts.

Orientation plays a vital role in how well a building performs. Profuse sunlight in winter and ample shading in summer can reduce energy bills by as much as 80 percent.

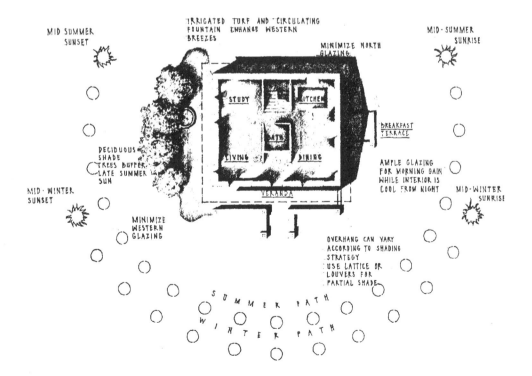

MID SUMMER SUNSET

MID-SUMMER SUNRISE

IRRIGATED TURF AND CIRCULATING FOUNTAIN ENHANCE WESTERN BREEZES

MINIMIZE NORTH GLAZING

STUDY   KITCHEN

BREAKFAST TERRACE

BATH

DECIDUOUS SHADE TREES BUFFER LATE SUMMER SUN

LIVING   DINING

AMPLE GLAZING FOR MORNING GAIN WHILE INTERIOR IS COOL FROM NIGHT

MID-WINTER SUNSET

VERANDA

MID-WINTER SUNRISE

MINIMIZE WESTERN GLAZING

OVERHANG CAN VARY ACCORDING TO SHADING STRATEGY USE LATTICE OR LOUVERS FOR PARTIAL SHADE

SUMMER PATH

WINTER PATH

Another advantage of solar heat over forced-air systems is the effective distribution of heat in the room. In a solar/thermal mass application, the energy that is not utilized directly is stored primarily in the mass of the floor. When needed, it is gently and silently dispersed into the room, creating the warmest conditions along the floor itself. Feet first, that is, and warm feet send comforting signals to the brain. As the distance from the floor increases, the effectiveness of the radiation and convection decreases, thereby presenting cooler air (better working conditions) for the lungs and head. Forced-air systems, with registers located either in the floor pointing upwards or at the top of the walls, blow heat haphazardly around the room, either up our skirts and pant legs or in our faces. The distribution pattern of forced-air heat is exactly reversed from that of radiant heat. The warmest air is near the top of the room, surrounding our heads and negatively impacting the processes of thought and respiration.

(Facing page, top) Low-angled winter sun can be brought deep into the living spaces through careful design of overhangs and placement of skylights.

A less definable quality of a home bathed in sunlight is the impact it can have on us psychologically. In addition to the tangible benefits of warmth, light, and clean air, there is also the positive effect of a living in better balance with the environment. Letting the sun back into our lives allows us to recognize the symbiosis that exists among all life on the planet. The global awareness of the need for a sustainable architecture will be enhanced as people directly experience the benefits that the sun can bring to their homes and pocketbooks.

In short, if we plan our house to take full advantage of the sun's path throughout the different seasons of the year, we benefit from lower fuel bills, lower mechanical system costs, a quieter indoor environment, healthier air quality, and a more harmonious and sustainable lifestyle.

Winter Winds and Summer Breezes

(Facing page, bottom) Overhangs, arbors, and skylight shutters can provide much appreciated shade when the summer sun is high in the sky.

Regional architectures evolved throughout the centuries in response to wind patterns as much as they did to sunlight and rainfall. In the harshest of winter climates, houses "turned their backs" and "hugged the ground," letting the cold winds roar overhead. Sometimes houses were even built partially into the ground, to lessen the wall surface exposed to the wind and to take advantage of the warmth of the earth. The low linearity of Frank Lloyd Wright's prairie houses are examples of 20th century vernacular architecture, appropriate to the climate of the Midwest.

In hot, humid regions the movement of air through a building is absolutely essential to maintaining human comfort. Here houses are frequently built up off the ground to catch the breezes and allow for air circulation under the floor. Porches are used to create shade and increase the cooling capacity of the wind

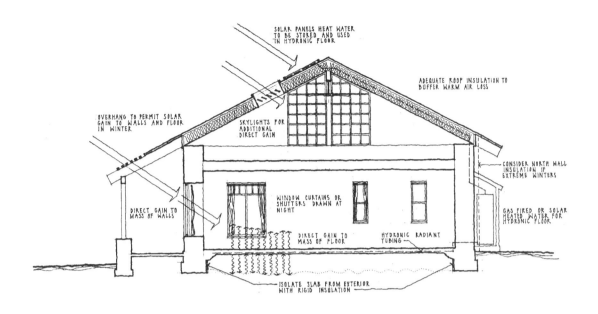

SOLAR PANELS HEAT WATER
TO BE STORED AND USED
IN HYDRONIC FLOOR

ADEQUATE ROOF INSULATION TO
BUFFER WARM AIR LOSS

OVERHANG TO PERMIT SOLAR
GAIN TO WALLS AND FLOOR
IN WINTER

SKYLIGHTS FOR
ADDITIONAL
DIRECT GAIN

CONSIDER NORTH WALL
INSULATION IF
EXTREME WINTERS

WINDOW CURTAINS OR
SHUTTERS DRAWN AT
NIGHT

DIRECT GAIN TO
MASS OF WALLS

GAS FIRED OR SOLAR
HEATED WATER FOR
HYDRONIC FLOOR

DIRECT GAIN TO
MASS OF FLOOR

HYDRONIC RADIANT
TUBING

ISOLATE SLAB FROM EXTERIOR
WITH RIGID INSULATION

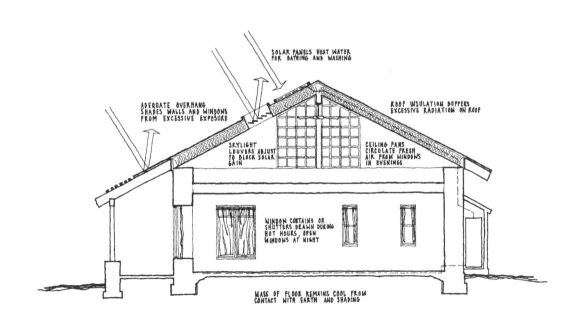

SOLAR PANELS HEAT WATER
FOR BATHING AND WASHING

ADEQUATE OVERHANG
SHADES WALLS AND WINDOWS
FROM EXCESSIVE EXPOSURE

ROOF INSULATION BUFFERS
EXCESSIVE RADIATION ON ROOF

SKYLIGHT
LOUVERS ADJUST
TO BLOCK SOLAR
GAIN

CEILING FANS
CIRCULATE FRESH
AIR FROM WINDOWS
IN EVENINGS

WINDOW CURTAINS OR
SHUTTERS DRAWN DURING
HOT HOURS, OPEN
WINDOWS AT NIGHT

MASS OF FLOOR REMAINS COOL FROM
CONTACT WITH EARTH AND SHADING

Overhangs play an important part in decreasing heat gain by shading south and west walls from direct summer sun (or north and west walls in the southern hemisphere).

through the house. Walls are lightweight and openings are large, allowing for unrestricted cross-ventilation. Frequently, openings in the roof near the peak augment the natural flow of air through the house. Think of a Polynesian house with its nearly nonexistent walls and double open-ended gable roof. To the Pacific Islanders access to wind is as critical as access to sun was to the ancient Greeks.

In dry desert regions, where the air and the wind are hot, houses with thick walls and small windows are built close together. The buildings shade one another, and the desert sky at night cools the thick earth walls. The narrow, winding streets capture the wind off the desert. The shade and the cool walls refresh the wind as it passes by. Stairways opening onto flat roofs work as exhaust ports, pulling cool air off the street and through the house. Like a milkman on his early morning rounds, the desert wind deposits daily sustenance at every doorstep.

So vital is the breeze to comfort in the desert that in regions east of the Mediterranean builders evolved an architectural tool for capturing the wind. Mudbrick towers rise above the flat roofs, their open sides facing into the prevailing winds. As hot desert air enters the scoop of the windcatcher, it cools and

Hassan Fathy's village of New Gourna in Egypt exemplifies desert architecture.

falls to the base of the tower, freshening adjacent rooms before rising to exhaust through the stairwell. The concept of the wind tower has recently been employed with success in the deserts of the American Southwest.

With certain techniques, it is possible to create a breeze where there is none. The fabric and skin tents of the Bedouins, black on the inside with white exteriors, utilize the principle of the thermal differential to stimulate air movement through the tent. Likewise, air can be induced to accelerate through flat ceiling spaces by painting soffits black and using white roof coverings, a technique used, among other places, in Thomas Hibben's rammed earth houses in the experimental Mt. Olive project.

One of the primary intentions of this book is to serve as a reminder that, long before the invention of mechanical systems that wrestle for domination over the environment, sustainable solutions for moderating climate were already in use. Our current dependence on petroleum to control comfort is extremely short-sighted and is in effect the "lazy" solution. By attempting to ignore or deny the diverse weather conditions that exist around the world, we are allowing this dependence on nonrenewable resources to destroy our vernacular heritage as it contributes to the homogenization of global architecture.

The form and style of new houses should reflect the general climate of the region and the microclimate of the site. Just as the optimization of sunlight controls a portion of the design, so too does the wind.

If you are still looking for property and have the luxury to choose from more than one parcel, make two of the factors in your decision-making process the exposure of the property to cold winter winds and the access to evening summer breezes. If the choice of land has been made and your parcel is large enough to offer more than one building site, wind patterns should play a part in the selection of the right location. Remember that cold winter winds can sap valuable heat from a thermal-mass house. Even with windows and doors closed, exposing too much of a wall's face to the cold will affect the size of fuel bills and the comfort level inside the house. If possible, choose a location where natural features, such as large trees or small hills, will buffer the house from winter winds. For summer enjoyment, remember that a well-sited house and an evening breeze can work energy magic by refreshing both the occupants and the thermal-mass walls.

Finding the right location on a building site to benefit the structure in both winter and summer may require making compromises. In some areas, cold winter winds and evening summer breezes blow from the same direction, in which case the windbreak that works to advantage in the winter may be stifling to a summer afternoon's enjoyment. Select the best house site within the critical parameters, then modify the design of the structure and its landscape to mitigate harsh weather conditions and to enhance the desirable ones.

Though not as important in the design of the "natural" house as sunlight, winds do have a very significant effect on comfort and efficiency, in both winter and summer. Just as the importance of orientation for winter sunlight was climate-driven, siting for maximum winter wind protection will take precedence

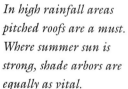

In high rainfall areas pitched roofs are a must. Where summer sun is strong, shade arbors are equally as vital.

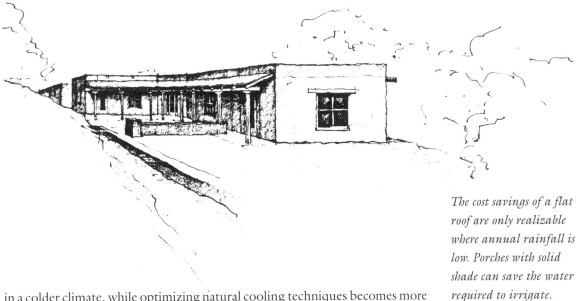

The cost savings of a flat roof are only realizable where annual rainfall is low. Porches with solid shade can save the water required to irrigate.

in a colder climate, while optimizing natural cooling techniques becomes more important in hot climates.

The emphasis throughout this book is on the refinement of methodologies to make the most efficient and sustainable use of natural resources. Although we normally think of construction materials and the energy used to power our dwellings as consumable (but renewable) resources, we need to realize that the most local (and therefore most efficient) resources have been shining on and blowing across our particular piece of land since the beginning of time. As we begin the design process of the house and its landscape, we will see that the relationship between site and structure is critical if we are to achieve our goal of symbiosis.

Thermal Performance of Earth Houses

The most frequently asked questions about building a house of earth are "What happens when it rains?", "What happens in an earthquake?", "How much do they cost?", and "What is the R-value?" How many times have I wished I could answer, "Nothing, nothing, not much, and a lot."

In reality, the answer to each of these questions is far more involved. The resistance of the walls to rainfall is a factor of the soil type, the rate of stabilization, the degree of compaction, the amount of protection afforded the wall, the drainage at the base, and the climate. The resistance to earthquake damage is dependent on the strength of the wall, the design of the building, the quality of construction, and the force of the earthquake. The cost of a rammed earth house is affected by the design of the building, the slope and accessibility of the site, the percentage of owner-supplied labor, and the degree of finish work.

The R-value question is even more complex. The concept of an R (for *resistance*)-value was developed as a means of quantifying the resistance to heat transfer of various insulating materials. Prior to the Energy Crisis of the early 1970s, very little attention was paid to heat loss in houses. As the costs of oil and electricity climbed, however, and as the public became more aware of the environmental side effects of wasted energy, Amory Lovins and other energy experts began to argue the economics of buildings constructed to conserve energy. Lovins pointed out that saving energy could actually increase profits for power companies. Reducing consumption could eliminate the need for the construction of new power plants, meaning less air, water, and soil pollution.

States began to enact legislation establishing minimum energy performance standards for all new construction. Annual energy budgets, expressed in Btus per cubic foot of interior space, were set for both residential and commercial buildings. Before a permit for new construction could be issued, the designer or owner had to verify that either the required insulation was specified for walls, floors, and ceilings (the minimums varied according to climate zone), or that the building as a whole would perform according to the standards. This legislation, along with utility-company incentives and tax credits, generated a huge new market for the manufacturers of synthetic insulation. The R-value scale became as familiar as the Richter scale.

Dense materials such as adobe, concrete, stone, brick, and rammed earth have R-values roughly equivalent to .25 per inch. So 18-inch-thick earthwall would appear to have a total R-value of only 4.5—far from adequate to meet today's strict performance standards, even in mild climates, where R-11 is the minimum wall insulation. If this is true, how can it be that an adobe house feels "warm in winter and cool in summer," as is so often reported?

There are three reasons for the exceptional performance of thermal-mass buildings despite the low per-inch R-value of the wall components. First (and most easily documented) is the heat capacity of the mass itself, known as the *K-value*. Rather than resisting the flow of energy from outside to inside, as an insulated wall does, a mass wall *stores* heat energy for return to the living spaces as it is needed. This concept is often described as a "thermal flywheel." In your car, a heavy rotating disc, located between the engine and the transmission, stores mechanical energy to even out the pulsing action of the crankshaft and provide energy to the wheels even after the explosions in the cylinders have ceased. In your house, a heavy wall can store heat energy to even out the temperature swings from day to night and provide the occupants with comfort long after the sun has set. (More on thermal flywheels in cold, gray climates later.)

The second reason a thermal mass house can boast a high comfort level is the effect that heat transfer through radiation has on our bodies. When we stand, sit, or walk near a mass wall, the energy in the wall will cause direct sensations of warmth or coolness, regardless of the temperature of the air in the room. Direct radiant energy provides a soothing, subtle, and effective alternative to forced-air heat and mechanical air conditioning.

There is possibly a third explanation for how a low R-value material can perform as well as it does: a reason that has not been explained in the laboratory, but nevertheless has been documented through centuries of satisfactory performance. It might be thought of as "strength in numbers." To illustrate, the Zen teacher holds one small twig between the thumb and forefinger of each hand and with a slight twist snaps the twig. He then gathers eighteen twigs together in a bundle, and finds that his thumbs and forefingers no longer have strength enough to snap the gathered twigs. The combined strength of the twigs is greater than the sum of their parts. In our case, 18 inches of R .25 are effectively greater than R 4.5. If so, how can this be?

I like to think of this phenomenon as "the dance of the Btus." Of course, Btus are only units of measurement and don't really "dance." However, as the individual molecules that make up the mass of a solid earthwall heat up, they do increase their rate of vibration, and transfer a part of that vibrational energy to adjacent molecules, which do the same, all the way through the width of the wall. The speed at which the molecules pass their energy on to one another, and the rate at which the ones nearest the wall surface give up their energy, depends upon the temperature differential between one side of the wall and the other. This differential changes every hour of the day depending on factors such as sunlight, wind, and outside air temperature. As some of the molecules lose energy, their movement becomes random, blocking the swifter molecules. The dance degenerates from choreography into chaos, and the increased resistance prevents heat accumulated in the wall from being lost.

The metaphor of the dance can help us visualize how actual thermal performance can exceed the mathematical predictions. In other words, the insulation value of a wall system is not the only determinant of comfort. Computer programs that have been developed to predict energy performance in new buildings recognize this fact, and require the input of data for the thermal mass of the wall as well as for the R-value.

The dance of the Btus may be used to explain why actual performance exceeds the mathematical R-value predictions, but there are many other factors that combine to affect the overall energy efficiency of the building as a whole.

The single greatest factor is climate. In some climate zones and with good design, thick earthwalls can provide all of the resistance to heat transfer necessary to maintain comfortable indoor conditions year-round. In regions where temperatures are extreme, the addition of supplemental insulation may be required to counteract excessive heat loss during the winter or excessive heat gain during the summer. Extremely cold or oppressively hot outside temperatures will render uninsulated thermal mass ineffective. In these climates, some barrier to the direct flow of heat through the wall is essential and will generate more than enough savings in energy bills to offset the cost of installing and protecting the insulation.

Exactly which climates demand insulation, what strategy is appropriate, and how much energy savings can be expected? In very cold regions, where winters are long and average outside temperatures are below freezing, an exposed, uninsulated wall will become cold even with a supply of warm air on the interior surface. The cold walls will "wick" heat out of the living spaces, adding to the fuel bills as energy is expended in an attempt to offset the heat loss. Despite warm air temperatures, the walls will also create the sensation of cold through a constant radiant heat loss between the occupants and the wall mass. In these situations, insulation, either embedded within the wall or applied to the outside surface of the walls and protected with stucco or paneling, is economically justifiable. Say the cost of installing 2-inch rigid insulation board and a stucco protection totals $10,000 (or you do it yourself for $2,000). If this will save an average of $100 per month for six months per year on your winter heating bill, then in just under seventeen years you will have paid for the insulation and will begin to realize the economic gain on your investment. (Knowing full well that fuel prices are going to rise, you will in fact pay off the insulation in fewer than seventeen years.)

In climates where temperatures are not as cold and the winters not as long as in the example above, the annual savings on fuel will not be as great. The payback period will be longer, and the cost of installing manufactured insulation and hiring a stucco contractor will be harder to justify.

In moderately cold climates, insulation embedded directly in the walls may be the most economically feasible strategy. Although not as airtight as external insulation, rigid insulation boards buried in the wall will vastly improve the thermal resistance. To embed insulation, 2 x 8-foot strips of rigid insulation board are held in place in the center of the formwork while earth is compacted on both sides. Additional 2 x 8-foot strips are stacked on top of one another as the level of the wall is raised. This technique demands careful work at the door and window jambs, along the top of the wall, and around the electrical and plumbing runs. The advantage to embedding insulation is that it eliminates the need for a protective covering on the outside of the wall, saving not only the initial cost of the stucco, but also the maintenance it will require. Remember, a properly designed and built natural earthwall only gets better with age.

In mild climate zones, but where some winter protection is helpful, it might make sense to explore alternatives to insulation, especially if an uninsulated wall can work to your advantage in maintaining cool temperatures during a long, hot summer. Some of these alternatives might involve altering your design to provide greater solar access if winter heat is your predominant requirement; or adding a wide porch if summer cooling is the higher priority. If your winters are cold but short and sunny, perhaps the most feasible alternative would be the addition of solar panels to heat water for circulation through the floor slab, thereby offsetting the heat loss through the walls with inexpensive heat gain. If the summers are hot and dry, consider installing a nighttime evaporative cooler to force-ventilate the house and chill down the walls. If you live on rural property, try stacking bales of hay or straw against the north side of the house during the cold winter months, then using the straw for summer mulch on the garden.

Whether you rely on an attached greenhouse or an annual straw bale blanket, there are a wide variety of alternatives worth evaluating before buying into synthetic insulation and stucco protection. Even in the coldest of climates, you might decide to build your house without exterior insulation and test how well it performs for a year or two. You can always add the insulation and stucco later if the heating bills are too high.

In the end, any discussion of thermal performance is best concluded with testimonials from people who live in the houses. As we listen to the stories of our clients, we are reminded of Goldilocks and her visit to the house of the Three Bears. In some stories, the house is too hot, in some it is too cold, but for the most part the temperature is just right. If we correlate the testimonials of the responding residents to their design style and type of construction, we find that the critical factor is not the extent of insulation, but rather design and orientation. A well-designed and properly sited house of earth, insulated only when essential, will provide its occupants with a lifetime of appreciation.

Topography and Terrain

Another important factor in the site-selection process is the "lay of the land," that is, the direction and severity of the natural slopes. Of course, on small urban lots or perfectly flat parcels, topography does not enter into the formula, but on larger pieces or where the land is steep, working with the slope rather than against it will both facilitate construction and improve the performance of the building. Understanding how the intensity of the sunlight varies depending on its angle of incidence with the hillside, or how cold air falls downslope and winds blow strongest near the top will allow us to use the terrain to our advantage.

A sloping site presents both opportunities and impediments. On the positive side, a house built on a southern or southeastern hillside, exposed more directly to the sun's rays, will warm up more quickly in the morning. From a financial standpoint, this results in lower overall fuel bills. From a psychological point of view, it can help induce a "brighter" outlook on the day. Likewise, the soil on a south-facing hillside will warm up more quickly in the spring, stimulating more vigorous plant growth, which translates into earlier yields from the vegetable garden.

The difficulties and extra expense of building on a steep sidehill may in some cases be justified by a spectacular setting.

Hillsides can stimulate air movement independently from the prevailing breezes. Just as hang gliders ride thermal currents generated by warm air moving upslope, a house that is well sited on a sidehill can "ride" the warm air

currents to better energy performance. A house should not be located too far down the slope, as cold air gathers at the bottom of the hill. Farmers know all too well that cold settles in the lowlands, freezing crops on the valley floor while those on the hillsides remain undamaged.

Neither should a house be situated too far up the slope, as wind velocity increases near the top. In some areas, winds are strong enough across the tops of hills to dictate that these sites should be avoided if possible. If there is a view from the top of the hill so spectacular as to warrant building a house there, make provisions in the design of the structure or in the landscaping on the site to protect the house as much as possible from the high winds.

The fact that a fantastic view can justify a less-than-optimum energy orientation is just one example of the many compromises that will inevitably be a part of the site-selection, and later the design, process. As we have already seen, maximizing winter solar gain may result in higher summer cooling loads. Orientation for summer breezes may mean unwanted exposure to winter blasts. Priorities differ from climate to climate and in fact from person to person. The advantages and disadvantages of the site must be catalogued and then evaluated in terms of their effects on the lifestyle of the homeowners.

Hillsides which slope to the west tend to be hotter in the summer, oriented as they are to the late afternoon sun. North-facing slopes are colder in the winter, when the rays of the low-angled winter sun glance off the face of the hill. North slopes are also slower to warm up in the spring, which results in a longer heating season and a shorter growing season. There are situations on north-facing slopes where the hilltop behind the house can rise so high that it will block out the sun entirely during the middle of winter, leaving the house without any solar gain. It goes without saying that such locations should be avoided.

The severity of the slope and the access to the building site are two important factors to be considered during the selection process. As we have observed in our discussion of sun angles and air currents, in some cases gently sloping land can actually enhance the performance of the building and the gardens, but remember that the complexity of the construction increases in proportion to the severity of the slope. Driveways on steep sites can be expensive to build and to maintain. They may even prove hazardous on rainy nights or frosty mornings. Diverting storm water may add expenses to the project.

Simplest of all sites to work on is the completely flat pad, where no grading is required and all foundations and stem walls are of equal depth and height. On a flat site, the tradespeople and their pickups can access the project from all sides, thereby reducing the time spent hauling materials and carrying tools to and from the truck. On the other extreme, a very steep site will require significant extra work and money to build retaining walls and stepped foundations, not to mention additional structural engineering and possible special inspections. All building materials must be off-loaded and stored at one side of the project rather than where it is most convenient, then carried or hoisted up- or downslope as needed. The parking area is typically on the other side of the material-storage area, which means every trip to the truck takes minutes rather than seconds. When all the additional costs for materials and manpower are factored into the equation, steep sites may become prohibitively expensive.

Once again we are confronted with the issue of compromise—in this case, to build on flat ground or a hillside. The steep site may be priced lower than alternative parcels, it may have a great view, or it may have some special inspirational quality that simply beckons you to build there. Assess the long list of advantages and disadvantages rationally, make your decision, then confidently proceed.

Winter Rain Considerations

Water is the lifeblood of the soil, but it can wreak considerable havoc if the building and the site aren't prepared for a deluge. Low-lying building sites are subject to flooding. Driveways and pathways above a house may channel water into a doorway. Wind-driven rain can beat against window frames with enough force to creep around the sash. Saturated earth walls tend to lose their thermal efficiency and may become subject to accelerated surface weathering.

Depending on the amount of annual rainfall in the region, water-related issues may play a very big part in the site-selection and design processes. Where winter rains are extremely heavy, great care must be taken to ensure rapid run-off away from the building. If positive control systems are not installed, water may back up against foundations and floor slabs, eventually migrating underneath the structure and generating unhealthy conditions in the house, or possible settling of the foundation walls.

The first and most important line of defense against groundwater damage is careful siting of the house. Study the land for signs of water flows. Avoid sites that are clearly water drainages. The picturesque arroyo, today a peaceful habitat for yucca, sagebrush, rabbits, and quail, was originally gouged out of the land by water. The water will come again.

Low, boggy areas make poor building sites for several reasons. Wet ground stays cold longer in the spring. Driveways are expensive to construct and maintain. Foundations must be made more extensive. Buildings can become uncomfortably damp and expensive to heat.

Another drawback to building on a steep site, besides construction logistics, is the need to divert the water that runs off the hillside above the house. Make certain that natural drainages remain free-flowing.

The second line of defense against water-related problems is the finish grading around the building. Ground should always slope away from the house on all sides so that water will run away quickly from the building and never towards it. If water is allowed to back up against the walls it will eventually work its way into the house. In some cases water can build up enough pressure to actually dislodge a building from its foundation. Drain lines can be buried at the base of the walls as additional diversionary measures, but surface drainage is always critical. Lastly, take special precautions to ensure that neither driveways nor walkways create natural watercourses leading towards the doors. Even a little footpath can become a streambed after a downpour.

The third level of protection, which, like grading, relates more to construction than to the selection process, is the team of roof overhangs, gutters, downspouts, and underground drain lines. In high rainfall or snowfall areas, overhangs and gutters are absolutely essential. Where the soil is heavy or drainage poor, use underground lines to carry the water from the roof away from the building.

Unlike the considerations for sun, wind, and terrain, which vary significantly from site to site, rainfall remains relatively uniform within any given bioregion. Annual rainfall will govern certain aspects of the design, but within the parameters we are establishing for choosing a building site, our biggest concern with groundwater is how it affects the stability of the building.

Site Selection with the Garden in Mind

When a farmer looks for land, the number one concern is the quality of the soil—its fertility, depth, and tilth. When the prospective homeowner of a sustainable dwelling looks for land, soil quality should be viewed as a significant selection criteria. Healthy, productive gardens provide fresh, nutritious food for the table, they enhance the performance and comfort within the building, they improve the quality of the living spaces surrounding the building, and they help establish a symbiotic relationship between the land and its stewards.

Symbiosis is the mutually beneficial relationship between dissimilar organisms, in which the by-product of one species contributes to the development of another. On the macro scale this is exemplified by the oxygen/carbon dioxide cycle shared by the plant and animal kingdoms. Animals depend on the oxygen transpired through plant growth. Plants in turn utilize carbon dioxide, the by-product of respiration. On the micro scale, the decay of single-celled organisms contributes to soil quality and provides the nutrients necessary for healthy plant growth. In geologic terms, this perpetual growth and decay of

When looking for property, try to visualize the final relationship between the built space and your use of the land around the house.

The successful integration of a house with its site can enhance the symbiosis between the inhabitants and the rest of the natural world.

microscopic life over millennia is the force behind the creation of living soil from solid rock.

Symbiosis occurs at all levels of life on earth. The relationship is so incredibly complex, in fact, that the study of these interactions has led to the formulation of a concept of the earth itself as "the" living organism. In the Gaia theory air, water, and soil are the major components of this one organism, Planet Earth. What we have always thought of as life—the plants and animals that inhabit the earth—have evolved merely to regulate the chemistry of the biosphere. Humans are insignificant participants, far less important to the life cycle than termites. Even the imbalances that we are currently creating through our overconsumptive lifestyles may be corrected through biological regulation once humans become extinct.

If we think of soil as the "skin" on Planet Earth, we can understand how important its health is. It is easily understood that the erosion of topsoil, whether the result of overgrazing, clear-cutting, or desertification, lessens the productivity of the land. We now know that soil abuse also has devastating effects on the environment as a whole: fisheries are strangled by the buildup of silt in the rivers, air is polluted with windblown dust, and even the chemical balance of the atmosphere is altered with excess carbon dioxide.

When we were considering topography as a factor in choosing a building site, we saw that there were compromises to be made between the flat, easy-to-build-on site and the steep site with the great view. Typically the price of the land reflects its accessibility. When we consider soil as a factor in the selection process, unless we're looking at farmland, price is not typically affected. Just as you evaluate the parcel for its solar access and wind exposure, study the surrounding vegetation for indications of soil quality. Lush growth and green grasses that linger into summer are indicators of deep and healthy soil. Bare earth and stunted growth are signs of shallow or poor soil. Take a shovel with you and while you're on the property studying the quality of the setting sun one evening, dig a hole as deep as you can. Is the soil loose and friable? Is it a rich brown color? Does it have a good smell? These are some of the characteristics of a soil ripe for gardening. On the other hand, if the ground is so hard you can't dig it with a pick, or the soil so sticky you can't shake it off the shovel, be aware that the gardens on this site will need extra work if they are to prosper.

In the next section, as we develop the architectural plan, we'll begin to see how interrelated the house and garden become. The symbiotic relationship that is critical to the optimization of site resources and to the health of the occupants depends on the flow of positive energy between inside and out. Think of this energy flow as respiration, and think of the house as alive, its walls expanding and contracting slightly with each breath. Into the lungs and the bloodstream flows air fresh from the gardens, filtered and rich in oxygen. Through the house and back to the garden comes air laden with excess heat and moisture, good air for plant growth.

With Planet Earth alive, according to the Gaia theory, why not design our dwellings to be alive as well? If we take this approach, then the search for sustainable solutions to architecture becomes even more critical. We can develop a set of criteria for building materials that evaluates their "livelihood." How respectful to the environment is the manufacture of any given material? How effectively does it contribute to the conservation of energy within the structure? How completely does it recycle or decompose once it has exhausted its useful life? As we discuss the selection of appropriate building materials later in the book, we'll discover both the possibilities and the pitfalls that confront us. Just as no single building site provides all the optimum characteristics, no single building system presents an "ideal" solution. Our obligation is to study all of the available resources of the building site, and carefully consider how each resource might best be utilized in the construction of an environmentally responsible habitat.

CHAPTER THREE

The Architectural Plan

IN ADDITION TO "FITTING" THE SITE, a dwelling must also fit the lifestyle of the occupants. Rather than designing a building for its outward appearance, consider how to create spaces that bring comfort, security, happiness, efficiency, and functionality. Allow the architectural plan to evolve from the site and from the needs of the residents. Remember, designing a house that is right for you and your family takes a great deal of time and a thorough understanding of your lifestyle.

Considering Climate

During the process of site selection, we evaluated several different resource categories: sun, wind, water, terrain, and soil. Within each category there were positive and negative factors affecting the final decision of placement, but one factor that affected all of the categories was the climate of the region. As we will see, climate governs the design of the building even more strictly than it does the selection of the building site.

For most of the five decades following World War II, our society has been infatuated with the development of increasingly sophisticated machinery to dominate nature. Engineers and entrepreneurs continue to invest enormous quantities of time and money in devices that essentially do no more than expend nonrenewable energy in a battle against climate. With cheap energy and no pollution concerns, those efforts seemed valid at the time. But today, with petroleum nearly as extinct as the dinosaurs that created it and the entire planet in jeopardy, our concept of mechanically manufactured "comfort" is ludicrous beyond belief. Just think. We burn coal to boil water to generate electricity, and

46

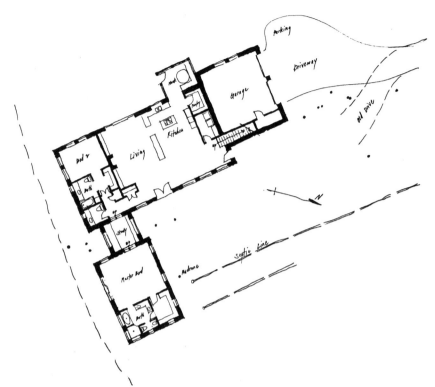

A floorplan begins to take shape around the site and its access.

then transport that electricity hundreds if not thousands of miles through copper and aluminum wires in order to run a machine that lowers the air temperature inside a building by maybe ten or twenty degrees.

With better design and a willingness to accept the reality of seasonal weather patterns, we can live in buildings that maintain comfortable conditions without a dependence on nonrenewable energy sources. If we study proven vernacular techniques for controlling comfort and refine those techniques in combination with the most efficient applications of modern technology, we can learn to work with the climate rather than against it.

Which vernacular solutions might accomplish the maximum utilization of resources available on site will vary from region to region. In a hot, humid climate, wide porches and large screened windows for cross-ventilation are the most effective architecture for maintaining indoor comfort. In a hot, dry climate, thick walls, small windows, and nighttime ventilation will reduce cooling loads by using the thermal mass of the walls to counteract daytime heat gains. Rather than opening the structure to the day's heat, windows are kept closed and the sunlight minimized. The walls then use the coolness they "harvested" during the previous night to maintain a comfortable indoor temperature throughout the day.

In climates where the demand for winter heating exceeds that for summer cooling, design strategies will change. If the winter days are typically clear and sunny, large south-facing windows and thermal mass floors will reduce heating loads. In regions of the country where winters are long, cold, and gray the best approach is to build small, well-insulated buildings with low ceilings and a minimum of exterior wall surface exposed to the weather. Use the shape of the building or the natural topography and landscape features to protect the house from the brunt of winter storms.

In actuality, most regions of the country experience a wide variety of weather patterns over the course of twelve months. Climate-appropriate architecture should be a reflection of that variety. Think of the design of your house as a work of art or a piece of music composed to respond to the seasons. In winter we seek warmth and a sense of coziness and security. In spring we want to throw open a window, inviting sunlight, birdsong, and the fragrance of the garden into our home. During the hot summer months we seek the shade of the porch and the breath of the afternoon breeze. And, finally, when autumn approaches we enjoy the fall colors and the quality of the light as the sun drifts towards solstice.

Not only do the necessities of climate govern the design of a structure, a building must respond to the lifestyle and aesthetic preferences of its residents. Keeping in mind that fiscal and environmental responsibility are the watchwords in good design, we nevertheless have a veritable cornucopia of possibilities available to us as we begin the design process.

The Home Program

Almost unconsciously, we seek out spaces in which we are most at ease. If we are cold, we move towards light and warmth. When we are hot, we seek the refreshment of shade. Throughout the day

Architecture changes in response to the climate. In Florida, shade and a cooling breeze are essential to comfort.

S. D'ORMANO/CRATERRE

Where winters are severe, the design of the building as well as the mass of the walls result in greater interior comfort.

and the year sunlight, shade, and wind have different effects on our dwellings. By anticipating the character of each season and by considering our personal preferences, we can build spaces that work for us in different ways at different times. The patio where I drink my morning coffee in April, for instance, would be unpleasantly hot in August.

Sunlight moves around the house throughout the year, just as the occupants do. Here, spring sun warms geraniums on a southeastern patio.

The process begins with what's called a *program*. This is basically a list of the features you want to include in the house, except that the list should be much more inclusive to your needs than merely "two bedrooms, two baths, great room, country kitchen," etc. A comprehensive program for the design of a site- and lifestyle-specific, resource-efficient, healthy house should list the basic spaces you require (bedrooms, bathrooms, etc.), and then it should include a description of how you intend to use each space and during what times of the day. For example, one person might write: "Master bedroom—an intimate, remote corner of the house where the two of us can feel private in the evenings, and where we can lie in bed as the sun comes up, listening to bird sounds and making plans for our busy day." A different type of person might describe the master bedroom in this way: "Big enough for a sofa, a comfortable chair, and a big screen TV which we can see from bed; close enough to the kids to hear them during the night; protected from the morning sun so we can sleep late on the weekends." (See Builders' Resource B: A Sample Home Design Program, pp. 233–37.)

In the previous section we undertook a thorough evaluation of the building

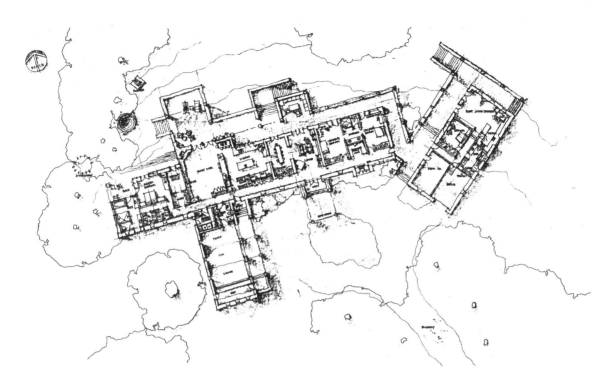

*Complex floor plans
respond to complex
programs as well as the
site and its restrictions.*

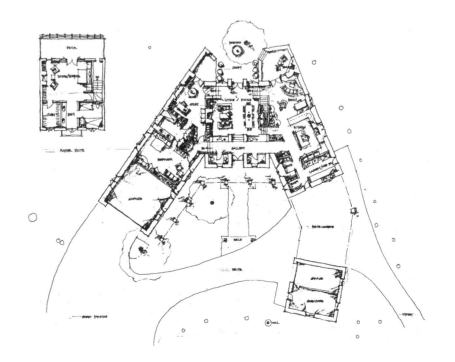

site in terms of available resources. The design program is an even more thorough evaluation of living spaces in terms of personal expectations. With a truly comprehensive program come two rewards. First, it provides you with the information necessary to create living spaces that make positive contributions to your daily life. At the same time, the exercise of evaluating your lifestyle and needs in terms of physical space presents the opportunity to learn more about yourself, the ultimate objective being to construct an environment that results in greater peace of mind and a more healthy attitude towards life.

What you will likely find as you perform your self-evaulation is that your moods change with the seasons. Winter doldrums, spring fever, and summer boredom syndrome are all terms coined from real life. Try to pinpoint the source of your own discontent, if any exists, and build an antidote into your design.

Capturing, Enhancing, and Deflecting Solar Energy

Just as a proper diet will improve your physical health, the right environment will improve your mental health. Sunlight is the primary nutrient in sustainable architecture and our greatest resource. Not only does it drive the biosphere, the sun powers our psyches as well. Our architecture fails if it does not maximize the energy of the sun. Well-placed windows capture wanted sunlight. Well-placed shade prevents unwanted summer heat buildup.

As we begin to arrange the rooms in our house design, our first consider-

Design concepts respond in different ways to the sunlight on the site. One begs for sun, the other for shade.

ation is that the spaces we use during the daytime should be located on the sunny side of the house. Flooded with low-angled sun during the winter, these rooms will be the warmest in the house and require less electricity for lighting. During the summer, with proper overhangs and shading, they'll be comfortable and well-lit. Obviously, the degree to which the rooms concentrate on winter heat and light rather than summer shading and ventilation is a factor of the general climate in the region.

The kitchen is a day-use space in nearly everyone's program. With windows on the east side, it will warm up quickly in the morning, and with windows on the south it will capture additional heat throughout the day. Very often the kitchen is the most frequently used room in the house, and for this reason it should be given priority placement on the site and in the light.

Depending on how large the house will be (or more likely on your construction budget), you might consider building a nook off of the southeast corner of the kitchen in which to eat breakfast. Plan it so that a door or window opens onto the kitchen garden. This way your spring morning reverie may be accompanied by the fragrance of herbs and flowers, and, with luck, the sounds and sightings of songbirds. With an abundance of glass, this breakfast nook may even perform supplemental functions as both a winter herb garden and a solar heater.

Which other rooms warrant priority locations will vary from family to family. In one program, sun-critical spaces might be the living room and study. In another program the family room, den, workroom, or dining room may

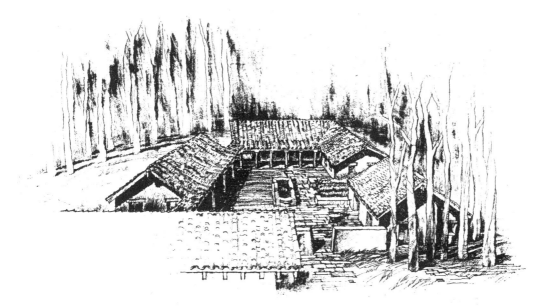

A sunny kitchen with a view to the garden may be the highest priority for many homeowners.

Rooms should be arranged so that sunlight floods the spaces used during the day.

command the best exposure. Your objective is to make decisions based on your own requirements and daily patterns. Think in terms of where you work, relax, contemplate, or concentrate. Create a place or places to enhance those particular activities. If your site has a special geographic or landscape feature, consider how to develop the relationship between this feature and one of your living spaces.

Relegated to the solar backwater, that is, the north side of the house, are the night-use spaces. Logically, these are the rooms to sleep in. Because the majority of time spent in the bedrooms is post sunset, it just makes sense to place them on the dark side of the house where there is less light but plenty of air. Every bedroom must have good air movement, preferably with windows on two sides for natural cross-ventilation. Fresh air is a natural sleep enhancer. Good ventilation is as important in the bedrooms as sunlight is in the kitchen.

In colder climates, windows on the north side should be small to reduce heat loss, and windows on the west should be shaded to reduce heat gain in summer. It shows bad planning to have a bedroom still baking from the afternoon sun just about the time you're ready to go to sleep. Bedrooms located on the east side of the house should be reserved for the early risers in the family.

Other night rooms, if your planned house will be large enough to encompass more than the basics, might include a library, study, music room, computer room/office, or a media room. Window placement should follow the same rules as for bedrooms: small on the north, shaded on the west. In terms of fresh air, cross-ventilation is less critical in the occasional-use night and evening spaces than in bedrooms. For one thing, air movement through these areas can be less restricted by the partition walls and doors which provide the privacy normally required for bedrooms. An open floor plan, which will allow air to move freely from one end of the house to the other, is not only less expensive to construct, but also allows one space to overlap into another, thereby reducing the overall floor area to build, heat, clean, and pay taxes on.

Sunlight and wind are only two of the site resources to consider when deciding where to place rooms. In some climates, a third resource, shade, can be as critical as sunlight. Late afternoon summer sun can beat through west-facing windows with such intensity that unprotected rooms become unpleasantly warm. If trees are growing on the site, try to position the building in such a way that they will shade the west wall. Better yet, locate the west-side windows precisely where shade will fall around five o'clock on the afternoon of the summer solstice.

If there are no trees on the site, position the building to take maximum advantage of the other important resources, then plant trees in exactly the right

The north-side rooms should be those that warrant less daylight. For some people, a cool, dark space in which to sleep late is essential.

Small windows on the north side of the house will reduce heat loss and save energy.

Even when the front entry is on the north, resist the temptation to use excessive areas of glass.

Building in the shade of existing trees not only helps to cool the house, but trees can also give the house a sense of belonging to its site.

locations. Shading west windows with arbors or well-placed trees is the single most effective contribution towards reducing energy costs in hot climates, regardless of the method of construction. To illustrate this point, take a drive (or, better yet, walk) through an old neighborhood with tree-lined streets on a hot summer day, then head for the parking lot at the mall for comparison. The difference in these two environments is so noticeable it's hard to believe tree planting isn't one of the top priorities for every energy management program.

Energy studies indicate 50 to 80 percent savings in air-conditioning costs for buildings utilizing well-placed shade trees. By shading the walls, trees reduce the demand for mechanically assisted cooling, thereby decreasing monthly fuel bills and improving the environment. Not only do trees filter dust from the air, convert carbon dioxide to oxygen, and improve the general aspect of the outdoor spaces, they eliminate (or at least greatly reduce) the noise and exhaust heat of the air-conditioning unit itself. What's actually taking place during the air-conditioning process is that a motor, consuming electricity produced by burning a fossil fuel, is compressing CFC-laden freon gas to create cold air, which is then blown into the building with fans (consuming more electricity). Not only is the air conditioner heating the immediate environment as it works to cool the inside of the house, but temperatures at the power plant are into the 1,000 degrees F range. Compare the energy wasted in this method of mechanical cooling to the simple system of shade trees and natural ventilation. It's like the difference between a powerful but gas-guzzling V-12 engine and a simple but elegant perpetual motion machine: there is simply no comparison.

When shade is utilized in combination with thermal mass walls, additional cooling benefits result. American Indians used fire-heated rocks to

If trees are not an option to create needed shade, build an arbor and plant it with deciduous vines.

The timeless, pre-industrial solution to natural cooling—an earthwall in the shade of a mature tree.

Vines growing directly on an earthwall provide supplemental cooling.

gradually bring water to a boil. Applying this same principle in reverse, shade-cooled mass walls can bring inside air temperatures down. According to the laws of thermodynamics, energy states are constantly moving towards equilibrium—heat from the rocks is transferred to the water in the pot, and heat from the air in the living space is transferred to the mass in the walls. By designing so that the walls will be shaded as long as possible during the summer days and cooled down at night with good ventilation, the building will maintain comfortable temperatures around the clock. In many regions, these passive techniques will provide all of the cooling required. In very hot climates and in high-humidity areas of the country, a small amount of mechanically assisted cooling may be required. If so, an evaporative cooler, rather than an air conditioner, can be used at night to help bring down the temperature of the walls. An evaporative, or "swamp," cooler works by blowing air across a wet mat. It uses the same principle as the wet handkerchief draped behind a French legionnaire's cap. The only mechanical parts in a swamp cooler are the fan and the small pump used to recirculate the water. New-generation, high-efficiency evaporative coolers can provide supplemental cooling with very little energy expense.

It is the coolness stored in the walls which works to maintain comfortable temperatures throughout the day. Cool walls absorb heat, and the function of a mechanically assisted cooling system is to help the walls release their excess heat. The most efficient time to run the evaporative cooler is at night when outside temperatures are lower. In some areas of the country, utility rates are also lower at night, further improving efficiency.

Remember, our goal is to use the energy forces and resources the site has to offer, in conjunction with responsive design, to achieve a comfortable and energy-efficient environment.

Feng Shui: Energy from the Fourth Dimension

There are other forces at play on the site. Less tangible than sun and wind, these forces are nevertheless potentially very powerful. For centuries, the Chinese have practiced an art of building placement which draws on an invisible energy force called *ch'i* (pronounced "chee"). According to Taoist theories, ch'i is the force that links people and their surroundings; a sort of cosmic wind blowing through our bodies, the atmosphere, and the earth. Maintaining good ch'i is essential for physical, environmental, and emotional balance.

Feng shui (pronounced "fung shway") is the art of placement to improve the flow of ch'i around the building and site. Proper placement will enhance the flow of personal ch'i for the occupants, thereby improving every aspect of

their lives. Expressed another way, by locating a building to be in harmony with the energy of the site and by designing the building for comfort, security, and vitality, the home will become a source of well-being and prosperity for its occupants.

The idea of placement for the best ch'i is really no different than placement for the best sun exposure, except that ch'i is invisible. If we can accept the idea of ch'i as a "cosmic wind," then it follows logically that by properly directing this wind we can improve the metaphysical harmony within our dwelling, in the same way that directing a prevailing summer breeze can improve a building's physical comfort. Think of feng shui as architectural dowsing. In the same way that a water witch can detect the flow of underground water, a feng shui expert is sensitive to the flow of ch'i.

While some elements of the art of fung shui, relying as they do on symbolism and the yin/yang duality of Taosim, may be challenging to skeptical Western thinkers, many are grounded in pure common sense. These elements are very much within the realm of the layman. They deal mostly with light, space, and circulation. For example, sunlight can make us feel comfortable, but shouldn't be too bright. Breezes can make us feel refreshed so long as they're not too strong. Open spaces create a sense of expansiveness and confidence, but still must provide a sense of protection. Small, narrow spaces can be restrictive and oppressive, but if designed properly they may recreate the security of the mother's womb.

The design and placement of a house can respond to natural energy on the site, enhancing the lives of the occupants.

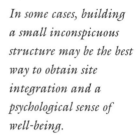

In some cases, building a small inconspicuous structure may be the best way to obtain site integration and a psychological sense of well-being.

Many of the rules of feng shui deal with reinforcing this sense of security. After all, security is one of the most important functions of shelter. To help the occupants maintain the psychological confidence that they are safe from intruders, doors—especially the entry door—should be placed in such a way that no one can enter the house without being seen. Since in reality this is difficult in a large house, try to arrange rooms so that the front door can be viewed from the kitchen, the heart of the house. When called in for some cosmic realignment of an already built house, feng shui experts often use mirrors hung in strategic locations to give a view of the front door when a direct line of sight doesn't exist. In the case of a new design, you can arrange for a view of the entryway from a window or through a hall.

The bedroom is the place for rest and rejuvenation, and often the room where major decisions are made. Good energy in the bedroom is essential to the harmony and well-being of the occupants. The bedroom should be uncluttered and free of anger—full of fresh psychic air in other words. It should be a place for confidence-building. Try to locate the bedroom in a good position on the site, but not out in front of the rest of the house. A bedroom that is too exposed can make the occupants feel vulnerable. Arrange the bedroom so that the door can be seen from the bed, and hinge the door in such a way that a person entering the room is immediately visible. This will enable the occupants to feel more secure while they sleep.

In our lives today there are a multitude of hazards, both physical and psy-

Given as much time as we spend in our bedrooms, the correct placement in relation to the rest of the building and a proper orientation with respect to the sunlight is essential to maintaining personal balance and a healthy relationship.

chological, threatening our sense of well-being. The origins of feng shui date back to an ancient time, when life was perhaps less psychologically threatening, but when people were truly at the mercy of the elements. In early China's agrarian society, everyone from the peasant to the emperor was dependent on the weather and the harvest. If buildings and fields were not placed in auspicious locations, crops did not prosper, sickness prevailed, floods destroyed houses and even entire villages. From generations of experience, rules of placement evolved: south-facing sites warmed up earlier in the spring; gentle slopes prevented soggy soil; hillsides were safer during floods than the valley floor; buildings were warmer when they turned their backs to cold winds; children grew strong and healthy in houses full of sunshine and fresh air. Families who followed the rules of placement grew wealthy and more prosperous than those who didn't.

An in-depth study of the art of feng shui is beyond the scope of this book. The principle upon which it is based, however—building to harmonize people with their environment—is the purpose of the book. The common thread is common sense.

Small Is Beautiful (and Costs Less)

A final consideration in the design process, one in which common sense again comes into the formula, is project size. Throughout history, a building's size has most often been limited by available resources, typically the financial resources of the owners. Today, the argument can still be made that size should be governed by available resources, environmental as well as financial.

For all but the most affluent, the construction budget will govern design decisions as firmly as does sunlight, and one of the primary factors governing the budget is the overall size of the project. Essentially, the larger the building, the more expensive it will be to construct. There are other considerations, such as the difficulty of the site, the complexity of the construction, and the refinement of the finishing specifications, but none are as simple to calculate as size. If you can restrict the volume of built space to the minimum that meets your needs, you can reserve money for other uses, be they retirement accounts, college tuition, or extensive landscaping. Not only does building smaller reduce upfront construction costs, it also saves on maintenance, insurance, permit fees, property taxes, and interest payments. As anyone who has studied the cumulative effects of mortgage interest knows, borrowing money for twenty or thirty years can be very expensive indeed, often exceeding the face value of the loan several times over. Servicing a debt is in a way like maintaining a house. Interest and utility bills are both paid monthly. By reducing the size of the

In some instances, a very small house may provide all the living space we need.

A simple cottage with a porch for shade and a bedroom or two tucked under the roof might be more than adequate.

house, you can reduce the amount of borrowed money, thereby lowering interest payments; and by heating, cooling, and illuminating fewer square feet you can reduce payments to the utility company. A smaller house also saves proportionally on the periodic maintenance expenses associated with paint, plaster, caulking, roofing, downspouts, and gutters.

From the standpoint of sustainability, appropriately sized dwellings are the most responsible. A smaller house requires fewer materials to build, thereby causing less of an impact on the earth's finite resource pool. It will also require less energy to maintain comfort year-round.

Building with the Planet in Mind

Thinking in terms of environmental responsibility leads to the realization that a house built with the health of the planet in mind—that is, one that uses appropriate materials in a sensitive manner—will also last longer than a house thrown together without a thought as to where the materials came from or how they were manufactured. By outliving its shoddy counterpart, a well-built house can make a very significant contribution to the conservation of resources. When a building reaches the end of its useful life, it has to be torn down, buried in a landfill somewhere, then reconstructed using new materials, which must be harvested, processed, and transported. By surviving for just one generation longer, a well-built house saves 5,000 to 10,000 board feet of lum-

At 200 years of age a building, like this one in France, should merely be entering its midlife.

ber, 500 or so gallons of diesel fuel, countless pounds of solid, liquid, and gaseous hazardous manufacturing by-products, and roughly 200 cubic yards of landfill space. If a house can last twice as long as its planned-for-obsolescence counterpart, enough time will have passed for 10,000 board feet of lumber to have grown from seed and 200 cubic yards of waste house to finally decompose back to usable soil.

A construction budget is one of the sustainable designer's most important tools—one of his governing factors, really. To illustrate this point, consider the space known as the guest bedroom. Many of our clients list a "separate bedroom for guests" as one of the requirements in their design program. Yet if you calculate the cost of constructing an additional 300 square feet, add fees, maintenance, interest, etc., you'll discover a startlingly high number. Thinking in terms of a cost-to-value ratio, one would be far better off investing the money that might be spent on building a guest room in a savings account. Interest income could then be earmarked for housing the occasional visitor in the local bed-and-breakfast and the capital retained for other uses.

When you consider that permit fees, property taxes, and insurance rates are all based on the size (or replacement value) of the structure, the logic pointing to downsizing is irrefutable. Make the building small to control costs, then try to maximize the use of outdoor spaces such as verandas, courtyards, patios, and screened porches. Outdoor spaces are not included in permit fees nor appraisal rates, and they are considerably less expensive to construct than indoor spaces. And it goes without saying that outdoor spaces require no investment in supplemental heating or cooling.

Money isn't the only reason to design your house for outdoor living, however. In fact, it isn't even the most important one. Health is. Enhancing the interactions between the natural and the built environment is as important to the health of the occupants as cost reduction is to their pocketbooks. Imagine yourself living in a the midst of a lush garden, replete with sweet fragrances and the quiet splash of flowing water. Compare this image to the thought of a sealed box plopped down in the center of an asphalt pad. Now try to guess in which environment you would feel more comfortable, more in tune with the universe.

When you invite plants, birds, and healthy soil into the spaces surrounding

A private courtyard or a sunny patio can easily become one of the most important "rooms" in the house.

your house, you improve the symbiotic relationship between people and the planet. Allowing indoor spaces to flow into outdoor "rooms" further enhances that relationship. In most climate zones, the weather is mild enough for many months of the year that outdoor living can be very comfortable. Quiet morning reading and early evening entertaining are two activities perfectly suited to a porch or patio. Think of the design for your house as having two parts—a small, solid inner core, where inclement weather cannot penetrate; and a thin outer shell full of light, air, and life. In this respect, a house on its site is like the planet in space. Gravity decreases and the atmosphere gradually thins as the distance from the earth's core increases. A house should be designed so that the human influence gradually decreases as the distance from the core increases. At the center is the fully enclosed, built and conditioned space, surrounded by the less defined indoor/outdoor spaces, leading through the gardens and pathways, and eventually to the "outer" space, the world beyond.

Sketch of the Elm Street bungalow.

In a way, this notion of housing is a bit like the Gaia theory, which reverses the commonly held idea that the planet is just lifeless rock and people are the most important inhabitants. According to the Gaia theory, Planet Earth herself is the one (albeit huge) living organism. Soil, water, air, and rock are the structure of the organism; plant and animal species living on earth are no different from the microscopic organisms living in our bodies. These proteins and bacteria inhabit and regulate our tissues, bones, and fluids in much the same way that algae, termites, and rain forests regulate the earth's water and atmosphere. Try thinking of your house as a living organism, responding to the weather, the environment, and the occupants.

A successful integration of architecture and landscape is no easy task. As we learned in the previous chapter, the selection of land and a building site demands thorough investigation, careful evaluation, and (ultimately) numerous compromises. The design of a house and its gardens is no different. It requires a thorough understanding of site resources, a carefully constructed program, and just as many compromises.

Environmental responsibility, appropriate technology, sustainable materials, feng shui, and common sense. These are the guidelines for our buildings.

CHAPTER FOUR

In Preparation for Building

S ITE CHOSEN, PLANS DRAWN, major decisions behind us. It's time to begin the process of building an environment. Our goal is to create a dwelling place that maximizes site resources both during and after its construction, ultimately improves the land on which it is built, and in the long term contributes to the health of the planet.

Like a garden, a house is not really planted in undisturbed ground, but rather on a carefully planned and prepared bed. The work of preparing the building site, although virtually invisible in the finished product, is just as critical to the ultimate success of the house as soil preparation is to the garden. Preconstruction work on a building site primarily entails grading for control of water runoff; laying underground lines for drainage, utility services, and waste disposal; trenching for foundations; and preparing of the subgrade for the building pad.

Let's carry the analogy of a living house one step further. Fruits, flowers, and vegetables all thrive in fertile soil—loose and well-drained—where roots can easily absorb vital nutrients. Plants need exposure to the proper amount of sunlight, air circulation, and an ample supply of water. A house must be planted in the right type of soil as well: firm for good bearing, yet well-drained for a solid foundation. Underground services such as water lines and utilities—the "feeder roots"—supply the house with vital "nutrients." Exposure to sunlight, good circulation, and the right amount of moisture in the air improves the functioning, or "respiration," of the house. In other words, when saying "site prep," think "seed bed."

Compostus Gigantus

Nothing short of drought or toxins inhibits plant growth to such a degree as compacted soil. Roots must expend so much energy trying to bore their way through hardpan that their very survival is in question. Nutrients are inaccessible and water runs off before it percolates downward into the root zone.

Nothing compacts soil around a job site so effectively as truck tires and tradespeople. Pickup trucks, work boots, sawhorses, and scaffold legs can convert once loose soil into hardpan in a matter of weeks. Trying to landscape hardpan is nearly as difficult as trying to landscape asphalt. Yet time after time we see houses completed, the debris hauled to the landfill, one-gallon plants stuck into two-gallon holes in the hardpan, bare ground dressed with an inch of redwood bark, and the project then deemed "fully landscaped." Like the roots in the soil, the life force of this type of house must struggle for survival.

The reality is that construction and equipment in this modern age are heavy. The soil around the building site will without doubt become compacted by the time the house is complete. The only prevention would entail extensive fencing, barriers, and hazard tape, all at the expense of construction efficiency, time, and money. Even with these precautions, however, some soil improvement after the construction has been completed would be required.

Let's strike a compromise with construction. If we accept the fact that soil compaction during construction is inevitable, we can at least protect the valuable topsoil by moving it out of the way, storing it in some safe place until we're ready to use it. In other words, let's plan so that our first step in the building process, preparing the building pad, relates to the last steps, planting the gardens and bringing the house to life.

Knowing the damage that construction can inflict on soil vitality, we've developed a point of view that sees an undisturbed job site as the ingredients for an enormous compost pile. This approach to site preparation is like brushing back a mound of leaves in the forest to make yourself a bed for the night. Visualize the bulldozer on the building pad as two hands delicately scraping grasses, fertile soil, and a million living organisms out of the way, to protect them from a herd of stampeding buffalo.

Compost is an extremely rich and fertile soil amendment created by the breakdown of organic material. In the same way that airborne yeasts convert sugar into fine wine, microscopic organisms in the soil convert vegetable matter into rich nutrients. When properly prepared, compost has an aroma as fine as a Napa Valley Chardonnay.

The first gentle swipes across the building pad will yield a valuable resource—topsoil—which should be saved for reuse later in the landscaping process.

Although compost is normally made out near the garden in small batches, this compost pile we are making will be as big as a house. Backyard compost piles are built of vegetable scraps, leaves, grass clippings, and possibly manure, with a little bit of soil added as an activator. Our big pile will be built of weeds, grasses, roots, and a bit more soil. Left to ferment for the duration of the construction, and turned and watered once or twice if possible, the revitalized soil will be ready for replacement around the house just about the time you're putting the finishing touches on the interior.

Your dozer operator will build this compost pile. Make sure he knows what your intentions are. You want him to "buff" off the site, that is, scrape off the groundcover and an inch or two of the soil. Determine where on the job site the pile will be out of everyone's way throughout construction. If it's late in the year and the soil has begun to dry out, add water to the pile as he's building it up. If you don't have water on site yet, consider hiring a water truck while building the pile. Moisture will greatly facilitate the decomposition of the organic matter; the pile will heat up better, and worms and microorganisms will multiply. Turning and watering the pile at least once during construction, when a tractor is on site for other purposes, will improve the homogeneity of the finished soil.

We'll discuss returning the reinvigorated earth in Chapter 12 of this book. For the next few months, maintain the image of your mountain of earth teem-

70

A well-instructed dozer operator can separate the topsoil from the less fertile mineral soil, yielding an eventual gold mine of compost.

ing with life—all of it living, dying, and decomposing for the benefit of the gardens.

The Catacombs—Underground Services

Underneath the well-planned sustainable house of the future, unseen by the naked eye, is a maze of access routes. Water comes and water goes. Winter rains can be stored for summer use. Conduits carry power, communications, and even two-way access to the information superhighway.

Planning is extremely important at this stage. You don't want to dig up the landscaping and gardens later on to add a forgotten service line, or regrade the site to divert an unanticipated seasonal creek. Some projects are large or complex enough that the local jurisdiction will require a grading and drainage plan drawn up by a licensed civil engineer before issuing a permit. On small projects, an experienced equipment operator, one with an engineering contractor's license, can determine drainage requirements and grade the site accordingly. In some situations water can be diverted around the building on the surface, in swales and ditches. In others, sumps, interrupter drains, and buried culverts may be called for. Whichever case applies, take the time and commit to the expense necessary to positively guarantee that rainwater runoff during a downpour will not back up against the building or (worse yet) flow into the garage or the front door. These are protective measures you can take on your own building site. For protection against more severe water problems (the river flooding or the dam breaking, for instance), build on high ground.

With grading and drainage accounted for, the other important element to site preparation is underground services. Although electric lines and phone lines used to enter a house draped from a power pole to the roof, more and more frequently these services are being placed underground along with water, gas, and sewage lines. The trenches for the electric and gas lines should be laid out over the shortest distance between two points, since losses due to friction can affect power output and necessitate an increase in pipe or wire size. Water line trenches should be laid out to service various stations along the way from the well or city meter to the main house. Sewage lines must connect to all fixtures within the house before heading straight for the septic tank or city connection. Drainage lines connect to roof drains and catch basins, then run downhill to "daylight," that point below the house where water from the pipes can flow on the surface.

If possible, dig all the trenches for both foundations and underground service lines during the first stages of construction.

The planning and mapping of these different service lines will vary considerably from project to project. Usually the septic tank is on one side of the house and the well on another. Frequently the outside services originate from a third direction. Anywhere lines cross, changes in trench depth must be accounted for. Power lines and water supply lines can vary in their distance from the surface, but sewer lines and drain lines must maintain a uniform "fall" from source to outfall. Prepare a diagram of the site with all of the service lines indicated. Use different colored pencils to represent each type of line.

Power lines and phone lines, typically buried 24 inches deep for protection from garden spades and tillers, run directly from the source of origin to the main panels in the house, the single greatest power demand. Other trenches then carry smaller conduits to the various shops, wells, garages, and outbuildings. Even within the building, shallow trenches and conduits may provide a shorter route from the main panel to subpanels and points of use than wires strung through the attic and frame walls.

Water lines are usually routed differently than power lines. Rather than running in a straight shot to the house before distribution, the main water line is tapped for branch lines, standpipes, and valve boxes along its way from the well or city meter to the point of entry at the house. Especially when gardens are an integral part of the built environment, thoughtful layout of irrigation systems at the planning stage will save time and money. Trenches are easy to dig on a wide-open site without the obstructions of buildings and walkways, and PVC pipe is inexpensive and simple to install. Try to plan for every location where you might want a hose bib, irrigation valve, or future water supply. You'll want water near the compost pile as well as in the garden, orchard, workshop, and fountain. Any trenches that service valve boxes, recirculating pumps, or sprinkler manifolds should also include a separate conduit for electricity. Automatic sprinker systems conserve both time and water by allowing irrigation to be programmed for the most advantageous hours of the day, typically early morning when evaporation rates are lower.

A final consideration for the underground service lines might be an attempt to second-guess the future. The relatively small expense of an additional 1-inch conduit in key trenches may prove very useful as your requirements for power or communications increase over time. Certainly, an extra service conduit from the utility company's power pole directly to the house, to be used for additional phone or cable lines, would be a wise investment.

Well laid-out and properly installed undergrounds at the start of construction will prevent trouble and extra work later on.

Pre-construction Organization

A construction site can be a real mess if you let it get away from you. On the other hand, careful planning and ordering of materials, timely delivery schedules, and frequent cleanups can save both time and money.

It's surprisingly easy to let the mess accumulate—a trench left open here, a box of nails there, a bucket of miscellaneous tools, reject 2x4's, form stakes, extra hardware, receipts stuck into nail bags rather than into a file, not to mention plain old trash. Before you know it, you're running out to the hardware store to buy another one of those "it was around here somewhere," the soda cans are mixed in with the wood scraps, and bent nails and lunch bags are everywhere.

Help! Not only is this mess unsightly, discouraging, and even depressing, it can be a safety hazard as well. Open trenches and carelessly discarded nail-laden boards can lead to accidents. In fact, safety is the most important reason to keep the job site clean, more important in the long run than efficiency or economy. Injuries, even minor ones, result in lost time, enthusiam, and productivity.

There are several important factors in job site organization. The first consideration is the arrival of building materials. Designate an area where supplies will be dropped off. This should be a location as close to the building as possible in order to shorten the distance materials must be hand-carried, but not so close that lumber piles may crowd the construction. Large items such as lumber, rebar, or palleted goods are usually safe left outside. Smaller items, such as bolts, hardware, fixtures, etc., are easier for someone to carry off and may require a lockable storage box. If your project does warrant a storage box or job shed, make sure to pick a location that won't crowd either the access to delivery trucks or the construction. A spot that's close to the temporary power pole is always convenient if possible. That way you can have light in the shed and possibly rig up a power distribution point that needn't be disassembled every evening.

Materials should be ordered far enough in advance to ensure all necessary items will be delivered and on hand for each given construction phase. Plan deliveries so that a second shipment won't inconvenience access to an earlier one. Also, try to separate orders so that materials required for the rough-in stages of construction will be fully utilized and the drop-off area cleaned up before you take delivery of finish materials. With good planning, the finish materials can be off-loaded directly into the structure, saving time and possible damage from weather or vandalism.

74

A clean, flat, easily accessible area near the building can save time as well as frustration.

Discipline yourself to complete each phase of construction before moving onto the next whenever possible. Complete the underground service lines with stubs on all conduits and piping so that trenches can be filled. Clean, pull nails, and oil the foundation forms after stripping; then stack them neatly, well out of the way for eventual reuse. Backfill and grade around the foundation when it's finished. Throughout the project, try to maintain a sense of completion and order. You'll have to struggle at times to avoid the temptation to jump to the next phase before the nuts are tightened, the framing clips nailed off, or the manifolds connected. Think of your endeavor as a sort of Zen and the Art of Housebuilding. Not only will you make fewer mistakes and lose less time, but you'll experience a sense of completion and accomplishment at key points along the way. These periodic milestones can re-energize you for the work ahead.

One possible scheme to assist you in keeping your project under control is to set aside a portion of one day every week to organize the site and finish up loose ends. Every Monday morning or Friday afternoon (or Saturday morning if you're as driven as we are), you might schedule a job site cleanup. This will be your chance to monitor progress, verify that construction details are being

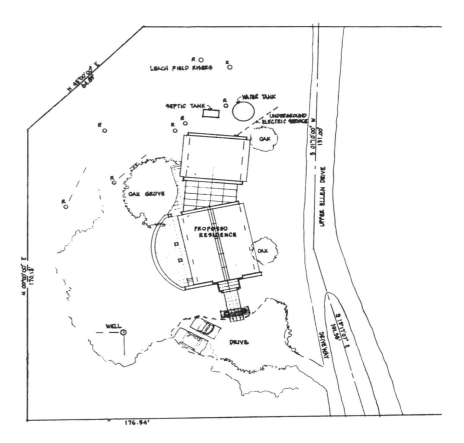

Sketch of a typical site plan.

completed, ascertain whether the required supplies for the week's work are on-site, jot down some notes and lists to yourself, check the site for safety hazards, and make a run to the dump. Frequent cleanups, although a hassle to people in a hurry, save time. They even add a sense of accomplishment to an undertaking that might otherwise border on the overwhelming.

CHAPTER FIVE

Foundations

(Facing page)
Foundation formwork
ready for concrete.

T̲HE FOUNDATION IS THE BASE on which the building stands. Its importance cannot be overemphasized. A business, a belief, and a building each need a strong foundation in order to survive. An earthwalled building, even more than a lightweight frame building, demands the strength and protection afforded by a well-designed foundation.

In one sense, the foundation is the anchor which secures the building to its location and restricts movement of the walls. In order to be effective, this anchor must be buried in the ground, its sides restrained by the inertia of the undisturbed earth which surrounds it. Just as the other aspects of vernacular architecture have evolved over time through a lengthy process of trial and error (the "survival of the fittest" notion), foundations, too, have been refined to accommodate the resources and requirements of the users.

The simplest and least expensive of foundation systems involves nothing more than locking the base of the wall into the earth; essentially beginning the construction of the wall a certain distance below grade. This approach works only in cases where either the climate is very dry or the wall material is not subject to deterioration from contact with moisture or soil organisms. Also, the ground under the wall must be firm enough to resist differential settling.

A more traditional and permanent foundation system involves the excavation of a trench somewhat wider than the wall and deep enough to extend below the depth of winter freezing. The trench is then filled with a matrix of large and small stones, to achieve good weight distribution, and the wall is built on top. In masonry construction, whether block or mortared stone, the irregular surface on top of the stone foundation results in a strong mechanical bond with the wall, an important consideration in seismic areas.

A variation on the rock foundation which has been used effectively in many applications is the "rubble-filled" trench with a poured-in-place concrete grade beam on top. The "rubble," normally gravel, road base, or crushed stone, uniformly distributes the weight of the walls over the full width of the trench. The concrete grade beam ties the wall system together at its base and makes the required strong connection between the walls and the footing. Where groundwater is significant or winter freezes severe, drain lines should be installed at the bottom of the trench and the water diverted either to daylight or to dry wells. The concrete beam should be poured high enough to lift the base of the walls above the surrounding ground to protect them against saturation.

In areas where the ground freezes during the winter, the rubble-filled trench type of foundation can yield major savings in both labor and materials. When wet soil freezes, it expands with enough force to lift even a heavy building. If moisture is allowed to accumulate underneath a foundation, and that saturated soil then freezes, serious structural damage can result. The greater the frost depth, the deeper the foundation must extend into the ground to be certain no freezing occurs underneath it. In some parts of the world, the frost depth is 8 feet or more. Compare the cost of filling a 9-foot trench with cracked rock to the expense of pouring concrete footings 9 feet into the ground and then constructing an 8-foot-high, water-impervious wall merely to bring the building to the point of starting the actual house walls!

Deep frost lines were a major contributor to the evolution of the full basement. If, in order to protect the building against possible frost damage, a foundation had to extend deep into the ground, why not make those foundation walls perform the additional function of defining a usable space? Rather than excavating only the trench to the required depth, builders began to excavate the entire building footprint, pouring foundations at the bottom of the trench, then constructing masonry walls to grade. The full basement became a furnace room, coal bin, root cellar, tornado shelter, and general storage room. It did, of course, add expenses to the overall project, but this extra cost was easily justified in that the homeowner benefitted in extra space from what would otherwise be merely solid underground walls built with only one function in mind.

Frank Lloyd Wright was an early proponent of the rubble-filled trench, especially because one of his goals was to simplify residential construction practices in order to reduce costs and make quality housing more accessible to the common man. Elimination of the full basement was a big step in that direction. Since many of Wright's early commissions were from clients in the upper Midwest, where frost lines are deep, his experiments with alternatives to solid foundation walls, specifically cracked limestone in deep trenches, resulted in big savings. Wright's "Usonian" house concept, refined throughout his career, achieved his goal of simplicity and affordability.

Concrete Foundations

The most common foundations today are built of reinforced, poured-in-place concrete. A concrete foundation typically is comprised of two parts: the spread footing and the stem wall. The footing distributes the weight of the building onto the earth below grade. The stem connects the walls of the building to the footing. The width of the footing is a factor of the load-bearing capacity of the soil on which the building is anchored. In very strong soils, the footing may be no wider than the wall itself, while in very weak soils, the footing may be twice or even three times as wide as the wall. Standard engineering guidelines assume soil strengths in the weak range, from 1,000 to 1,500 pounds per square foot (psf) bearing capacity. On the other hand, site investigations and testing by certified geologists may discover soil strengths on the order of 2,500 psf or greater. A significantly stronger soil, one that could justify narrower footing widths, allows you to pour narrower footings, thus saving money on concrete costs. Soils reports can be expensive, however, so before contracting with a geologist, try to determine the potential savings in concrete you could expect. Obviously, the larger the project, the greater the savings.

The footing can either be poured separately or in conjunction with the stem wall. Where frost depths require a deep footing, it is simpler to excavate the trench to the precise width designated by the engineering design, install the required reinforcing steel, and then pour concrete to the specified thickness directly into the trench. Form boards or form panels can then be set on top of the spread footing to the dimensions specified in the engineering. Where footings are shallower, it may be possible to complete the whole foundation system in only one concrete pour. In this case, forms for the stem wall are suspended above the footing trench on stakes which are pulled before the concrete in the footing has fully set.

Both the spread footing and the stem wall require horizontal reinforcing steel tied continuously around the perimeter of the building. Typically, three $\frac{1}{2}$-inch rebar are spaced evenly across the bottom of the footing trench, and two $\frac{1}{2}$-inch rebar are suspended 3 inches from the top of the stem wall. Intermediate horizontal courses of reinforcing steel are required if the distance between the top and bottom steel exceeds 18 inches. Unless engineering design or special seismic considerations warrant it, vertical reinforcing does not extend above the top of the stem wall.

After the building pad has been prepared, chalk lines indicate the building perimeter.

Trenches for the footings are dug to the width determined by local soil bearing pressures and the depth prescribed by local frost lines.

The distance between the form boards for the stem wall would normally be equal to the thickness of the wall to be constructed on top. To simplify erecting the cumbersome formwork for an earthwall, however, we have found that casting a narrow ledger into the top of the stemwall both increases the accuracy of the wall system and speeds up the construction. To create the ledger, a thin strip of wood is attached to the upper inside face of each top form board. We use either 1 x 2-inch lathing or strips of ¾-inch plywood ripped to 1½-inches. Nail the strips to the form boards once all the formwork is secured in place. The ledger strips allow you a final opportunity to ensure that the final grade is accurate and level. Remember to take into account the thickness of the ledger strips when setting the spacing between the form boards, and to include the thickness of the ledger when setting the outside building line. If plans call for a building that is 24 feet wide by 40 feet long, and your ledger strips are $\frac{3}{4}$ inch thick, then the outside form boards should be set at 24 feet, 1$\frac{1}{2}$ inches by 40 feet, 1$\frac{1}{2}$ inches apart.

An alternative to forming both sides of the stem wall is to pour what is known as a slab with thickened edge. Excavate the footing to the required width and depth, form only the outside perimeter of the building, then pour the concrete slab and footing at the same time. This method does have some additional complications associated with it—subgrade preparation and slab edge insulation among others—but in many cases it may prove to be more economical. Setting the formwork for the earthwalls becomes more complex without the stem wall and ledger to clamp against, but time and money saved in formwork and floor finishing may justify the extra time in form setting.

The strength of the connection between the earthwalls and the concrete foundation is a result of both mechanical bonding and the weight of the wall. To improve the mechanical bond between the base of the walls and the top of the stem, the concrete should be left very rough after it is poured. The deformations in the concrete serve as a field of mini-keyways into which the earth is locked as it is compacted. We prefer this roughened top to the alternative of casting a keyway in the concrete. Rebar dowels as a supplement to the roughened concrete are useful in high-wind or seismically active areas, but they also present a potential safety hazard. Unless they are critical to the security of the wall system, rebar dowels protruding from

With the trenches excavated and cleaned of loose soil, the reinforcing steel for the footing can be installed. Note the extremely heavy reinforcing schedule for this earthquake-susceptible location.

A stem wall is that portion of the foundation which extends above the ground. The earthwalls rest on the stem wall. Reinforcing dowels connect the wall to the foundation to resist movement in the event of a large earthquake.

82

In some cases, it is most economical to pour the foundation and the concrete slab floor at the same time. Here, one outside form board encircles the entire building perimeter, with reinforcing steel in place for both the slab and the wall system.

the foundation both complicate the ramming process and add risk to the construction.

A complete description of the steps involved in forming, pouring, and curing concrete foundations is beyond the scope of this text. Yet the quality and accuracy of the foundation work is of major importance to the success of any earthbuilt home. For all but the simplest of building designs, especially for projects on steeply sloping sites, obtaining the services of an experienced concrete contractor is strongly recommended. If, however, you do elect to construct your own foundation, or want to play an active role in supervising the contractor you hire to do it, we provide the following reminders and checklist:

The project begins to take shape with the foundation, both in form and in organization. You can set the tone of how well the project will be run by how smoothly you put together the various elements of the foundation and the underground services. This is one place where experience has taught us some valuable lessons, the first one being the importance of getting pipes, conduits, and other services into their permanent locations before any concrete is poured. Also, the efficiency with which the foundation is formed, poured, and stripped can have a big effect on your attitude. The most important aspect, of course, is how accurately the foundation is laid out, as mistakes at this stage will haunt you nearly every step of the way.

In some cases, the foundation is poured in stages: first the footing, then the stem wall, then the slab. In others cases, the footing, stem, and slab are poured as one unit. Which approach to take depends on several different considerations: wall construction system, site logistics, and flooring finish to name a few. The checklist below relates most closely to the system of pouring footings and stem wall as one unit, with the floor slab treated as a separate phase.

1. Meet with the plumber and electrician to clarify what portion of their work they want to install before the foundation is poured. Give them a schedule of the work.

2. Meet with the backhoe operator to make sure he understands the dimensions and depths of all trenches. Explain that you want the soil moved away from the foundation trenches, but left near the service trenches.

3. Check the batterboards for accuracy before digging.

4. Use a laborer working with the backhoe to keep all trenches straight-sided and flat-bottomed.

5. Check the depth and width of the trenches frequently. They must meet the dimensions on the plan, but should not exceed them. Foundation trenches that are too deep waste concrete. Trenches for plumbing waste lines must have the correct slope or "fall."

6. After completion of all excavations, reset string lines onto the batterboards and check that the trenches are accurate enough to accommodate the form boards.

7. Begin setting the form boards. First set, align, and brace the outside perimeter. Check line and level. Second, set the inside perimeter, using stakes to the ground and spreaders off the outside forms.
   Note: Drop the required pieces of horizontal reinforcing steel into the trench before beginning to set the inside form boards or else the spreaders will be in the way.

8. Oil the form boards before tying steel.

9. Install reinforcing steel. Set the bottom course on dobes (small manufactured concrete blocks, typically 3-inch cubes) and hang the upper course with tie wire. Maintain proper overlaps at all splices.

10. With the forms accurately in place, have the plumber and electrician install all of the required service lines.
    Note: Although chases can be placed in the bottom of the trench, we have found it more successful to install the services themselves before the pour.

11. Check that all the trenches are clean and that the steel is placed properly and not touching either the earth or the forms. Check all dimensions, especially column placement and door openings.

12. Call for inspection.

13. Order concrete and pump after passing inspection. Calculate concrete and add 10 percent as a margin of error. It is less expensive to purchase extra concrete than to run the risk of paying standby time for the pump and the labor while waiting around for a clean-up load.

14. If possible, set up an early morning pour to allow plenty of time for pulling stakes and cleanup.

15. Wet down trenches prior to the pour.

16. During the pour, make sure the reinforcing steel remains in its proper place.

17. Settle all concrete, either with a concrete vibrator or by tapping firmly and frequently on the form boards.
18. Make sure forms are full to the top. Use a wood float only on the top of the stem to ensure a good bond with the earth wall.
19. Clean up all spills and boils from the bottom of the form boards. Make sure all sleeves and exposed plumbing lines are free of concrete.
20. Pull all embedded stakes as soon as the concrete set allows.
21. Wet down concrete, spray with curing compound, or cover with plastic.
22. Clean up all tools and the site before departing.
23. Leave forms in place as long as is practical. Continue to cure concrete with water for at least seven days.

CHAPTER SIX

The Essential Soil

(Facing page) This
"geologic wall" at the
California Academy of
Science was created by
ramming different-
colored soils into strata
that resemble
sedimentary rock.

THE PLACE TO START with any type of earth construction is an understanding of soil, the friable material that covers the planet's land surfaces. Soil is a product of the decomposition of solid rock. Wind, water, ice, and microbes all act ever so slowly to turn rock into soil. So slowly, in fact, that the evolution of rammed earth, from hand tampers and heavy wooden forms to the technologically sophisticated wall systems of today, has, by comparison, occurred in the blink of an eye.

In nature there are three basic types of rock: igneous, sedimentary, and metamorphic. *Igneous* rock, as its name implies, is created through heat and fire. It was, before cooling and hardening, molten lava. *Metamorphic* rock has undergone structural change and reconsolidation due to extreme heat and pressure. It is basically a composite, a conglomerate material. *Sedimentary* rock has been created over thousands and millions of years through the gradual deposition and consolidation of loose soil. Rammed earth construction is very much like the natural creation of sedimentary rock. Layer by layer, soil is deposited and consolidated back into solid rock. The difference is that what nature has taken millennia to construct, tractors and pneumatic tampers can do in a minute, creating in effect an "instant antiquity."

All the different types of rock vary in their hardness, strength, and density. Simply speaking, the best soils for building rammed earth walls are those derived from the strongest rock. Granite, which is igneous in origin, is one of the hardest of rocks. Decomposed granite, if properly moistened and adequately compacted, can be rammed back into a granite of sorts, with cement stabilization replacing the high-temperature fusion that occurs within the earth's crust. Sedimentary rock types are not as strong as igneous, but soils derived from sedimentary rock also can be transformed into very adequate and durable walls.

Fine-grained soils yield smooth-surfaced walls. Gravelly or rocky soils can be compacted into strong walls, but the finished walls will have a coarser surface. Some rocks, such as shale and claystone, are neither durable in their natural form nor strong when reconstructed into rammed earth walls.

Soil Classification

Soil is classified by the size of its individual particles, not by its parent rock. Generally speaking, there are five basic soil types: gravel, sand, silt, clay, and organic. The five soil types are rarely found separately in nature. Rather, various combinations of particle sizes blend together over time to create soil mixtures: silty sand, clayey gravel, sandy gravel, etc. Which soil to use in constructing a rammed earth wall is a matter of availability, economics, and climate. Some soils, of course, are far more suitable than others.

Soil particles range in size from microscopically small to 3 inches in diameter (particles larger than 3 inches are called boulders or simply rock). The smallest of soil particles are clays, which are less than .0002 inch in diameter. The largest soil particles are gravels, ranging from $\frac{1}{2}$ inch to 3 inches in diameter. Between these two are the silts and sands. Individual particles of silt are too small to be seen with the unaided eye. They are powdery to the touch, like wheat flour. In fact, silt is sometimes called "rock flour." Sand particles vary in size from about $\frac{1}{4}$ inch to the smallest grain you can see with the naked eye. Organic soils are a product of the decomposition of once-living matter. They are dark and spongy, virtually impossible to stabilize, and, in all but the smallest percentages, totally unsuitable for earthwall construction.

To recombine into a strong and durable rammed earth wall, a soil should be a well-graded blend of different-sized particles. Large particles provide the bulk of the matrix, while the smaller particles fill in the spaces. With ever-decreasing particle sizes, virtually all of the air space within the wall matrix can be eliminated, resulting in the densest wall possible. Density is one of the contributors to ultimate wall strength.

Clay

The first soil component to investigate is clay. In traditional rammed earth, clay was the binder that held the other particles together. It is a natural, earthy material that is sticky when wet but hard when dry. Clay expands with the addition of water and shrinks as the water evaporates. Individual particles of clay are actually flat, like a dinner plate. These plates are electrically charged and act like small magnets to attract water molecules to the surface of the plates. The expansion that takes place within a clay soil when it is moistened is a result of the accumulation of water between the individual plates of clay.

There are many different kinds of clay. Some of them will shrink and swell enormously, while others are dimensionally stable. Clays that do not shrink and swell extensively, such as kaolinite, laterite, and montmorillonite, are excellent binders for a rammed earth wall. Bentonite clay, on the other hand, which is so expansive it is frequently used to stop water leaks in ponds and retaining walls, is unsuitable for building rammed earth.

The proper proportion of clay in the soil is essential to the ultimate quality of the wall. Correct percentages of clay bind the other, structural soil components together in a dimensionally stable matrix, resulting in a durable and long-lasting wall. Too little clay and the soil components won't hold together. Too much clay, and the wall will shrink and crack as it dries. Although shrinkage cracks do not in themselves result in a weakening of the wall, when the wet season returns and moisture penetrates into the cracks, the soil will re-expand. After only a few seasons of expansion and contraction, the wall will begin to experience accelerated deterioration.

Clay particles actually work in two different ways to strengthen the soil in a rammed earth wall: one chemical, the other mechanical. Chemically, clay acts like a glue to bind together the other components. The clay-and-water solution actually envelops each of the soil particles (much like Portland cement and water in concrete). As the solution dries it creates a very strong bond between individual grains of sand and gravel. It has locked them together with a chemical glue.

Mechanically, moistened clay works like a lubricant to allow the other particles to slip and slide against each other under the repeated blows of the rammer. The better the lubrication, the tighter the final configuration of the individual particles within the matrix and the denser the finished wall.

Silt

Silt is composed of microscopically small particles of pulverized rock—hence the descriptive imagery of silt as "rock flour." Unlike clay, silt is chemically inactive. It does not have a magnetic charge to attract water, and thus it will not expand when wet. Particles of silt will contribute to the overall density of a wall, but, since they are not sticky, they do not contribute to the binding together of the other particles nor to the ultimate strength of the wall. Actually, too great a percentage of silt in the mix will weaken the wall, for two different reasons: one mechanical, the other purely mathematical. Mechanically speaking, individual grains of silt are not angular enough to lock together against other particles. Silt particles, which are more or less rounded, just don't have the edges, bumps, shoulders, and various other surface deformations that sand and gravel particles have. Building a wall of silt is a little like trying to stack up a pile of marbles.

The mathematical case against silt as a strong wall component is based on the fact that the total combined surface area of all particles in any given volume of material increases factorially as the average particle size decreases. In other words, the higher the percentage of small particles (silt) in the soil, the greater the surface area to be covered with the clay-and-water (or cement-and-water) glue. When silt content exceeds a certain proportion, there just isn't enough glue to go around.

Sand

Sands are the fine grains broken or eroded from various types of rocks, most commonly from quartz, a very hard mineral composed of silica (SiO_2). Sand particles range in size from $\frac{1}{4}$ inch in diameter to the smallest grain that can be seen with the naked eye. They can be almost any shape: round, flat, or angular. When compacted, sand particles create a dense soil matrix. By themselves, sands will not hold together, but when glued with either cement or clay, they are the primary structural aggregate in a rammed earth wall.

Pure sand is found in streambeds, on beaches, in deserts, and in areas once covered by glaciers. Sand, in some proportion or other, is found in almost all soil blends.

Gravel

Gravels are the coarse pieces of cracked or broken rock. They range in size from $\frac{1}{4}$ inch in diameter and upwards. At a certain size, somewhere between about $\frac{1}{2}$ inch and 3 inches, people quit using the term "gravel" and start calling it simply "rock." At most quarries we deal with, "pea gravel" is $\frac{3}{8}$ to $\frac{1}{2}$ inch in diameter and "drain rock" is $\frac{3}{4}$ inch to 2 inches. Material larger than 2 inches might be called cobbles, boulders, or rip-rap. For the purposes of rammed earth construction, gravel is that component with particle sizes larger than sand and small enough that you don't feel the impulse to pick up individual pieces with your hand and toss them out of the mix.

Each grain of sand or gravel possesses the structural characteristics and strength of the rock from which it came. Strong individual soil particles contribute to a strong earthwall, as does a well-distributed variety of particle sizes. As stated earlier, the best earthwalls are built with a well-graded soil.

The Quest for Suitable Soil

The proper selection of soil is critical to the quality of a rammed earth wall. Some soils may yield walls that appear to have good characteristics when first completed, and yet over time prove to be unsatisfactory.

The logical point to begin our research into which soils are best suited for building new rammed earth walls is to look at old walls. What is the typical composition of the soil that was used to construct walls that have survived for a century or more? It turns out that most of the world's oldest rammed earth walls were constructed with basically the same soil composition—roughly 70 percent sand and 30 percent clay. Need we look further?

The answer, unfortunately, is yes we do. Most of the world's soil is not composed of 70 percent sand and 30 percent clay. In fact, soil varies enormously from region to region, even from one side of a valley to the other, and from the top of a hill to the bottom. Finding a suitable soil right beneath the spot on which you have chosen to build your house is like finding money buried there. The reality is, most of the soils we have encountered in our work are too high in clay content to be used as they naturally occur. Hence the need to understand the range of suitable soils and the means to amend those soils that are less than ideal.

To use some of the terminology spoken around the counter at the local farm supply store, we can say that sandy clays or clayey sands make good walls. Even gravelly clay will work. Loams and other agricultural soils are typically too fine-grained to be made durable, without excessive cement stabilization. "Gumbo"—a fine, silty soil that forms a sticky mud when wet—is totally unsuitable. The terminology used by geologists and civil engineers to describe soil is different from that used by farmers, and it focuses on structure rather than tilth.

In concrete construction, sand and gravel are the structural aggregates, while cement and water make the glue. In rammed earth construction, sand and gravel are also the primary aggregates, and clay and water act as the glue. Portland cement added to a soil mixture will contribute to increased strength, durability, and moisture resistance, but it is not an absolutely necessary admixture in constructing durable walls, as history has shown us. French pisé de terre structures have lasted for hundreds of years in extreme weather conditions with no stabilizers other than those that occur naturally in the local soil.

When a soil available on or very near a building site has roughly suitable characteristics for wall building—some sand, a little silt, and a bit too much clay, for instance—it can be modified by the addition of a small amount of extra sand at a reasonable cost. A soil with too much sand and not enough clay can be modified either by blending with another soil which is too high in clay or by the addition of cement. Within limits, both financial and geographic, marginal soils can be made suitable. If, on the other hand, your building site yields pure sand or pure clay, the soil may require so much amendment that you would be better off rejecting the site soil altogether and searching for other sources.

There is one other reason, separate from structure and durability, to launch a quest for the ideal soil: looks. The physical appearance—both color and texture—of a raw earth wall is one of the primal delights of building with rammed earth. When walls are left unplastered, they impart a "natural" character to interior spaces that really can't be duplicated by any other material or system. Variations in color and texture are seen as enhancements, signatures of the process. Bare walls reveal the layering of the soil strata, the subtle imperfections, and the human hand. They tell their own story.

A soil with all the right characteristics, both structural and aesthetic, for building walls that need no further surface treatment represents major financial as well as aesthetic benefits. The walls are essentially finished as soon as the formwork is removed. No time or money need be invested in either plaster or paint. Best of all, with costly wall treatment avoided in the first place, there is never the need for repairs or for repainting. Over time, the cost of this periodic maintenance can mount up, not to mention the inconvenience of protecting the landscaping against the building during painting. Natural earth walls, built properly, need no more maintenance than do brick walls. Plant material can be allowed to envelop the house if desired. Imagine the freedom of owning a building whose walls never need painting!

The jar test for determining rough percentage of fines in the soil.

Narrowing the Quest

How do we find this dream soil? First, look close to home. In our discussion in chapter 2 on choosing a building parcel, we listed soil as one of the important criteria for a good home site—a healthy, organic soil for vigorous plant life, and a strong mineral soil for free wall material. If you're very lucky, both soils will satisfy your requirements.

The organic soil (the topsoil) is relatively easy to assess. Feel it, smell it, look around and see how vigorously plants grow in it. The mineral soil (or subsoil), on the other hand, demands a more thorough and involved evaluation. Samples must be carefully obtained and tested for composition and strength. Simple field tests are a legitimate point of beginning, but verification of the field observations by geotechnical testing laboratories should be completed before you undertake any major construction.

The mineral soil, your hoped-for wallbuilding material, lies beneath the relatively thin layer of topsoil and on top of the bedrock that forms the earth's structural plates. The topsoil layer varies in thickness from region to region; in some places it is no more than a few inches deep, in others several feet. Mineral soil also varies in depth, but in most instances it is clearly differentiated from the topsoil.

To obtain samples of the mineral soil on any given site, dig down through the topsoil layer, using either a shovel or posthole auger. At the bottom of this topsoil layer, either the color or composition of the soil will visually change. When you have reached the mineral layer, gather a small amount of the soil to be evaluated (a five-gallon bucket's worth is adequate), and label the sample with its locale and depth. The soil may change with depth. Keep all samples that appear different labelled separately. Samples should be taken from several locations on the proposed site. Cut banks along driveways or gullies may provide easier access for gathering samples than boring through topsoil.

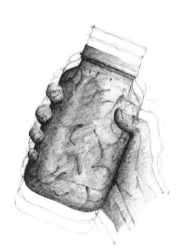

Soil Testing in the Field

An important first piece of information to look for when evaluating a soil is the ratio of coarse particles to fines. A simple technique for obtaining a preliminary assessment of the percentages of clay and sand in any given soil is the "jar test." It can be performed easily and quickly on a number of soil samples. Here's how we do it:

> Place about 2 cups of the soil to be tested into a quart jar. Fill the rest of the jar with water, shake it until all of the soil is in solution, and then let it stand for a few hours or until the water is clear. The sand particles will settle to the bottom more quickly because they are heavier. The silt and clay will settle out more slowly, resting on top of the sand. The line between the sand and the clay/silt layers should be clearly visible. By measuring and comparing the thickness of the two layers, you can roughly determine the ratio of fine to coarse particles.

In this admittedly rough and preliminary test, it is difficult to differentiate between clay and silt since both settle slowly, rest on top of the sand, and are virtually indistinguishable from one another in appearance. Broadly speaking, if the layer of fine particles is roughly one-half to one-quarter as thick as the layer of sand, then the material can be considered a contender in the suitability contest. The next round of testing can then be scheduled.

If, however, the jar appears to have no fine layer at all, or, conversely, appears to be all fines, with the water still cloudy a day after shaking, then you will need to seek alternate sources of soil for building. If the layering in the jar shows a nearly suitable ratio, and the color is right for you, then the alternate sources to investigate would be in the form of an amendment material: clay soil if the jar test shows too great a percentage of sand, or a sand supplier if the jar is too full of clay. If the ratio of coarse to fine in the jar is far from suitable and the color is also not right, then the alternate source should be a soil that is usable on its own as a building material, not merely an amendment.

In some lucky instances, the results of the jar test may be encouraging enough to allow you to proceed directly to the construction of sample blocks and cylinders. The blocks will be used to test weathering characteristics, and the cylinders will be used to test wall strength. They'll also start to give you an idea of how the finished walls might look.

In unlucky instances, the results of the jar test are inconclusive or downright discouraging. At this point, you may decide to enlist the aid of a geotechnical testing laboratory to assess the properties of your soil. On the other hand, as a future earth builder you may feel compelled to become more knowledgeable about soil in general. Certainly as an owner of an earth house you will be called upon more than once to tell the story of its creation. What better way to begin your story than with a scholarly discussion on the nature of soil?

To further your knowledge of soil mechanics, please take the time to read Appendix A at the back of this book. It includes an informative and understandable excerpt from the *Handbook for Building Homes of Earth*, Bulletin #21 of the Texas Transportation Institute, authored by Professors Wolfskill, Dunlap, and Gallaway. I first met Dr. Wayne Dunlap in 1980, at a gathering of earthbuilding enthusiasts in Tucson, Arizona. His complete understanding of soil mechanics was enlightening. His thoroughly enjoyable presentation, on what might otherwise been a rather dry subject (no pun intended), has to this day inspired my own interest in the science of soil.

Laboratory Testing

The procedures described by Professor Dunlap and his colleagues in Builders' Resource C, in conjunction with the data in the table on pages 244–46, do provide the necessary information to select a suitable soil. Even the simple jar test yields enough raw data to undertake a small pilot project. Certainly, throughout the history of rammed earth building, preconstruction testing was virtually unknown. A soil was dug, a building was built, and time was the test. Where soils were naturally suitable, rammed earth became the construction method of choice. Where soils were unsuitable, buildings deteriorated after only a few years, and the contractor either sought a new profession or left the area.

Today we have the advantage of very sophisticated laboratory-testing procedures available at a reasonable cost. These tests can determine not only the composition of the soil, but also the shrinkage characteristics, the moisture requirements, the density, and, best of all, the ultimate compressive strength of the finished wall. For the investment of a few hundred dollars, you can establish with relative confidence that your "free" building material will consolidate into wall components that will serve the needs of your family and of generations to come.

For most of our projects in California, where seismic safety is critical, we are required by local building departments to provide test data on the wall material prior to construction. We enlist the services of a geotechnical testing laboratory to perform a *sieve analysis* (also known as a *grain size distribution test*) and compressive tests of cylinders made from the proposed mix design. Specifications that accompany all construction documents submitted for building permits define the range of suitable materials and the minimum compressive strength of the test samples. In addition to preconstruction testing, during the course of wall construction we compact test cylinders from the various batches of soil being placed in the forms and then test these cylinders after they have cured for a month. In some counties, we are even required to take cores from the finished wall and test the cores to verify that the material in place conforms to the stated design strength. In other words, the engineering design approach for building structural walls of earth in earthquake country is extremely conservative.

To be conservative when building with earth is a wise thing. It involves careful testing, construction in accordance with the proper procedures, and protection of the finished walls with adequate drainage and roof overhangs. To be *extremely* conservative, however, can often prove expensive. We are mandated by current design guidelines to pour extra-wide footings, incorporate reinforcing steel in the wall system, and decrease the spacing on the bolts anchoring the roof to the wall. Yet, in California today there are perhaps a hundred earthwalled buildings that have survived earthquake damage for a century or more—all built without cement, steel, or roof bolts, and some without even

On-site testing of the soil mix during wall construction is performed by a special licensed inspector.

foundations. To be sure, some earth buildings (more precisely, some *parts* of some earth buildings) have not survived the earthquakes. Engineers can study these failures (or partial failures) and use the lessons learned to improve design procedures for new earth construction. They can extract pieces of the old walls, test these pieces in the lab, determine their composition and strength, and then make recommendations for new mix designs.

Another thing the laboratory can test for is the shrinkage characteristics of the soil. Since a sieve analysis does not differentiate between clay and silt, a further series of tests are necessary when the ratio of fine particles in the soil exceeds 30 percent. The *Atterburg limit tests* will determine the amount of clay in the soil and whether this clay will be harmful in construction. Two separate tests are involved: The *liquid limit test* measures the moisture content in percent of dry soil weight at which the soil changes from a plastic to a liquid state; the *plastic limit test* measures the moisture content in percent of dry soil weight at which the soil changes from a solid to a plastic state. The numerical difference between the liquid limit and the plastic limit is a value known as the *plasticity index*. The lower the plasticity index, the less the shrinkage of the finished wall.

A final test that either you or the laboratory may conduct is a *lineal shrinkage* test. Basically, a rectangular wooden mold like a bread pan, approximately 2 inches square and 12 inches long, is filled with the proposed soil mix and allowed to dry. The shrinkage is measured and calculated as a percent of the length of the mold. This percentage will allow you to predict the shrinkage in the full sections of wall.

Our recommendation to prospective earth builders is to approach the selection of suitable soil with patience and thoroughness. Gather various soil samples from your building site and other nearby sources. Study these samples using the jar test and the procedures described by Professor Dunlap (see Builders' Resource C) in order to increase your knowledge and familiarity with soil science, and to make a preliminary determination of suitability. Construct test blocks and cylinders from what you believe are the most promising of the soils or soil blends. Then, after selecting what appear to be the best of the best, send samples of this material and the cylinders to the laboratory for confirmation of your own findings.

Constructing Test Blocks and Test Cylinders

Test cylinders are tubes of compacted earth that are round in cross-section (as the name implies). To conform to standard testing procedures for concrete, their height should be twice their diameter. We typically cast 3 x 6-inch cylinders in either special plastic molds purchased from our testing laboratory or in 6-inch-long sections of 3-inch ABS sewer and drain pipe. Although the lab is more used to handling the 3-inch cylinders, a smaller mold—2-inch ABS pipe cut into 4-inch sections—will allow you to obtain a greater number of samples from a given batch of material. Make one saw cut lengthwise down the ABS mold to allow for extraction of the sample after casting. During compaction, the mold is held together with two or three stainless steel hose clamps.

The samples must be cured slowly to accurately represent the wall. The plastic molds come with caps so that curing takes place within the mold. To cure the samples extracted from the ABS molds, wrap them in plastic or place them in sandwich bags. Samples are typically broken at seven, fourteen, and twenty-eight days. The early breaks are to determine that strengths are adequate to continue with construction. The last breaks are called the "ultimate" strength, although in fact rammed earth continues to increase in strength with age.

Test blocks are helpful to the decision-making process for a number of reasons. The flat surface of a block is much more representative of the finished wall than a cylinder. The texture and color of different samples are easier to compare flat than round. The flat blocks can be used to evaluate different surface sealers and treatments, and (perhaps most importantly) the blocks can be subjected to various accelerated exposure and weathering tests to determine how the walls will hold up over time and how they might look after a few decades.

The test blocks are made in a wooden form held together with ½-inch bolts. The small wooden form is made of the same components as the full-size wallbuilding form, with the exception that walers are not required if the block is 12 inches or less in width. We make two different-sized test blocks for different applications. One is about 5 x 6 inches x 1½ inches thick, the other about 12 x 16 inches x 3½ inches thick. The small ones sit around on tables and desktops as examples of the range of soil types. We ship them to potential clients who ask about available colors. The larger ones sit out in the garden, wetting and drying in the rain and the sprinklers. If a test block begins to erode when subjected to a heavy spray from the hose, and the soil is intended for building in a rainy climate, this soil should be stabilized.

Sample blocks give homeowners a chance to see some available wall colors.

Stabilization

Stabilization is defined as the elimination of change, the creation of a steady physical state. Within the context of rammed earth construction, stabilization is the elimination of the change in volume that occurs in a soil as it absorbs and discharges water. Stabilization does not always mean the addition of cement, because in some soils and under ideal conditions, it is possible to compact the soil tightly enough to create a wall which will resist moisture absorption and hence the tendency to expand in volume.

The key word here is ideal. An ideal soil is one in which colloidal cementation supplements thorough compaction. Colloids, although not specifically defined in our description of soils above, are a sort of natural "gelatin" found in clay soils. Ramming earth massages the colloids into action in much the same way that kneading bread dough works up the gluten in flour. Compaction and colloidal cementation have proven successful in all the world's ancient rammed earth structures.

In another, very broad sense of the word, the addition of soil amendments can "stabilize" a soil against volumetric change. For instance, if a site soil is so high in clay content that it cannot be made to resist expansion when wet, the addition of an appropriate amount of sand will bring the blended soil within a range where compaction and natural cementation will result in stabilization. Conversely, a sandy or gravelly soil, although certainly not susceptible to expansion when wet, will just not hold together without some sort of glue. Mixing the proper proportion of a soil high in clay with the sandy site soil can create a usable blend which will prove adequate without other stabilizers.

Within the modern context of earth construction, however, a stabilizer is not raw clay, but rather manufactured or processed additives, such as asphalt emulsion, hydrated lime, or Portland cement. The primary function of these stabilizers is to increase the resistance to moisture of the finished wall. Asphalt emulsion, used mainly in adobe brick construction, reduces absorptivity, but does not appreciably increase the strength of the bricks. Portland cement, used in making pressed blocks and in rammed earth, both reduces absorptivity and increases strength. Hydrated lime reacts chemically with clay to alter its expansiveness, which in turn improves its natural stability.

For practically all of our work in the United States, we add Portland cement to the soils we use. Relatively small percentages of cement, one to two sacks per cubic yard of earth, can increase the strength of a finished wall by as much as five times what it would be if composed of raw earth. This increased strength is demanded by engineers, building officials, and most homeowners, especially where seismic activity is prevalent. To be sure, the historical record of raw earth buildings indicates that unstabilized walls do survive earthquakes when constructed following certain design principles. Cement stabilization, however, provides a much needed psychological and mathematical safety factor.

In high rainfall areas, cement stabilization can make the difference between an enduring building and a mishap. Many people think of earthwalled structures as primarily suited to dry climates. In fact, earthbuilders from antiquity to the present have claimed that "all an earthwall needs is a good hat and a good pair of boots." The truth is that, with ample roof overhangs (hats) and raised foundations (boots), clay walls have long endured the wet weather prevalent north of the forty-second parallel. It's just that cement can help make a secure wall even stronger, again providing an important psychological safety factor.

Cement stabilization also allows for the use of earthwalls as garden elements. Without the protection afforded by a roof, freestanding walls made of raw rammed earth would deteriorate too rapidly to justify their construction. They might survive a few years in some regions, a few decades in others. In either case, without cement they would begin to lose their edges and surfaces, sloughing onto the paths and plant material at their base. But with cement, earthwalls can be permanent and wonderfully harmonious in a landscape design. Small garden projects are actually a great way to experiment with rammed earthbuilding and learn its techniques.

The Case for Importing Soil

There are those situations where the soil on-site is just not suitable for wallbuilding without extensive modification. It may be too rocky, too heavy in clay, too contaminated with tree roots and other debris, or have some other problems that make it more costly to use than it would be simply to import all the soil from elsewhere. Screening rocks and roots out of soil can require days of labor and equipment. Amending a site soil with sand can be expensive, since clean, washed sand, purchased from a gravel plant, is sometimes twice the price of other quarry products. Certain soil types, especially fine-grained silts and clays, take a long time to mix and are slow to compact. They require greater amounts of water for optimum compaction, which in turn increases their likelihood of shrinking and cracking as the walls dry.

For these reasons, the costs of cleaning or amending an on-site soil should be carefully compared with the cost of importing a ready-to-use soil material. Soil purchased from a quarry is usually not very expensive as long as it has not been washed. The single biggest expense of an imported soil is typically transportation. With luck, a suitable soil may be found very near the job site and hauling costs will be minimal. In some instances, local excavators or swimming pool contractors may be working on projects where they have material to dispose of and will deliver the overburden to your job site for little or nothing.

Next to structural composition, the appearance of the finished wall system is perhaps the most important consideration in selecting a soil. Color and texture vary widely from one soil type to another. Finding a good import will take some looking. Throughout our years of searching out soils that yield both durable and attractive earth walls, we have found quarries to be the most reliable source. Most quarries sell a product classified as road base or structural backfill, composed mainly of sand and gravel with 10 to 20 percent clay. These soils usually require cement as a supplemental binder, but they result in strong finished walls, albeit somewhat coarse in appearance due to the gravel. Road base and backfill materials cost considerably less than clean sand that has been washed to remove the clay and silt. Of additional value is the fact that, in many cases, the quarry will have test data on the grain size distribution of the materials they sell.

Another product we have found good for wallbuilding is "quarry fines," a leftover from screening decorative rock. The fines—actually a blend of clay, silt, fine sand and small gravel—are what remain after the saleable rock has been shaken out of the bulk soil. These quarry fines are higher in clay than road base, but are usually within the acceptable range. Even if they are slightly above 30 percent clay, a small amount of added sand will control the shrinking. The real benefit of the quarry fines we buy is the price. Since it is a waste material, we can buy it for less than half the cost of road base or backfill.

There are several other advantages to using quarry-produced materials for building cement-stabilized walls. One is the experience factor. Using a familiar material eliminates the preconstruction testing and the uncertainties that accompany a new soil. Multiple projects using the same material give wall builders the chance to become knowledgeable in the specific idiosyncrasies of the material, specifically optimum moisture level for ideal compaction.

A second advantage to using road base and backfill materials is their dependably low clay content. Low clay ratios virtually guarantee that the soil is nonexpansive and will not stick to the forms or crack as it dries. Cement will compensate for the low clay content.

A third advantage to road base, backfill, and amended fines are that they tend to mix and compact more quickly than clod-filled site soils. Shorter mixing and compacting times means lower installation costs, especially when equipment is being rented and laborers are being paid. In some cases, importing soil may actually result in lower overall wall costs. If walls built from site soil are so visually unattractive that they require plaster, then importing may prove by far the least expensive option.

One final advantage to importing is the opportunity that using a known material affords the builder in negotiating new projects. With completed wall systems available for inspection, the architect and future client can make informed choices.

The Environmental Side

Importing tons of soil dozens of miles in diesel-guzzling trucks seems to fly in the face of the environmental side of building with earth. The rationale behind importing material, though, is based on the full life-cycle cost of an earthwall constructed from an ideal soil. Take the total cost of fuel to transport 200 cubic yards of soil from a quarry 20 miles from our job site; say, $250. Add a "green tax" to the price of the fuel to compensate for environmental pollution; say 100 percent. Then divide the total, $500 (let's call them greenbacks), by the number of years the wall system can be expected to remain serviceable, say conservatively 500 years. The resulting number, one greenback, is the cost per year of wall life attributable to transportion cost.

This number takes into account only the expenses associated with the one-time transportation of the soil material. Maintenance expenses can also affect the overall life-cycle cost. Say we used a site soil to build the walls, saving the initial 500 greenbacks. But if the walls built with site soil were unsatisfactory to the degree that they needed stucco or plaster, then we would have an additional investment in greenbacks for the interior and exterior coating—transportation, metal lathe, sand, cement, fuel for the plaster mixer, etc. Worse yet, stucco and plaster need to be repaired and/or replaced periodically, say once every fifty years, adding more greenbacks each time.

Environmental doomsayers predict that the rate of inflation of the greenback will be exponential in the decades ahead. Investing in long-term, low-maintenance systems today is a wise strategy. In other words, the payback on greenbacks is good.

Pondering the question of the appropriate soil.

A Final Word on Soil

As a building material, earth can't be beat. Inexpensive, available, healthy, it can be converted into durable wall systems that will survive for centuries. Working with earth is simple in one sense, but very complex in another. Soil is so diverse, its properties and reactions so widely variable, that to fully understand its uses and limitations, and to build with it successfully, takes years of study and experience. Civil engineers understand density and moisture content. Agronomists comprehend porosity and tilth. Geologists speak of composition and classification.

Earthbuilders must know it all. Take your time.

CHAPTER SEVEN

The Art of Formbuilding

F{OR CENTURIES}, the forms used to build rammed earth structures have varied little: two wooden side pieces, no larger than two men could easily move, and two end pieces the width of the wall, all held together by post-and-rope crossties. This formwork is still in use today in parts of Asia and Africa, and was used as recently as the 1960s in America, with the substitution of steel bolts for the rope ties.

Building with rammed earth is a little like making adobe bricks, except the forms are larger, the earth is drier, and the bricks are never moved. Sundried adobe bricks are poured into molds set on the ground, left to cure, then laid up into a wall with mortar. Rammed earth is pounded into forms set in place on the foundation. Once the form is full, it is moved to a new position along the wall. The blocks of earth are never moved, nor is any mortar required to bind them together. The force of ramming provides the bond between adjacent sections of wall.

Formwork is a major part of building with rammed earth. In fact, the time spent setting, aligning, and stripping the forms is usually greater than the time spent transporting and compacting the earth within the forms. For this reason, the efficiency of the forming system is key to the quality and affordability of building with rammed earth.

The traditional approach to building rammed earth has been used on every continent except Antarctica, and has remained essentially unchanged for two thousand years or more. The perimeter walls of the building are defined on the ground, either by constructing some type of foundation or by marking a line in the dirt. The two form panels and two endboards are erected at some chosen starting point along the building line. Layers of moist soil are then placed into

106

CRATERRE

CRATERRE

(Top) Traditional rammed earth formwork, such as this in use in Morocco, was comprised of simple components. (Bottom) Once the form was filled and compacted, it was moved horizontally along the wall.

the formwork and compacted until the form is full. Once full, it is disassembled and repositioned along the building line, one end clamped against the section just completed, the other end closed off with an endboard. This process is continued around the perimeter of the building to complete the first level (course) of wall sections. The formwork is then lifted to rest on top of the first course and the process is continued around the perimeter a second time, followed by a third, a fourth—as many passes as necessary to obtain the desired wall height. Each successive circumnavigation of the building results in raising the walls approximately 2 feet. The higher the walls, the more difficult setting the formwork becomes and the greater the inaccuracies in plumb and line.

My personal attraction to the rammed earth method began with a self-imposed challenge to improve the formwork. The first time I built with rammed earth, I used the traditional formwork; heavy wooden side and end panels held together with ½-inch threaded bolts spaced 2 feet apart in each direction. The walls we built on that first project were fine—magical in fact—but setting and disassembling the formwork was so slow and cumbersome that it must have taken three times as long to set each section of wall as it did to ram it. There had to be a better way. As a university-trained industrial engineer, I saw the opportunity to redesign the forming system for rammed earth construction, and by so doing make affordable housing once again available to humanity. You might say I took it on as my "calling."

Twenty years later, the formwork has been redesigned (several varieties in fact), and a revitalized rammed earth construction is indeed available to humanity. The affordability issue, however, has not quite been solved. Rammed earth is a labor-intensive method of construction. High labor rates in

This series depicts the evolution of the Rammed Earth Works (REW) forming system, from heavy wooden forms with bolt connections through the various refinements of the pipe clamp and wide waler approach.

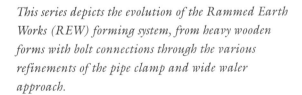

this country keep the cost of a rammed earth wall comparable to or even higher than wood-frame construction. On an owner-builder project, where "sweat equity" can reduce mortgage investment, rammed earth can result in significant cost savings; but as long as timber production fails to reflect its true costs to the environment, contractor-built rammed earth will remain at premium price levels.

Modern Formwork

Advances in forming technology have increased the efficiency and quality with which rammed earth walls can be built. Today, with the help of front-loading tractors, pneumatic tampers, and well-designed formwork, earth walls can be built in a fraction of the time it used to take. Under good conditions it is possible for a crew of four workers to complete 300 square feet of wall per day, compared to the 40 or 50 square feet per day typical for a four-person crew working with hand tampers and baskets.

Rammed earth builders in Australia and the American Southwest use a type of formwork similar to that employed for poured-in-place concrete. Form panels are normally 2 x 8-foot sheets of plywood mounted on steel frames; form ties are either steel bolts or straps installed every 24 inches horizontally and vertically. The Australian rammed earth builders have had more success at re-introducing earth construction to the marketplace than any group of builders in the United States. Over the past twenty years the industry there has grown to capture as much as 20 percent of the new home market in some areas. The reliability of the Australian formwork is a big part of this success.

The Australians build individual freestanding panels of solid earth that extend to the full height of the finished wall. Adjacent panels are keyed together on the sides and spanned with a continuous wooden sill plate at the top. The form system is comprised of tall endboards and 2-foot-high face panels. The endboards are first set in place along the foundation, defining the length of the wall section to be built, then secured plumb using adjustable form-aligning braces. The first pair of face panels are set directly on the foundation and clamped tight against the endboards. Tapered steel rods, threaded on both ends, pass through both face panels every 24 inches, one course of rods near the bottom of the panel and another near the top. Once this first level of formwork has been set and braced, it is filled and compacted with the prepared soil mix, one layer at a time, until it is nearly full. Then a second set of face panels is set on top of the first, clamped tight against the endboards, then filled and compacted. The process is repeated until the desired height of the wall is reached.

(Facing page) Sections of the Australian forming system, known as "stabilform," erected to build an angled wall 18 feet high at its peak.

The unique and useful detail incorporated in the Australian formwork is a tongue-and-groove assembly that locks each of the face panels together as they stack. This eliminates one row of bolts in each panel except the first, and results in a clean and tight seam between panels. This forming system is so widely used throughout Australia that architects now design their rammed earth buildings to accommodate the dimensions of the formwork, another factor contributing to the success and rapid growth of the industry.

The forms that we use in our work are somewhat different, having been developed for the special considerations of building in highly seismic areas like California. One of the big differences is our elimination of 75 percent of the form ties, which both facilitates compaction around the required reinforcing steel and reduces the number of holes through the finished wall. Whereas the other systems use thin section supports for the back side of the form panels, thus requiring ties at frequent intervals in order to resist bowing, we use wide back supports, allowing us to space ties at intervals of up to 10 feet.

The story behind the evolution of these two different approaches to formwork is, in a way, similar to the "survival of the fittest" concept we've

110

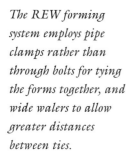

The REW forming system employs pipe clamps rather than through bolts for tying the forms together, and wide walers to allow greater distances between ties.

used elsewhere in this book. Both systems began at the same starting point: two sturdy yet cumbersome side panels, two endboards, and a method of resisting the outward forces of compaction. Both systems were confronted with the same challenges in trying to gain acceptance for rammed earth as a viable construction alternative: the traditional formwork was slow to assemble, especially as wall heights increased, and it was difficult to maintain in-plumb walls with straight lines. The systems diverged on their evolutionary paths in response to differing geographical conditions, primarily the likelihood of earthquake activity.

To both increase speed and improve accuracy, the Australians used the same basic panel size, approximately 2 feet high and 8 feet long, but rather than building wall sections horizontally around the building perimeter as in the traditional way, they built sections vertically to the full height of the wall. With this method, there is always a solid base to receive each successive section of forms, thus eliminating the inaccuracies that accompany setting free-floating formwork. The plumb of the wall is maintained by the tall, fully-braced endboard. Form bolts are run through the wall at 2-foot spacings, and because the form panels are only 2 feet high, there is little difficulty in lifting the heavy rammers up and over the form ties. Because there is no significant seismic activity in Australia, no horizontal reinforcing steel is needed to connect one section of wall to another, nor is a perimeter concrete beam required on top of the walls.

The California forming system, like the Australian, evolved in the vertical direction. The mutual (although non-collaborated) consensus was to build walls in the vertical rather than the horizontal direction. As in Australia, endboards are full-height and, for walls over one story in height, the forms stack one on top of another. The two biggest differences between the California and Australia systems are that form ties are spaced 8 to 10 feet apart rather than 2 feet apart, and the form panels are 8 to 10 feet high rather than 2 feet high. Spacing the ties farther apart and extending the form panels much higher results in a form that is essentially a deep, empty box. As with all rammed earth, soil is compacted in layers until the form is full. In the California system, once the forms are set, layering and compacting takes place uninterrupted until the desired height of the wall is reached.

(Above and right) Long wall sections can be constructed using stabilform components by connecting the 2-foot-high panels together end to end. Architects have learned to respect the forming system in their designs.

The REW system relies on one pair of pipe clamps for each set of walers, allowing the rammers to work inside the form without all the ties in the way. The wide walers also serve as both ladder and scaffolding.

(Left and bottom) In one approach to forming, long runs of wall are set up before any earth is placed, allowing for delightfully complex detailing.

The obvious drawbacks to setting full-height panels are that all of the soil must be lifted up and over the top of the forms, and that the workers must reach down into the formwork for the first few courses. The advantages are that, with fewer form ties, the rammers can move freely down the wall, and with large sections of wall being formed at one time, vertical and horizontal steel can be installed as required for earthquake safety. When long sections of wall are formed at once, the concrete bond beam, a requirement in seismic design, can be poured directly on top of the earth walls without having to set additional formwork.

Both the Australia and the California systems have been tested for nearly two decades and through that time refined to produce stabilized earthwalls of a consistently high-quality, both structurally and aesthetically. The Australia walls display horizontal seams at 2-foot intervals and vertical expansion joints at roughly 8-foot spacing. The California walls display vertical seams at 4-foot intervals and vertical expansion joints at roughly 30-foot spacing.

California Forming

The form panels we use in our work are typically 4 x 8-foot for 4 x 10-foot sheets of HDO (high-density overlay) plywood with no permanently attached supporting frame. Form ties are ¾-inch pipe clamps spaced between 6 and 10 feet apart in the horizontal direction and 15 to 24 inches apart in the vertical direction. The distance between pipe clamps is spanned by 2 x 10-inch or 2 x 12-inch wooden planks (called *walers* in forming language). The walers used in forming concrete are typically 2x4's, with ties spaced 2 feet apart. It is the extra width of the walers in our system that allows for the wide spacing of the form ties; and it is the wide spacing of the form ties that reduces the work of compacting the soil with the heavy backfill tampers.

Once erected, the formwork presents a big open box into which workers can compact as much as 8½ cubic yards of prepared soil without stopping. If the "continuous form" system is used (explained later in this chapter), the volume of material that can be compacted in a day is limited only by the number of workers on the crew. Volume building affords the opportunity to utilize more efficient and sophisticated mixing systems, thereby reducing cost and improving quality control.

With earthquake safety as our foremost concern and flexibility as our second, we have evolved three different approaches to forming the rammed earth walls, all of which use the basic full-height form panels. Which approach to use on any given project depends on several factors: the complexity of the archi-

When short sections of wall are built one at a time, the formwork for the lower portion is filled first, then the upper sections are stacked as the height of the wall is raised.

114

*Long sections of
formwork can be
employed for certain
high-production jobs or
for complex designs.*

tectural plan, the availability of manpower and equipment, and the amount of
formwork available.

The *freestanding panel system* yields individual blocks of rammed earth,
which are locked together in the final product with cast-in-place concrete
posts. This is the simplest of the forming systems we use for building the
rammed earth portion of the wall. It does, however, necessitate additional time
and money for forming and pouring the concrete columns. One big advantage

*Individual blocks of
rammed earth can be
built quickly and
without any form ties
penetrating the wall.
Spaces between blocks are
later poured with
concrete.*

to the concrete columns is the degree of earthquake safety they contribute to the wall system. The columns and bond beam take most of the lateral loads of the building, vastly reducing the stresses taken by the earth portion of the wall system. Reduced stresses in the earth panels allows for lower wall strengths, thereby greatly increasing the range of usable soils. The final appearance of this system, unless all walls are plastered, is that of a post-and-beam (timber frame) wall with infill panels of earth.

The *panel-to-panel system* utilizes the simple formwork of the freestanding system without the additional expense of the concrete posts. Blocks of rammed earth are built individually, as in the freestanding system, but, in this case, the blocks are locked together directly through keyways cast in the rammed earth and a continuous concrete bond beam poured on top. The panel-to-panel system develops its resistance to earthquake damage primarily through the mass of the wall. Secondary seismic design utilizes an integal steel reinforcing grid and a rigid roof diaphragm securely attached to the concrete bond beam.

When a wall system is constructed as a series of individual wall panels, keyed and locked to the adjacent panels, one set of forms can be used to build an entire perimeter wall.

The final appearance of this system is a continuous earthwall interrupted at intervals of approximately 8 feet with vertical grooved expansion joints. The concrete bond beam on top of the wall system is formed with 2x10's, which can be left in place to hide the seam between rammed earth and concrete. If the bond beam is exposed in the final treatment, the seam is generally somewhat unsightly. Holes where the pipe clamps passed through the walls must be patched or plugged. Done carefully, the holes become virtually invisible.

The *continuous-wall system* eliminates the frequent vertical expansion joints and yields a very clean seam between the concrete bond beam and the top of the rammed earth. It is the method which results in the most attractive finished wall system, but it is also the most difficult to install and requires a large quantity of forming materials. The continuous wall system is primarily recommended for contractors intending to specialize in rammed earth construction. Forty linear feet or more of full-height wall is formed at one time, before any earth is mixed or compacted. The crew can spend two or three days setting this much formwork, and only six to eight hours filling and ramming within it. Once the earth has been rammed to within approximately 9 inches of the top, the bond beam is poured directly onto the earth, within the same formwork, thus eliminating the time-consuming additional step of a separate form. Pouring into the same form, rather than stripping and resetting, results in a virtually flawless seam between the two materials. In fact, we emphasize the "floating" or sedimentary characteristic of the bond beam in this system. It's a signature of rammed earth in earthquake country. The individual courses of rammed earth, with their gray layer on top, appear to have settled naturally together, just as the layers of soil that make up sedimentary rock have settled on top of one another over billions of years. As in panel-to-panel walls, the continuous-wall system develops its strength in earthquakes through the mass of the wall in conjunction with the bond beam and roof diaphragm. (More on earthquake design later.)

REW (Rammed Earth Works) Formwork

The components to our basic formwork are: faces (or panels), endboards, pipe clamps, walers, and wedges.

Building single-story walls requires four full sheets of plywood for the form faces. Taller walls require additional sheets. The plywood can be either standard 8-foot sheets or special-order 10-foot sheets. The advantage to the more expensive 10-foot sheets is that they form larger panels of earth, resulting in fewer total setups. AC grade ¾-inch plywood is adequate, 1⅛-inch plywood subflooring is better because it deflects less between walers, but our preferred forms are built of ¾-inch HDO (high-density overlay) plywood. Specifically manufactured for architectural concrete forming, this type of plywood is stiffer and will deflect less under the pressure of ramming than other plywoods. A thin Formica-like overlay covers the grain of the outer veneer, resulting in smoother

(Top and right) Where extensive formwork is set, the walls can be virtually seamless, and the structural concrete bond beam can become an architectural element reflecting the methodology.

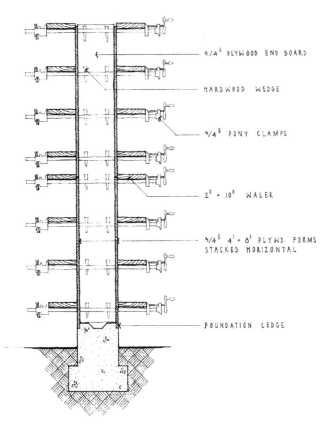

3/4" PLYWOOD END BOARD

HARDWOOD WEDGE

3/4" PONY CLAMPS

2" x 10" WALER

3/4" 4' x 8' PLYWD. FORMS STACKED HORIZONTAL

FOUNDATION LEDGE

The basic components of the REW forming system.

finished walls, less chance of material sticking to the forms, and a longer usable life. Expense is the only drawback to the HDO. At $55 or more per sheet, it's as much as two times the price of AC grade plywood.

Holes are drilled in the form faces to receive the pipe clamps. The smallest hole a ¾-inch pipe will fit through is 1⅛-inches in diameter. In the vertical direction, the holes should be spaced approximately 15 inches apart. Any greater spacing and the plywood will deflect between the walers. The distance between holes in the horizontal direction (along the wall) is determined by the length of the wall panels. Normally the spacing is 6 to 9 feet apart for individual panels and 10 feet apart for continuously formed walls. The actual distance between pipe clamps is determined by the exact length of the panels being built. A panel 6 feet long, built using 4 x 8-foot sheets of plywood and ¾-inch plywood endboards, would require that the holes be spaced 6 feet, 3 inches apart. A 9-foot panel, built using 4 x 10-foot sheets of plywood and the same endboards, would require holes spaced 9 feet, 3 inches apart. Generally, unless the endboards are thicker than ¾ inches, the distance between the center lines of the holes should be 3 inches greater than the length of the panel. The degree to which the perimeter walls are designed around a standard panel size will affect the efficiency and accuracy of the wall system. When all the panels are the same size, the formwork can be set up quickly, with little room for error.

When setting the forms, the full-height endboard and the lowest form faces are set first: lined, plumbed, and braced. (For freestanding walls and the panel-to-panel walls, plywood is set with the long side oriented in the horizontal direction). When walls are 8 feet or less in height, usually both the upper and lower form faces are set before ramming begins. This way the seam between forms is less visible and all of the mix can be prepared at one time, thereby lessening the chances of a color or textural change at the mid-point of the wall. As stated earlier, it is a bit awkward for the wallbuilders to compact the first foot or so of earth down in this deep form. We either use long-handled tampers, reaching over the top, or climb down inside the form, trying to stay out of the path of the soil cascading from above.

The endboards, like the form faces, are built of plywood. They are cut to the width of the wall thickness and the height of the finished wall. In other words, if the finished walls are to be 8 feet high, the endboards are cut to 8 feet; 12-foot walls require 12-foot endboards; 18-foot walls take 18-foot end-boards. It is essential that the endboards be as tall as the finished wall in order to maintain plumb and straightness. Endboards greater than one sheet of ply-wood in length necessitate the splicing together of two pieces. Use full-length 2x4's or plywood strips on the back side to support the splice, and remember to calculate the extra thickness of the endboard when determining the spacing between the holes in the form faces.

In each location where panels connect with one another, a full-length bev-elled 2x4 is attached to the front side of the endboard. This creates a keyway in the end of the earth panel, used to lock adjacent wall sections together. In the freestanding system, where columns are cast between each panel of earth, the keyways are poured full of concrete. In the panel-to-panel system, where sections of earth abut one another, the keyways are rammed full of earth. Looked at in plan view, the wall sections lock together in the same way that tongue-and-groove wood siding interconnects. The keyways are not used at door and window openings, where the ends of the wall panels are visible.

In constructing the panel-to-panel system, where the seams between sec-tions are exposed, small wooden chamfer strips should be attached to the sides of the endboards. These chamfer strips create a 45-degree bevel at the corners of the wall panels. At door and window openings the chamfered edges create a stronger corner, less likely to be chipped or broken. Without the chamfer, small rocks can occasionally find their way into the corner of the form, inhib-iting good compaction and resulting in weak and irregular edges. At the loca-tions where two panels of earth join one another, the chamfered edges create the first side of the expansion joint. The other side of this V-joint is created by lightly tacking additional wooden chamfer strips against the bevelled edge of the earth itself. The form faces are then set, filled, and rammed in the usual manner. When the form is disassembled, the chamfer strip can be carefully removed. The V-joint thus created is the point at which expansion and contraction, if any, will occur. The small amount of separation that may occur between panels, never more than $\frac{1}{16}$ of an inch, is recessed beneath the face of the walls and hardly visible at all. If the chamfer strips are not used where panels connect together, the seams will be very rough and ragged.

Holding the faces and endboards together are $\frac{3}{4}$-inch "pony"-brand pipe clamps. There are, of course, many other methods for holding formwork together: tapered bolts and snap ties specifically manufactured for concrete work, threaded rods, flat bars, and even heavy-gauge tie wire. In fact, pipe clamps are not normally used as form ties. We came upon their great suitability for this function almost by accident—a case of serendipity, really. As related previously, our early attempts at rammed earth construction utilized the existing forming technology, namely short panels and long bolts. The long bolts kept the faces from spreading, but we were having problems with the endboards shifting outward under the pressure of ramming. We thought the best way to restrict this outward movement was essentially the same method used to keep the faces from spreading—namely long bolts. Better yet, we thought, why not use the long, infinitely adjustable clamps from the cabinet shop? We used two clamps, grabbing the backs of the opposing endboards, one on each side of the wall. The clamps rested directly on top of the form faces, out of the way during ramming, and were moved upward with the forms as the wall progressed. Before we shifted to stacking forms on top of one another, we were even using the pipe clamps grabbing opposing endboards as temporary ledgers on which to rest the form faces before they were secured with the bolts.

You might imagine that all this—long pipe clamps, deflecting endboards, heavy form panels, long bolts continually being banged, bent, and cross-threaded, and wrenches lost in the overburden— would present a wide array of problems and continual frustrations. In retrospect, the solution was patently logical. At the time it seemed like genius: Abandon the threaded rods and the socket wrenches altogether, use the pipe clamps to hold the forms together, and—the real breakthrough—run the pipe clamps through the forms on the back sides of the endboards to keep them from spreading outwards. Not only did the pipe clamps solve the creeping endboard problem, but by substituting 2x10 walers for the 2x4's, we could span from one endboard to the other with no intermediate form ties and no bolts to lift the tampers over. The final coup de grâce to the old form system was the discovery that, by resting wide walers on pipe clamps spaced 15 inches apart vertically, we were building a ladder and scaffold arrangement, safe and secure enough for an army of earth rammers to climb on and shovel off of. The walers we use are Douglas fir, the common framing lumber in this area. When holes are spaced 8 feet or less apart, a 2x10 will span without deflecting; more than 8 feet and 2x12's are necessary. Grade #2, "standard or better," lumber is adequate, though #1, "select structural" grade, which is stronger and will warp less over time, may be worth the extra investment.

The last components to the REW forming package are the wedges; they are small but important. Each time the forms are set up, two tapered wooden wedges must be installed between each pipe clamp and the back side of the endboard. During ramming, the endboards are forced outward against the pipes so tightly that, without wedges, the pipes are virtually bound into the formwork. Extracting them requires too much effort and can damage the form faces. The tapered wooden wedges, on the other hand, typically about $1\frac{1}{2}$ inches wide and 4 inches long and cut from hardwood, make extraction of the pipes a breeze. After the wall has been completed, the clamps loosened, and the walers removed, a quick turn of each pipe with a pipe wrench causes the hardwood wedges to pop right out, loosening up the endboard as well. Hardwood wedges are far preferred over softwood ones, because they hold up better and last longer, and because the forces of ramming are strong enough to crush the grain of soft wedges, making them hard to pull. The tapered dimension on the wedges runs from about $\frac{1}{8}$ inch on the thin end to $\frac{3}{4}$ inch on the fat end. Oil the wedges for even easier extraction.

Setting the Basic Formwork

The formwork is clamped onto the foundation precisely where the wall panel is to be built. If a ledger was formed into the top of the foundation before it was poured, the form faces will sit directly on the ledger. This makes it easier to plumb and level the forms. Clamping the formwork tightly to the foundation helps maintain their alignment.

The normal procedure for assembling the formwork is as follows:

1. Set both form faces on the ledger, lean them back slightly, and temporarily support them with a shovel handle or a pipe clamp.
2. Set one endboard in place on the foundation.
3. Pull the two form faces against the endboard.
4. Insert the first pipe clamp through the third hole up from the bottom ("Number 3," we call it), slip on the backer (we call them "frogs"), and tighten the auger.
5. Set the second endboard in place, insert a clamp through the third

hole from the bottom ("Number 3"), slip on the frog, and tighten the auger. (These two pipes through Number 3 will secure the formwork assembly enough to keep it from falling over.)

6. Roughly plumb both endboards and the form faces using a 4-foot level held against the endboard. Loosen the augers just enough to allow the faces to slip against the endboard while reading the level. Once the bubble is within the lines, cinch the auger. Repeat for the other end.

7. Insert the remaining pipes through numbers 1, 2 and 4.

8. Set the walers on these three pairs of pipes, on both sides of the wall; shove the augers home, slip on the frogs, and lightly tighten the clamps.

9. Loosen Number 3 and set the final pair of walers.

10. Check that the back sides of the endboards touch the pipes. Tap them outward if necessary.

11. Check plumb in both directions, at both ends of the panel.

12. Install the wooden wedges, two per pipe, using a hammer to drive each wedge downward until the space between the pipe and the back side of the endboard is about ½ inch. The spacing should be identical at each pipe.

13. Check plumb a final time, then tighten all the augers.

14. Attach one diagonal brace from the top of each endboard to a stake driven into the ground.

This completes the procedure for setting the basic formwork. The bottom 4-foot section of wall is now ready for earth. Fill and ram to within a few inches of the top of the first form, remove the braces from the endboards, and stack the upper form faces following the procedure above. The bottom portion of the wall should be secure enough that bracing won't be necessary for the upper half. In much of our work, we prefer to stack the upper form faces before starting with the earth. When we do stack both faces together, the diagonal braces attach to the top waler rather than to the endboard.

Corner Forms

Corners are more difficult to form than straight sections of wall. The forces from ramming are compounded at the far outside corner of the formwork, and extra precaution is needed to keep a corner straight and the formwork tight. In fact, corners present such significant headaches that rammed earth buildings frequently are designed without earth corners altogether. That is, either door openings or full-height windows are positioned to butt against straight wall sections at the building's corners or else side walls extend beyond the ends of the building and the cross walls butt. (Viewed in plan, this configuration is in the shape of a T.)

The idea behind our corner is to construct a form which has to resist only perpendicular forces, just as in the straight-section form, but which yields two wings of equal length, the same thickness as the straight-section walls; and to do so without running pipes through the wall. The corner form we now recommend, having evolved the design through much trial and error, utilizes the same basic components as the standard form: form faces, endboards, pipe clamps, walers, and wedges. One difference between the straight-section forms and the corner forms is that the plywood for the corners is oriented vertically rather than horizontally. The form faces are each one full sheet of plywood with holes spaced 36 inches apart in the horizontal direction, and the endboards are cut 33 inches wide. (This 36-inch spacing and 33-inch width applies to forms built for the freestanding wall system in which a 6-inch-wide concrete column fills the gap between adjacent wall sections. Use a 39-inch spacing and a 36-inch endboard for the panel-to-panel system.)

The pipe clamps for the corner form must be at least 54 inches long; the walers can be 2x6's. Unlike the straight-section form, which is rectangular in plan, the inside of the corner form, seen from the top, is square; 33 inches on a side for one system, 36 inches for the other. Our goal is to create the two wings of the corner from this square section. We do this by constructing a full-height plywood box which fits inside the formwork, taking up the space in the formwork where we don't want earth. We call these boxes VDB's (volume displacement boxes) and use them to create spaces for doors, windows, and niches as well as corners. The dimensions for a corner VDB are calculated as the difference between the width of the corner form and the wall thickness. In other words, for an 18-inch thick wall in the panel-to-panel system (36-inch square corner form), the dimensions of the VDB would be 18 x 18 inches; for a 12-inch-thick wall in the freestanding system (33-inch square corner form), the dimensions of the VDB would be 21 x 21 inches.

The corner form is assembled in much the same way as the standard form with the exception that the VDB is set up first, before the faces or the endboards. Because the forms for the corner have to cross the foundation stem wall, which is raised $1\frac{1}{2}$ inches above the ledger, one of the faces and one of the endboards must be notched at the bottom where they cross the foundation. With the corner form endboards so wide, a third wedge is needed in the center

The basic corner form in use. Note the square VDB (volume displacement box) in the lower left corner, creating the two wings of equal length.

A miniature building, clearly illustrating the rule, "Build the corners first!"

of each of the long pipes to keep the endboard from deflecting. A chamfer strip should always be installed at the outside corner, and chamfers should be used at the ends of the wings in the panel-to-panel system.

Building the Walls

Constructing a complete wall system using the basic formwork is simply a matter of building one panel after another around the perimeter of the building. Panels are discontinuous at door openings and of partial height at window locations.

The first step, regardless of which method is used (freestanding or panel-to-panel), is to construct the corners. This way, the correct alignment of the walls can be maintained, corner to corner. String lines can be used to check alignment as each new form is set.

If concrete columns are specified in the design, each panel is spaced 6 inches from its neighbor. Where doors are to be installed, a panel is omitted, and where windows are to be installed, a partial-height panel is built. The simplest system calls for the door and window openings to extend to the height of the bond beam, thus eliminating the need for separate lintels. (More on doors and windows later.)

In the panel-to-panel system, where no concrete columns are used, wall sections are rammed directly against one another, end to end. When building this system, first mark out on the foundation the exact position of each of the wall sections. Door and window rough openings are calculated and marked out directly on the foundation. The mark actually specifies the positioning of the endboard for each setup. With all the sections laid out, first build the corners to provide a point of alignment for the walls, then form and construct

every other panel around the perimeter, leaving a full-panel gap between each section. The reason for the gap is that freshly constructed sections of wall are fragile, and, when forms are clamped onto green walls, there is a risk of cracking and other damage. By first making a complete circuit around the perimeter, building every other section, the walls will have enough time to cure, so that the seams will be clean and straight when the intermediate panels are built.

The first round of setups requires that both endboards are positioned directly onto marks laid out along the foundation, as described above. Pipe clamps and wedges are located on the back side of the endboards. The wall panels will have no obstructions in the way of the rammers except some electrical boxes and conduit in certain locations. The second circumnavigation of the building perimeter uses no endboards; form faces are clamped directly against the adjacent panels. Pipe clamps for these setups pass directly through the wall, the holes to be filled or plugged later. In order to get good compaction around the pipes, they should be spaced approximately 6 inches away from the adjacent panels. Either use a hand tamper in the space between the pipes and the wall, or lift the pneumatic rammer up and over the pipes as necessary.

Door and window openings are built in the same manner with the panel-

Individual panels of varying width and height make up the primary component of the freestanding panel system. Once the concrete columns and the bond beam have been poured, the walls are ready to receive the roof.

Finishing off the last of the infill panels for a house built using the panel-to-panel system. This window on the south end was so wide it required that two form sections be used end-to-end.

to-panel system as they are with the freestanding system. There are two differences, however: The bevelled 2x4's are removed from the endboards because we don't want keyways on the ends of the wall sections that double as jambs; and the rough opening dimension matches exactly that prescribed for the unit and does not include the width of the concrete columns.

To create a good clean seam between panels, attach chamfer strips to the endboards to bevel the edges of the first round of panels, then tack chamfer strips directly to that bevelled edge of the earth before setting the form faces. (Just a few 3d nails will hold it.) By recessing the seam between the panels, burying it in a V-joint, the slight shrinkage that may occur as the panels cure is barely visible. The shrinkage that does take place is made even less visible by the fact that it takes place along the hypotenuse of the chamfer, not at the point where the two triangles meet. When the chamfer is nailed onto the endboard, the long side of the triangle creates the bevel in the earth (approximately 1 inch in length). Then, when the chamfer strip is attached directly to the earth, the hypoteneuse faces outward, leaving the shorter sides (approximately ¾ inch across) buried in the earth. Without the chamfered edges, the seams between panels would be jagged and unsightly. Only when plastering both sides of the wall systems would it be acceptable to eliminate the chamfered seams.

Building a wall system one panel at a time will work for practically every design. Obviously, the more closely the layout of the perimeter walls accom-

In the panel-to-panel system, each of the individual sections of rammed earth fit tightly together, waiting for the cast-in-place concrete bond beam to provide the final tie.

modates the system, the simpler the work. By using just the two basic forms, the corner and the straight, you can minimize your investment in plywood, pipe clamps, and walers. The panel-to-panel system also provides an important opportunity to evaluate the quality of the walls being constructed, especially moisture, mixing, and compaction. Perhaps more importantly, building one panel at a time establishes milestones that are easily achievable. You can feel a sense of accomplishment and progress as each of those massive blocks of solid earth emerge from the formwork.

Forming Continuous Walls

The appeal of the basic REW forming system, as described above, is due to the fact that, with a relatively modest investment in formwork, there is practically no limit to the size of the project. On the other hand, there are several circumstances in which a given project can be completed more effectively through the use of extensive formwork.

For instance, if specifications call for varying wall heights, stepped foundations, or lines of soil stratification within a run of wall, continuous formwork might be appropriate. If the access to a site is so restricted that a crane is needed to deliver soil to the forms, then it makes sense to set all the formwork at one time before scheduling the crane on-site. The continuous forming method also eliminates the need for a separate set of forms for the bond beam, since with this method the earthwalls are completed before the top of the forms is reached. The concrete bond beam is then poured directly into the formwork.

To pour the bond beam on top of a section of continuous earthwall, the level at which the earth should stop must be clearly marked on the inside walls of the forms, either with a chalk line or with chamfer strips nailed to both sides. The chamfer results in a clean, sharp, straight seam between earth and concrete. The chalk line approach results in a "floating" seam between the two materials, since the top of the rammed earth is never precisely straight and level. Obviously, the floating seam is less work. Visually, it carries the layered look of the earth through to the top of the wall. Rammed earth is, in fact, manmade sedimentary rock, and the concrete bond beam is nothing more than one of the many layers. Structurally, the bond beam provides the critical seismic connection for the roof. Boldly expressed as it is in the continuous wall system, the concrete bond beam is a classic example of the dictum, "form follows function."

Although the investment in formwork is greater with continuous walls than with individual panels, a significant portion of the investment can be recouped by using the plywood as roof sheathing, the 2x4's for interior partition framing, and the 2x12's as roof rafters. Contractors who specialize in rammed earth can justify extensive formwork in money saved on the job through decreased equipment rental costs. When we elect to use the continuous-form system rather than building panel-to-panel, it is usually for one of two reasons: either for optimizing personnel and equipment, or for addition of a "strata" line of a different-colored earth throughout the wall system. In terms of efficiency, formwork is often most quickly set by experienced carpenters. Two people who know what they're doing can set, plumb, and brace form panels for a small building in two or three days. Too many formsetters actually decrease efficiency. Once the forms have been set, however, a crew of six or eight workers with four backfill tampers hosed to a 160 cfm air compressor and a front-loading tractor can mix, fill, and compact that same amount of formwork in less than two days. The same six-to-eight-person crew might complete a small set of walls using the panel-to-panel system in less than a week, but with the extra expense of additional days of equipment rental and payroll.

We form our continuous walls with either 4 x 8-foot or 4 x 10-foot sheets of plywood, oriented vertically. Each sheet has a framework of 2x4's attached to the back side, four footers at the top and bottom and full-length studs spaced 16 inches on center, with the 2x4 on each leading edge overhanging the plywood by ¾ inch to provide a back support for the adjacent sheet.

(Facing page, left) Formwork for the continuous-wall system requires a much larger investment in lumber and pipe clamps and is recommended primarily for specialty wallbuilding contractors.

The reason we use the 2x4 frame on each sheet of plywood is to increase the vertical spacing between pipe clamps. Without the 2x4's, clamps must be spaced no farther than 15 inches apart in order to resist plywood deflection. With the 2x4's, the clamps can be spaced 24 inches apart, thereby reducing the overall number of clamps and walers required, as well as decreasing the obstructions to compaction and the number of holes to be patched once the forms are stripped.

(Above) A closer view of the pipe clamps and wide walers. Fewer ties through the wall make it easier to move around inside the formwork.

The walers for the continuous-form system are longer than for the other systems. We typically use 2x12's either 16 or 20 feet in length. Pipe clamp holes only need to be drilled in every other form panel, leaving the distance between clamps at 8 feet. A 12-inch-wide waler will easily span 8 feet without deflecting. At the corners, drill the first set of holes 12 inches in from the inside face of the corner; use 2-foot walers to run by the outside and spike the walers together where they cross. This will keep the corner from bowing outwards.

The continuous-form system is cumbersome to erect the first time. It requires a good deal of forethought to utilize the panels appropriately, especially at the corners. A design consistent with the form module is also helpful.

The normal procedure for assembling the formwork is as follows:

1. Set the first inside form panel in place on the foundation ledger (or slab), and brace plumb with a 2x4 staked to the ground (or temporary plate).

To make certain that the walls remain plumb as the forms are being filled and compacted, diagonal bracing should be used at regular intervals. How much bracing is used depends on the level of caution of the individual builder.

2. Set the second form in place against the first. Screw or nail the forms together through the outside 2x4's.

3. Set the third form against the second, and so on, until the desired length of wall has been set for one side.

4. Set braces on every other panel. Nail the braces to one of the studs on the frame, making sure they will not obstruct the top waler.

5. Once the desired length of wall has been set for one side and braced plumb, nail one continuous 2x4 to the top of all the form panels to align and stiffen the formwork.

6. Set door VDB's where required against the inside formwork. Screw through the form panels into the sides of the VDB's.

7. Mark out all window VDB locations on the formwork. Attach ledger strips to indicate sill height.

8. Set all electrical boxes and conduit. Tie the first two horizontal courses of reinforcing steel.

9. Set the first opposing wall form. Make sure that the holes in the opposing form faces line up. Nail a temporary cleat across the tops of the two forms to hold them together.

10. Set the second form against the first, the third form against the second, and so on, until the end of the opposing panels is reached. Nail or screw the 2x4's of each form together on the sides and cleat each pair of forms across the top.

11. Once the panels are all set and endboards are located at each end of the wall length to be constructed, install pipe clamps.

12. Set the walers on each pipe clamp inside and out, and tighten the augers, firm but not overtight. Where two walers meet, either run one by the other for a minimum of 6 inches and use a full-height 2x4 between the clamp and the walers to support the splice; or make sure the walers meet directly on top of the clamp and use plywood cleats to reinforce the splice.

13. To firmly tighten the clamps without causing the formwork to bow inwards, use a 1 x 2-inch wooden spreader, cut to the exact wall thickness, at each pipe. (One person climbs into the formwork and holds the spreader in place while a second person cinches down on the auger.) The spreaders are removed as the wall is being built.

14. Secure the endboards with screws through the face of the form panels into the sides of the endboards. Install wedges or spacers to provide additional support to the back side of each endboard.

15. Make a final check for auger tightness and plumb.

This completes the procedure for setting the continuous formwork. It takes some getting used to, but it's now ready to receive a large volume of earth. Make sure the tampers are in good working order and the other equipment is full of fuel and well lubricated. A big crew can accomplish a great deal of filling and ramming in a relatively short period of time. Earth is rammed to the bottom of the windowsills, then window VDB's are lowered into the formwork, screwed in place, and ramming is continued to the bond beam line.

Speciality Formwork

In an attempt to accommodate some of the more commonly encountered architectural details, we have developed various special forming details and configurations. A sampling of these techniques are: window and door VDB's with bevelled openings, arches of different radii, curved wall forms, fireplace and chimney formwork, niche forms, flared wall tops, and gable-end wall details. In addition, we've been called on to design and install several different lintel configurations, each expressing a different architectural style. Although some of these techniques will be described later, a comprehensive description of the specialty applications is, unfortunately, beyond the scope of this text.

Once you perfect the art of form building, new doorways begin to open for you.

CHAPTER EIGHT

Soil Preparation and Compaction

(Facing page) A wall system under construction.

IN THE EARLY DAYS of earthbuilding, soil for a rammed earth wall was often taken from a pit adjacent to the building site and carried directly to the form in baskets. Under ideal conditions, when the ground was sufficiently wet from winter rains, the soil was neither mixed nor moistened prior to compaction.

As time went on, and as projects increased in scale, other methods of moving soil and obtaining optimum moisture contents were developed. Today, earthbuilders work with tractors, dump trucks, water under pressure, and large stockpiles of soil material.

When both water and cement are being added to a soil, thorough mixing of the ingredients before they are compacted in the forms becomes critical. A wall is, in fact, not much stronger than its weakest sections, and, when a soil is inadequately mixed, the advantages of adding cement are significantly lessened. Based on numerous observations in the field as well as laboratory testing, it appears that mixing, even beyond the point of visual homogeneity, plays a crucial role in obtaining the maximum strength attainable for any given soil formula. The fine particles of cement need time and agitation to incorporate themselves within the other fine-particle matrix of the clay-based soil.

Even in very low-budget or otherwise basic wallbuilding operations, the soil must be homogeneous prior to placement within the wall forms. Whether or not cement or other additives are part of the formula, it is imperative that the moisture be uniform throughout the mix. When a soil is too dry to result in good compaction, water must be added and the soil mixed to allow the water to be blended with all of the soil particles. In fact, it is advantageous to add the water to a dry soil several hours or, better yet, several days prior to compaction in the forms. It takes the clay particles a certain amount of time to fully absorb the free water, and, remember, it is the water-coated particles of clay that create the electrical bond with the rest of the aggregate.

There are several different methods for achieving uniform mix in the field. Drum-type cement mixers will work adequately when the soil is high in sand and gravel content, but this type of equipment, typically less than a cubic yard in capacity, is slow to produce mix and for this reason adds time to the wallbuilding process. The bucket on a tractor can be used effectively for some soils when operated with skill, but this technique can sometimes leave areas of the mix poorly blended. Neither the drum mixer nor the tractor bucket are capable of the thorough mixing necessary to obtain maximum benefits from the cement when used on soils with high clay content.

When using a drum-type concrete mixer, a plywood hopper constructed above the machine will allow for loading with the tractor.

A skilled operator using the bucket of a tractor can mix large batches of soil, cement, and water much faster than a drum mixer.

One type of equipment which does seem to be effective with all soils is the portable concrete batch plant. This machinery uses a combination of belt conveyor and two hoppers to combine the soil and cement in specified proportions. The ingredients are then blended together by a paddle auger in a semicircular rubber trough. A water bar along the trough adds moisture as the mix moves along the trough. The paddles on the rotating shaft are far more effective at combining the cement with the other fine particles than either the drum mixer or the tractor bucket. Earth and cement mixes must be "chopped up," in much the same way that two knives are used to cut cold butter into flour to form pie dough.

The only drawback to the portable batch plant is its price. At a cost of around $50,000, the only way to justify owning one is to be a full-time wallbuilding contractor or to have a ready-mix concrete business operating on the side.

Short of making such an investment, we have found that perfectly adequate and affordable mixing can be accomplished by using a rototiller mounted on the back of a tractor. Affordable, that is, assuming that a tractor is already part of your wallbuilding equipment. When either borrowing or renting a tractor isn't in the budget, rammed earth can be built using wheelbarrows and 5-gallon buckets, and a garden tiller can substitute for the tractor-mounted type. Just remember, it will take a lot longer. For speed and efficiency, the tractor is an important part of the overall success of the project.

The focus of the mixing process is the mix pad, a flat and clean area located

(Bottom right) The tractor-mounted rototiller is fast and very thorough. The powerful tiller can quickly blend cement with soil particles.

(Bottom left) A small garden tiller is a versatile machine. You can use it for mixing soil and cement during wall construction, then later use it to mix compost into your garden soil.

between the soil stockpile and the future walls. Each batch of material is measured and mixed on this pad before being transported to the wall forms. In order to keep the ratio of ingredients accurate, it is important that the surface of the mix pad be firm enough to work on without the risk of portions of the pad itself (or, worse yet, the soil under the pad) becoming a part of the mix. Digging up the mix pad alters the ratio of cement to soil, which was carefully measured as the batch was begun. Digging so deep as to bring up the soil underneath the pad can result in unwanted dirt clods or other blemishes in the finished walls.

Our recommendation is that every wallbuilding project begin with the construction of the mix pad. Choose a location with good access and, if you're using a tractor, plenty of room. If possible, choose a location that will become a future paving or parking area, because the mix pad and the area around it will be smooth, hard, and (as you'll see) difficult to remove, once wallbuilding is complete. With good planning, the area of the mix pad can serve as the drop-off and staging area for the other construction materials.

The pad itself is constructed in place, first by rough-grading the chosen area, then by making the first batch of mix. Three cubic yards of stabilized soil should make a pad 3 inches thick, approximately 20 feet in diameter. This is a

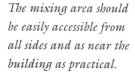

The mixing area should be easily accessible from all sides and as near the building as practical.

big mix pad, but it will prove very useful for efficient mix preparation as well as for temporary placement of construction materials and as a future parking area.

Use the tractor bucket as your measuring scoop. Buckets are typically ¼, ⅓, or ½ cubic yard measures. You can calculate the volume in cubic feet. Twenty-seven cubic feet equals 1 cubic yard. Cement ratios are usually given in terms of sacks per cubic yard. Standard 2,000 psi concrete is about four sacks per cubic yard. Extra strong concrete may be six or even seven sacks per cubic yard. Stabilized rammed earth contains on the order of one or one-and-a-half sacks of cement per cubic yard.

To make the mix pad, dump the required number of tractor buckets on the ground and knock the pile down so it's about 1 foot deep. Empty the contents of three or four sacks of cement into the bucket, then dump the bucket over the top of the pile, trying to spread the cement as you dump it. Use the bucket of the tractor to initially combine the soil and cement, then mix thoroughly with the rototiller. Turn the pile to bring the unmixed portion to the top, and mix again with the tiller. During the second mixing, a helper can begin adding water to the pile with a garden hose to bring the moisture content up to where it wants to be for good compaction.

Once mixing has been completed the blend will appear uniform in color. Spread it over the ground to a depth of approximately 6 inches and run over it with the wheels of the tractor until it is all packed down. Back-drag it with the bucket, spray it with water, and let it cure for a day or two. As work on the walls progresses, the mix pad will gradually get larger, thicker, and harder.

Tractor buckets vary in size. Once you've calculated the total volume of one full bucket, usually between 6 and 14 cubic feet, use this as your measuring device throughout. One sack of cement is 1 cubic foot.

Making the Mix the Tractor Way

The percentage of cement and other ingredients a soil may require to obtain its maximum stabilization will vary from project to project. Keep in mind that soils are incredibly variable. Even when the grain-size distribution of two different soils is identical, the shape of the individual particles as well as the chemical makeup of the clay can result in vastly different structural and weathering characteristics. Prior to commencing a project of any significant size, test samples of the proposed mix design must be evaluated either by a laboratory or by your own field methods. The results of this preconstruction testing will determine the percentages of stabilizer and amendments to be used on the job.

During the mixing process, in order to maintain uniformity of color throughout a wall panel, it is advisable (although not essential) to make batches of mix that are big enough to fill the wall form you have set up. In other words, if you are building a panel that is 8 feet long, 7 feet high, and 18 inches thick, the total volume inside the form is a little over 3 cubic yards (8x7x1.5÷27). Since most soils can be compressed to about 60 percent of their uncompacted volume, you'll need about 5 cubic yards of loose mix to fill this particular form.

Different soils have different "bulking" factors. A *bulking factor* is basically the amount of air that is trapped inside a pile before it has been compacted to its maximum density. Sands and gravels, soils which have low expansion/contraction ratios, will compact less than "fluffy," clay-rich soils. You'll need to experiment to learn the ratio of loose volume to compacted volume for the soil being used on any given project.

Calculating the amount of cement to add to the pile is based on the compacted volume of earth, not the loose volume. For example, the form panel we have set up has a volume of 84 cubic feet (8x7x1.5), or 3.1 cubic yards. Let's say the minimum adequate rate of stabilization determined from our preconstruction testing is 7.5 percent. Then by simple mathematics we know that the number of sacks that should be added to the mix pile is 6.3 (84 x 0.075 = 6.3). Each sack of cement is exactly 1 cubic foot. Regardless of how "bulky" the loose soil is, once it is fully compacted in the form it will have a volume of 84 cubic feet. Six and one-third sacks of cement will combine with that 84 cubic feet of soil, yielding the desired stabilization ratio of 7.5 percent.

Because this particular idea may be confusing, a further point of clarification is in order. Concrete, the gray semifluid product everyone knows (and often mistakenly calls "cement") is typically delivered to the job in a ready-mix truck. It is a combination of sand, gravel, water, and cement. Sand and gravel, the two primary components of concrete, have very low bulking factors. That is, they are virtually compacted as they sit in a stockpile. Even when they are compressed with vibrators or rollers, their volume changes very little. Therefore, if you have a pile of sand and gravel which is to be stabilized at, say, 15 percent, you'll need to add four bags of cement to each cubic yard. (In actuality, the amount of cement added at the batch plant is measured in pounds and is calculated as a percentage of the dry weight of sand and gravel.) Expressing the amount of cement in any given concrete mix as "sacks per yard," which has become common within the industry, is easy to comprehend.

A mound of soil, on the other hand, will occupy a bigger volume of space in a loose stockpile than it will when compacted within the formwork. A moist, fluffy, clay-rich soil may take up nearly twice as much space loose as it will compressed. This is because air was blended in with the soil when it was being piled up by the bulldozer or loaded into the truck. The amount of air in an uncompacted soil is the bulking factor. It varies depending on soil type, moisture, and how the stockpile was created.

The bulking factor must be taken into account when measuring the ingredients for each batch of mix. Cement should stay constant for each wall panel, but how many tractor buckets of loose soil will be needed to build each wall panel must be determined at the outset. You won't know how "bulky" the soil is until you've actually counted the number of buckets it takes to fill and compact the first form. You can make an initial determination by filling and compacting a small test panel using 5-gallon buckets to keep track of how much loose soil went into the form. Then use this information to make an educated guess at the number of tractor buckets of loose soil to use for the first batch of mix. After completing the first panel, adjust the formula as required. The sacks of cement should stay the same; only the number of tractor buckets will vary. You may actually find that, during mixing, the soil will become bulkier than it was in the stockpile. You may dump six scoops of soil on the mix pad, yet carry eight scoops to the form panel.

Here's the basic procedure we've developed for making mix with the rototiller on the tractor:

1. Begin by dumping the correct number of tractor buckets of soil onto the center of the mix pad.
2. If an amendment such as sand is being used, dump alternate buckets of material onto the pad.
3. Spread the pile out with the back of the bucket to a thickness of twelve inches.
4. Empty the contents of the correct number of cement sacks into the bucket, then dump the cement over the pile as uniformly as possible.
5. Roughly combine the cement and soil, then begin mixing with the tiller, being careful not to allow the tines to dig into the pad.
6. Continue mixing until the cement and soil have roughly blended together. (You'll still see color variation at this stage.)
7. Turn the pile over with the tractor bucket, bringing the unmixed soil from the bottom to the top.
8. Have your helper begin spraying the pile with water as the pile is being turned over this first time. (Watering too early will saturate the cement before it has been combined with the clay.)
9. Mix again with the tiller, continuing to spray water onto the pile until the soil is nearly uniform in color.

10. Turn the pile a final time with the bucket. Add water as necessary to any dry areas. Check that there are no unmixed areas.

11. Stack the mix into a high pile to conserve moisture while the wall panel is built. Use a tarp to cover the pile if the weather is warm or windy.

The soil mix is ready to carry to the forms when it is completely uniform in color and at the optimum moisture level. The soil sould have enough moisture to hydrate the cement and to lubricate the soil particles as they are rammed against one another, yet not so much water that the clay in the soil becomes expanded or sticky. It is always a surprise to people the first time they see how "dry" soil actually appears when it is right for ramming.

A good indicator of when the moisture content is right is the way the soil compacts under the head of the rammer. If the mix is too dry, it will not compact. It will stay loose and fluffy in the form. If it is too wet, it will ram down quickly, yet stay spongy. The tamper will leave distinct imprints in the top of the layer.

Proper moisture content is absolutely critical to a good rammed earth wall. When the moisture is correct and the soil is compacting properly, it is easy to tell, even for a novice earth rammer. The soil settles down with just one pass of the tamper around the inside of the form. Dirt and dust aren't flying around the base of the tamper. With a second pass, the material begins to lay down and the layer begins to sound solid.

Soil at the proper moisture level for good compaction appears drier than you might think.

After a bit of experience, it is possible to recognize optimum moisture content from the seat of the tractor. Until you attain that level of expertise, however, and in lieu of using the tampers in the form as the means of determining optimum moisture, you can employ a tried-and-true field test. This test has been passed on from one generation of earthbuilders to another, and is transcribed here in a version written in 1953 by the Australian earthbuilder and historian, George F. Middleton.

> With the two hands scoop up enough prepared moist soil to compress to the size and shape of a cricket ball; press it hard between cupped hands until it will not compress any more and becomes a hard ball. It should be compact enough for no part of it to fall away when it is held in the hand with the fingers spread apart round it (as if the operator were about to bowl a googly). Now hold it out about five feet from the ground and drop it on a smooth, hard surface; if it fails to fracture or breaks into only a few pieces it is too wet, but if it shatters into its former loose state it is just right.

Once you have determined the moisture content of the mix to be "just right," it is important to transport the stabilized earth to the formwork and accomplish the layering and compacting as quickly as possible. The cement in the mix will begin to hydrate as soon as water is added. It will start to absorb the moisture in the soil and, if not used in a relatively short period of time, this process will dry out the mix significantly enough to affect the compaction. How much time you actually have varies depending on the weather. If it's cool and cloudy, the mix will keep for a few hours. On the other hand, when it's hot and windy, the mix can become too dry after only one hour. If this is the case, you may even need to sprinkle and turn the pile several times as the wall panel is being constructed. You'll just have to keep your eye on the mix as you're building panels. Soils vary in how quickly they give up their moisture to the cement.

Batches of mix should be sized such they can be used within about three hours. As stated earlier, it is simplest if one batch of mix is prepared for each full-height form setup—approximately 3 cubic yards for a wall 18 inches thick. On jobs where the crew is small, it may not be possible to complete 3 cubic yards of wall in three hours. Or it may be that the method of forming you've chosen is to set and fill the lower half of a wall panel before stacking the upper forms, in which case stacking a form may take so long that the mix will dry out.

For these situations it will be necessary to make smaller batches of mix. Separate batches within the same wall panel are only a problem because the ratio of dry ingredients as well as the moisture content can vary slightly from one mix pile to the next, even with very experienced equipment operators. Variations in the mix will result in visible variations within the wall.

If you know ahead of time that the amount of material the crew is capable of compacting within three hours will not be sufficient to fill one full form, then adjust your mixing procedure. Instead of making one large batch, make smaller batches, one after another. Once half a batch is used and the next one started, blend the two together. This will maintain a more uniform color and moisture level, plus freshen up the cement.

Whether it takes one batch or two to complete a wall panel, it's important for both structural and cosmetic reasons to make every effort to complete each form setup within a relatively short period of time. Work for any given day should, ideally, be carried through to the completion of all wall panels undertaken. Otherwise, the issue of cold joints must be addressed.

Cold joints are the seams between a new layer on top and a dry layer below. They are not particularly visible if the formwork has not been readjusted. If no more than an hour or so has passed between layers, fresh mix can be placed on top of the old layer with no special considerations. On the other hand, when enough time has passed that the old layer is dry, some special precautions should be taken. Any loose material must be swept off the top of the old layer, and this layer should be moistened with water before the fresh mix is placed. Start with a thin layer of new material, settle it carefully along the face of the forms using a hand tamper or the handle of the shovel, then add more mix and begin the normal pneumatic compaction.

Rates of production vary considerably in building rammed earth walls, depending on the delivery system used for transporting the mix and the complexity of the formwork. With a tractor, pneumatic rammers, efficient formwork, and a crack crew, as much as 30 cubic yards of wall per day can be built. On the other extreme, with the old cumbersome forms, 5-gallon buckets, and hand rammers, 2 cubic yards of wall was a good day's work.

You'll have to gauge the scope of your own project. Assess your budget, the available manpower, and, most important of all, your personal energy level. Building with rammed earth can be a sort of magic, turning loose soil into stone. It can also be brutally hard work.

Alternate Mixing Procedures

A tiller on a tractor isn't the only way to make mix. I talked earlier about the drum mixer and the portable batch plant—one slow, the other expensive. However, another very affordable approach, one that we used for years, is a small garden rototiller. You might still want a tractor for measuring the ingredients, turning the pile, and carrying the prepared material to the forms, but a 5- or 8-horsepower tiller will be perfectly adequate for chopping up the soil and blending the cement and the water into the mix. It won't be as fast as the tractor-tiller, but it also won't be as big an investment.

Of course, it is also feasible to eliminate the tractor altogether. For the first few projects I built with stabilized rammed earth, I used a rototiller without a tractor. We measured out piles of soil by counting the number of shovelfuls, added the required number of cement sacks to the pile, mixed with the tiller, turned the pile with shovels, watered until the mix was ready, then shovelled directly into the forms. Hard work, but it proved effective and affordable.

On the least expensive end of the mixing-equipment spectrum is mixing by hand. This is a really slow process, but appropriate in very low-budget applications. It's hard to imagine situations in this country where even a garden tiller is too pricey for use in construction, but in other parts of the world, where labor rates are low, unemployment is high, and the cost of a gallon of gasoline is equal to an hour's wage or more, using a machine to do work that a human can accomplish and receive pay for is not appropriate. For the construction of the Los Carlitos Preschool in Leon, Nicaragua, we mixed by hand and moved by bucket over 200 cubic yards of soil. The workers on the project were paid in beans, rice, oil, and flour.

Delivery Systems

There are several different methods of delivering the soil mix to the wall forms. Which method to use depends on several factors: site logistics, production requirements, economic feasibility, and social responsibility. In developing countries, where labor is by far the most available construction resource, delivery by bucket or basket is the only appropriate method. Any alternative that would burn a nonrenewable fuel source, such as gasoline or diesel fuel, instead of human calories, should not even be considered an option.

Likewise, for a low-cost, owner-builder project in the developed world, 5-gallon buckets or wheelbarrows and ramps may prove to be the most economical approach. When a wallbuilding crew is so small that setting the forms and

For moving soil, plastic 5-gallon buckets or recycled food cans, like these on the job in Brazil, can be surprisingly efficient.

compacting the soil takes up the bulk of the time, renting a tractor to move the earth may represent too big a part of the budget. Although the prospect of moving a hundred cubic yards of earth in 5-gallon buckets might seem staggering, the truth is, it can be done. To move a mountain of earth one bucketful at a time, remember the words of Zen master Lao Tzu: "The journey of a thousand miles begins with the first step."

Progressing up the scale from least mechanical to most, we have several options. Our most frequently used method is to set a hopper (made of one full sheet of ¾-inch plywood with 2x12 sides) on the top waler of the forms, dump a full tractor bucketload onto this shelf, then shovel the material off the hopper into the forms as the rammers demand it. By using a hopper to store material rather than shovelling directly out of the bucket, the tractor operator has time to continue preparing fresh mix while the ramming is taking place. Otherwise, the tractor will be tied up during all of the ramming and won't have a chance to keep up with the mix. Also, just the time it takes for the tractor to drive to the mix pile and back can waste valuable minutes. The hopper can store enough material to allow for the roundtrip to the mix pile. You'll also find that the finished quality of the wall appears more uniform when the material is shovelled into the forms in thin layers rather than dumped directly from the bucket in thick loads.

When the crew is large enough to warrant additional equipment, we add a forklift to the project. You can construct a hopper for the forklift that will hold a cubic yard of mix, using a full sheet of plywood for the bottom and 2x12 sides and back. The forklift maneuvers near the mix pile, the tractor fills the hopper on the lift, the forklift positions itself near the wall forms, raises the hopper to just above the top, tilts forward slightly, and a shovelman empties the hopper into the forms as needed by the rammers. On average, it will take one shovelman and two rammers about fifteen minutes to compact a yard of mix, plenty of time for the tractor operator to continue the preparation of subsequent batches.

When walls are exceptionally tall or access is very difficult, filling the forms can become the most time-consuming and expensive part of the wallbuilding operation. You'll need to make a cost evaluation of your options. Choice number one, believe it or not, might be the bucket brigade. If only a small percentage of the wall panels are inaccessible, renting a special piece of equipment may not be economical. Second choice, especially for tall walls, is the fully extended tractor bucket and a person on the shovel. Shovelling over your head is hard work, without a doubt, but if the alternative is an expensive piece of rental equipment, a few hours of shovelling may be the best use of cash resources.

(Top left) A simple plywood shelf, resting on two legs and the top waler, can store enough soil material for several layers of ramming.

(Top right) A rental forklift and a 1-yard plywood hopper can free up the tractor for continuous mixing.

(Bottom left) The fully extended tractor bucket reaches to approximately 10 feet. From there it is only 7 more feet to the top of a two-story wall.

146

Choice number three is a rental crane or boom truck. By hooking a 1-yard concrete "bucket" onto the cable of the crane, we can reach far out over the hillside or way up in the air to fill very hard-to-reach formwork. A crane with an operator typically rents for $100 per hour, so it is imperative that, whenever a crane is hired, the formwork must be completely set, the crew large and experienced, and the mixing operation up to speed.

There are, of course, many other methods of moving bulk materials by mechanical means: conveyor belts, screw augers, pumps, and air-delivery systems. We tried a conveyor belt and found that it took up too much room on the site, was slow and cumbersome to reposition in front of each wall panel, and in general added time and expense to the wallbuilding process rather than saving it. The air-delivery system, like the conveyor, added rather than subtracted complexity. The compressor that was required to move the material was so large it burned too much diesel fuel per yard of soil transported. Even worse, the compressed air used to convey the material through the lines dried out the soil to such an extent that it was no longer properly moistened for good compaction. Screw augers, used with a great deal of success for moving grain from the bed of a truck to the top of a silo, are not very portable. They basically present the same problems as the conveyor belt, both being awkward to move around a rapidly evolving construction site. Pumping equipment only works when a material is wet and well-lubricated enough to move through the lines with a minimum of friction. A rammed earth mix is far too dry to be moved by a typical concrete pump.

A crane, delivering soil to the forms one full yard at a time, demands a ready set of forms and plenty of earth rammers to justify its $100/hour or more rental rate.

Ancient monument, Morocco.

Many pages of text, drawings, and black-and-white photos are a fine way to convey information, but what may be missing is the actual feeling. The color photos that follow capture to a greater degree the art and the essence of living in earth.

(Above, top) Passive solar home. Schmidt Builders, southeast Arizona. (Bottom) Sonoma, California.

(Above) The Chapel at
Holy Trinity Monastery.
Schmidt Builders,
St. David, Arizona.
(Left) A window framed
with sawn concrete
culvert pipe. Point Reyes,
California.
(Right) The Lenton Brae
winery. Built by Giles
Hohnen and Stabilised
Earth Structures,
Margaret River, Western
Australia.

(Above) Freestanding panels of full-height wall with short panels as infill beneath the window openings. Stabilised Earth Structures, Western Australia.
(Right) A covered entry on the western wall. A hint of strata line mimics the local geology.
(Facing page, bottom) A heavy timber roof, three-foot overhangs, solid redwood lintels, plastered earth walls, and clay tiles combine detailing from the mission, Santa Fe, and Craftsmen styles.

(Left) Courtyard walls and rustic wooden gates. Huston Construction, Albuquerque, New Mexico.

(Above) Exposed vigas, recessed lintels, and stepped parapets capture the regional style. Soledad Canyon Builders, southern New Mexico. (Right) The tools of the trade: clamps, shovels, and a hand rammer. (Facing page) Rammed earth columns support the grape arbor of this small cottage high on the ridge between Napa and Sonoma Counties, California.

Earth columns and vine covered
arbors create place without
enclosing space.

Deep recesses at all door and window openings are part of the magic of thick earth walls. (Right) Decorated in the style of Old Tucson. Rammed Earth Development, Inc., Tucson, Arizona.
(Facing page) Timbers, logs, and a terratile floor and hearth with plastered earth walls and fireplace. The curves in the chimney were created by carving the freshly rammed earth.

TERRENCE MOORE

*(Above) Hand-peeled logs,
turquoise windows, white plaster,
and a pine floor transport details
from Santa Fe to the Napa Valley.
(Right) Natural finished earth
walls with an exposed concrete bond
beam and cast-in-place soil cement
window sill.
(Facing page, top) Rising above the
blue oak and madrone, these 24-
foot-tall rammed earth panels
await the concrete post-and-beam
frame that provides such security in
an earthquake.
(Facing page, bottom left) A hand-
built hutch with doors paneled with
prunings from the vine, and a raw
earth wall. (Right) A tub in sunny
corner, with a view to the valley.*

In 1993, Pacific Gas & Electric selected this rammed earth residence with its thick walls and energy-efficient glazing to demonstrate the affordability of green houses. Gray strata lines flow through the rammed earth fireplace and interior walls, and hand-built trusses mounted on the plastered perimeter walls create huge open spaces.

The Kooralbyn Hotel Resort on Australia's Gold Coast. David Oliver of Greenway Architects calls his process Commercial Engineering Aggregate Construction (CEAC).

In summary, the most efficient and versatile equipment for transporting material, without doubt, is people and 5-gallon buckets. They're simple and uncomplicated and won't break down like expensive machinery has a tendency to do. When the buckets are not in use, the people can mix, shovel, ram, and interact with one another.

One small step up the scale from the pure simplicity of a project built by hand, is the tractor and the shovelman. In a developed country, where labor rates are high and a rental yard is around the corner, a tractor is an affordable, versatile, and logical addition to the team. Where the crane or conveyor must sit idle for precious minutes, the shovelman can also take down and set up forms, water the mix pile, go get lunch, and best of all, think.

Ramming the Earth

Think of rammed earth as a sort of "instant rock." The natural process of creating sedimentary rock occurs over a span of thousands and millions of years. An earth rammer, on the other hand, creates it in a matter of minutes.

Unlike most other tradespeople in the building industry, who work in relatively calm surroundings, the earth rammer plies his trade in an environment filled with the dust of soil and cement, the roar of diesel engines, and the staccato thump thump thump of backfill tampers reverberating within the form boxes. To some people, the idea of working so hard and with such an intensity of noise and energy is inconceivable. To others, and I count myself among them, it is magic . . . watching soil become stone beneath your feet, and knowing that, when the forms are removed, a well-built wall will be here that will survive the test of centuries.

Compaction is the force which turns soil into sedimentary rock. In nature, it occurs through the compression exerted by subsequent layers of soil deposition and the weight of the new soil layers on the old ones. In rammed earth, compaction occurs through impact, the force of a heavy object falling time and again on a recipient soil mass. This impact not only compresses the soil, but also encourages the individual particles within the soil to realign themselves. The jarring or vibratory action of the tampers forces the particles into the tightest possible molecular and mechanical configuration. Compression alone does not achieve the maximum ultimate strength of a given soil blend. Pounding the particles, bouncing them around against one another, is necessary to achieve the best results.

The historically proven tool for compacting soil is the hand tamper, a heavy block of wood fitted with a pole for a handle. Slow and tedious, tamping by

148

Around 99 percent of all rammed earth structures ever built have been constructed using a hand-ramming tool, much like this one pictured in use in Morocco.

hand is nevertheless extremely effective. Millions of yards of earth on six continents, have been rammed into stone under the repeated blows of a hand tamper. The average rate of production for a crew building rammed earth by hand, as documented in several older publications, is $1\frac{1}{2}$ cubic feet of wall per person per hour.

For our project in Nicaragua, we used four steel hand tampers per form, rotated the crews every 2 to 3 feet of wall height, and built 200 cubic yards of wall in eight days. With a total crew of forty workers and components for two complete sets of forms, the average hourly production was roughly 2 cubic feet.

The factors contributing to slightly better production were the faster-to-assemble formwork and the psychological motivation of a bigger crew.

A good hand tamper can be made with a 4 x 4 x $\frac{5}{16}$-inch steel plate welded to a 6-foot-long piece of 1-inch steel pipe. This results in a tool sufficiently heavy to achieve good compaction, while at the same time light enough to operate for long periods of time without tiring the arms. The 1-inch diameter of the pipe fits well into the hands.

For our work in the United States, we always use mechanical tamping equipment, powered by compressed air. The hand tampers are only used in tight spaces and around the plumbing fittings and electrical boxes. On a large project, we'll have four to six 30-pound pneumatic rammers in operation, all hosed to a 120 cfm air compressor.

The compaction process begins at the bottom of the form box, on a 4- to 6-inch layer of prepared soil mix. When tamping by hand, stand in the form box, and first settle the soil with your feet. Lift the tamper about 12 to 18 inches high and let it drop. Begin at one end of the form and work your way along the form from side to side.

Two or more people in the form—as many as can fit comfortably, in fact—will improve the overall rate of production. The rhythm of a team effort yields a psychological boost to the work. Lift and drop. Lift and drop. As the soil becomes compacted, the sound of the tamping will change from a dull thud to a ringing sound. When the layer rings, it's time for more earth.

When using backfill tampers powered by air compressors, some earth rammers prefer to stand outside the form box, where their toes are out of the danger zone. We've installed extensions on the handles of our tampers so that it is possible to reach all the way down into an 8-foot-deep form panel from the top. Whether in or out of the box, begin

Plenty of willing help and more than enough hand tampers to go around kept the enthusiasm high during the construction of the Los Carlitos preschool in Leon, Nicaragua.

An adequate supply of well-paid help and half a dozen pneumatic rammers finished this set of walls in short order. Where labor rates are high, speed is essential.

150

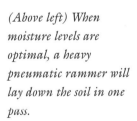

(Above left) When moisture levels are optimal, a heavy pneumatic rammer will lay down the soil in one pass.

(Top left) Long-handled rammers allow workers to reach to the bottom of a form when electrical and plumbing lines make climbing down inside impossible.

compacting at a corner, make a quick pass along one side, then across the end, and back along the other side to the starting point. Run the tamper down the center, then repeat the loop two times. Let the tamper linger a moment at each of the four corners.

The loud reverberation within the form may create so much extraneous noise that the ringing sound of a compacted soil layer will not be as detectable as with hand tamping, yet there still is a sound to be heard when the soil reaches full density. It is basically the sound of the formwork itself resonating. You'll learn to recognize the sound of well-compacted soil very quickly.

Once a soil layer has been completely compacted, shovel in another 4 to 6 inches and repeat the tamping ritual. Place layer upon layer, until the form is full and the top layer is hard. Because each of the layers benefits from the forces applied to it by the ramming of the layer above, you'll need to take twice as much time compacting the top layer as you did the others.

The above procedure for building a wall section, as you might guess, results in a "layered" look. Once the forms are stripped, the wall will display very visible horizontal lines between each of the courses, like sedimentary rock. The more level and consistent each of the loose courses are, the more uniform the layers in the finished wall. This layering is the traditional look of rammed earth. If desired, it can even be accentuated by increasing the thickness of each layer, from 6 inches of loose material to 8.

In our work, we've tried to move away from the strong layered look towards a more homogeneous wall. To achieve this, we continuously shovel material into the forms under the head of the tamper rather than working in clearly defined layers. The tractor dumps a bucket of mix on the hopper, the shovelman places it, one shovel at a time in the form, and the tamper is kept continuously moving back and forth over the soil. Each area within the form receives a brief pass from the tamper, and the soil becomes increasingly more compacted as additional material is piled on. None of the layers will appear to be solid, because full compaction actually takes place below the surface. The pressure from an upper layer delivers a surcharge to the layer below. The top layer, of course, must always be overworked to make up for the lack of that surcharge compaction.

Whatever method of ramming you choose to use for your projects—buckets and hand tampers, thick layers and pneumatics, or continuous delivery—the results are structurally very much the same. If the soil has been selected carefully, moistened properly, and well compacted within the formwork, rammed earth walls become like stone. And believe it or not, like stone they can become stronger with age.

(Facing page, top right) A shoveler fills the form as quickly as the rammer packs down the earth.

(Facing page, bottom right) Essentially reconstituted sedimentary rock, rammed earth takes on the appearance of the process that was used to construct it. Poured-in-place bond beams represent just another geologic layer.

CHAPTER NINE

Doors, Windows, Niches, and Nooks

(Facing page) Door and window openings demand careful and precise form work of their own.

T HE SOLID PANELS of rammed earth are in one sense the easy part of the wall system. Believe it or not, it can take longer to create the openings in the wall than it does to build the walls themselves. How can this be?

For one thing, a hole for a door or window, which we tend to think of as "the absence of earth exactly where we want it," may require forms that are actually more complex to construct than the standard wall forms. For another thing, installing this custom form takes extra time, careful measurements, and a scrupulous double check. Compacting uniformly on both sides of the opening demands special attention. Once the top of the opening is reached, the earth must be carefully levelled on both sides and the lintel beam must be lowered into the form to span the opening. When completed, disassembling the window or door form and removing it from the opening takes much longer than taking down the standard wall form.

A separate custom form, which we call a VDB (volume displacement box), must be constructed for each different-sized opening. In an average house, there may be two different-sized doors and four or more different sizes of windows. Each of the VDB's must be made square, sturdy, and to the *exact* dimensions specified by the manufacturer of the unit. If the size of the opening is wrong or out of square, it can involve hours of extra work either chipping the opening bigger or trimming it out.

This is the bad news: Fenestrations for a complex house built using the continuous-form system can be very time-consuming. The good news is that fenestrations for a house constructed using either the freestanding or panel-to-panel systems can be much simpler. For most openings, the VDB's can be eliminated altogether if the locations for the doors or windows are planned to

Small windows are punched out of the continuous-form earthwall. The bond beam spans the window as a simple lintel.

correspond with the panel layouts. Openings for small windows may still be created with VDB's dropped into standard form panels, but all the doors and the larger windows can be accommodated merely by accurately positioning the endboards for the wall panels that flank each opening. In other words, the distance between panels must match the rough opening width of the door or window unit. To create the proper rough heights, a lintel or bond beam spans the top of the opening and, for windows, a partial panel of earth is constructed below.

Before we discuss the construction of the fenestration VDB's and their use in the continuous-form system, let's clarify the procedure for the simpler method.

Creating Basic Rough Openings

In the freestanding system, each wall section is spaced 6 inches from the adjacent panels. This 6-inch space is eventually filled with concrete. Concrete columns also frame each door opening as well as the larger window openings.

This means that the spacing between the panels flanking these openings must be calculated to include the rough opening for the door or window unit plus the thickness of both columns and their trim. Smaller windows do not typically require the columns. Spacing between panels flanking small window openings should be calculated to match the specified rough opening.

When building the panel-to-panel system, the rough opening for each door or window unit will determine the space to allow between panels. First build one panel of earth with the end of the panel corresponding to one side of the opening. Measure over the exact dimension of the rough opening, say $39\frac{1}{2}$ inches for a 3-foot door, and position the endboard for the next setup so that the inside face of the endboard lines up with that $39\frac{1}{2}$-inch mark.

Window and door heights are important. Since either earth, timber, or concrete must span the tops of each opening in order to provide continuity to the wall system, it is simplest if door and window heads line up with the underside of the wood or concrete bond beam. With walls typically 8 feet tall and bond beams 9 to 12 inches thick, the tops of door and window openings should be 84 to 87 inches off the floor. A standard 6-foot, 8-inch door unit, with 2x6's attached to the jambs and head for mounting supports, will fit comfortably in the 84-inch-high opening. Casing and trim must be custom-cut.

Windows, on the other hand, fit into an opening created between the underside of the bond beam and a short section of rammed earth. Take the rough opening height of the unit plus $1\frac{1}{2}$ inches for a 2x6 at the top plus the thickness of the windowsill (wood, tile, or poured-in-place concrete). Subtract this number from 84 inches (to the underside of the bond beam) and the result is the height of the short panel of earth under the window. Normally, these infill pieces are the last sections of earth to be constructed in the wall system.

When individual panels of rammed earth constitute the wall system, window openings are created by building partial-height sections.

Creating Rough Openings Using the VDB

The function of the volume displacement box is to create a precise opening in a solid wall section. The VDB must be built strongly and accurately enough that the hole in the wall left after the box is removed is square and the unit will fit into it without modification.

The VDB must be strong enough to resist collapse or distortion under the forces of compaction and yet be removable from the wall after it has been compressed on three sides by rammed earth and concrete. After being removed from the wall, it must be reassembled for reuse. For multiple projects, a given VDB may be used a dozen times or more.

A VDB has two sides and a top, but no bottom. If timber or precast con-

An opening in a long section of wall is cast using a collapsible wooden displacement box.

crete lintels are to be dropped in rather than using rammed earth or poured-in-place concrete to span the openings, the top of the VDB can be eliminated as well. No bottom is necessary in any case because the door VDB's rest directly on top of the foundation or slab and the window VDB's are lowered on top of a section of compacted earthwall.

We build our VDB's out of the same plywood we use for wall forms—¾-inch high-density overlay (HDO). It's expensive, but lasts longer and stays straighter than CDX plywood. For just one project, the cost of HDO may not be justified. For multiple uses, though, and especially in cases where the VDB's will be stored for long periods of time between jobs, the more expensive plywood is well worth the extra investment.

The sides of the VDB are equal in length to the height of the rough opening. For square-sided openings, the sides of the VDB are just like short endboards, equal in width to the width of the wall. For bevelled openings, a detail frequently used in traditional thick-walled designs to allow more light to enter the room, the sides of the VDB's must be constructed differently. Three pieces of plywood are needed for each of the sides: a backer piece equal in width to the wall thickness, and two face pieces that create both the flat portion where the unit mounts and the angled inside piece. Study Figure 17 to see how these VDB sides are made.

To maintain the precise dimensions as well as the exact square of the VDB, we use solid plywood infill pieces (gussets) screwed to wood strips attached to the back sides of the backer pieces. (Hold the wood strips 3 inches from the top of the side pieces to allow for removal of the top piece.) For 18-inch and wider walls, you'll need three of the gussets to prevent the sides from bowing. It is possible to substitute a series of 2x4 braces for the

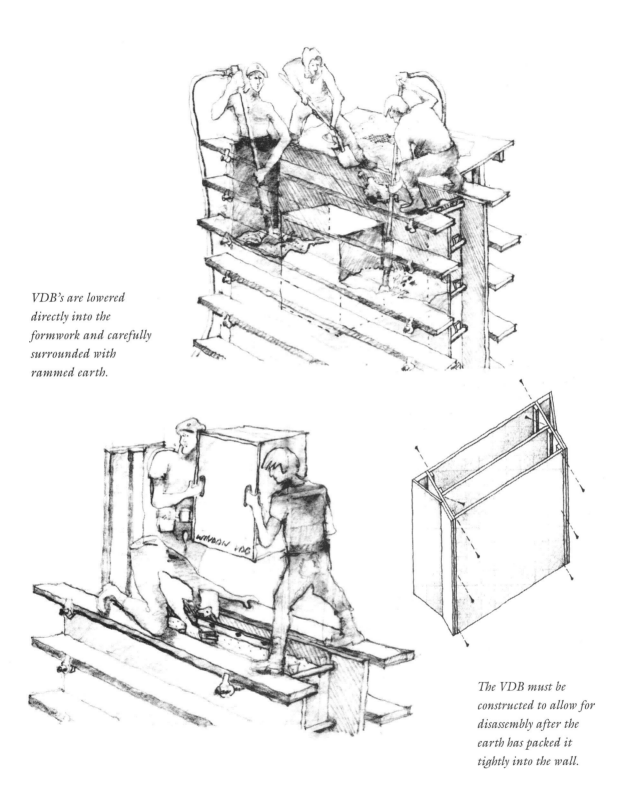

VDB's are lowered directly into the formwork and carefully surrounded with rammed earth.

The VDB must be constructed to allow for disassembly after the earth has packed it tightly into the wall.

158

gussets, but the solid plywood infills are your best guarantee that the opening will stay square.

If earth will be rammed or concrete poured across the top of the opening rather than using dropped-in lintels, then the VDB will need a plywood top strong enough to support the material above it. Because the VDB will need to be extracted from the opening once it is cast (a process that can be difficult if not thought through), the top should be made in a minimum of two pieces. We actually make the top out of three pieces: two short ones that are cut to fit the tops of the side pieces and the third piece cut to fit between the sides. To clarify: the length of the third piece is equal to the rough opening minus twice the thickness of the side pieces. The length of the third piece for the top will be equal to the length of the gussets or the 2x4 braces. Again, study Figure 17.

Once the VDB has accomplished its job, having been encased in earth and concrete, it must be disassembled and removed from the wall. First remove all three gussets (or all of the 2x4 braces), then pull the center top piece down and out, and, finally, remove the side pieces carefully. Re-assemble the VDB on the ground and it's ready to be used again.

Building the VDB on the ground and lowering it into the form as a unit is our preferred method. Another procedure that also works, albeit more slowly, is to install the components of the VDB one at a time within the formwork. First, mark on the inside face of the formwork exactly where the window or door is to go, hold the side pieces in place, one at a time, and have a helper screw through the face forms into the side pieces. Slip in either the gussets or the 2x4 braces, then drop in the top piece and tack it in place. Disassembly is the same for both setups.

Basically, VDB's are a lot of work for nothing:

(Top) A fully assembled VDB can be lowered into the formwork with either the tractor bucket or a forklift.

(Above) After the wall has been rammed around it, removing the VDB yields the finished opening.

nothing but a hole. It's ironic, but the measure of how skilled you are in rammed earth depends, to a great extent, on how efficiently and accurately you make the holes.

Door and Window Lintels

In designs where walls are to be taller than 8 feet, lintels are necessary to span the openings and support the weight of the wall above. Lintels can be of several types: precast concrete, timber, steel, or, for short spans, reinforced earth. The simplest to install is reinforced earth. Use steel reinforcing bars embedded directly in the rammed earth, placed approximately 3 inches above the top of the window VDB and extending at least 12 inches beyond the sides of the VDB. First layer 4 to 5 inches of prepared soil mix on top of the VDB and lightly settle it with the tamper. Lay three or four pieces of reinforcing steel directly on top of this bed of earth, shovel in another 3 or 4 inches of prepared soil, and compact thoroughly, just as you would for any other section of wall. Continue layering and compacting to the desired height.

Steel I-beams, checked for size by a structural engineer, can also be embedded in the earth to create hidden lintels. Like rebar, the I-beams extend 12 inches beyond the sides of the VDB. Unlike the rebars, which are buried completely in the earth, the I-beam rests directly on top of the VDB. When the

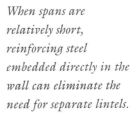

When spans are relatively short, reinforcing steel embedded directly in the wall can eliminate the need for separate lintels.

In some regions, wooden lintels are practically the signature of an earthwalled design.

window box is removed, the bottom flange of the I-beam is visible from below.

Exposed lintels are frequently used in earthwall construction. In fact, wooden lintels are practically a signature of the Santa Fe style. Lintels, whether heavy timber or precast concrete, are lowered into the formwork after the earth has been compacted to the top of the VDB. Make certain the bed for the lintel is flat, level, and hard. Set the lintel in place, extending 12 inches beyond the VDB on both sides, check for level, then continue filling and compacting to the desired height. To last forever, timber lintels should be either treated wood or a species which is naturally resistant to decay, such as redwood or cedar. From a sustainability standpoint, it is best to use recycled timbers.

When the formwork is stripped, timber and precast concrete lintels remain exposed as a part of the architecture. Reinforced earth or steel I-beams, on the other hand, are not seen; rather, the opening appears merely as a hole "punched" in the mass of the wall. When the continuous-form system is used in one-story applications, the exposed concrete bond beam encircles the building, spanning all door and window openings.

An arched opening, if it is not excessively wide, can eliminate the need for lintels altogether. As the Romans learned (and the Greeks did not), an arch allows for much greater spans than horizontal lintels, by placing all of the material in and below the arch into compression, the condition in which masonry is strongest. Like lintels in the Santa Fe style, arches are commonly asso-

Precast concrete lintels can actually be less expensive than solid timber. They also present an opportunity for custom castings

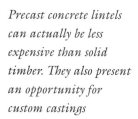

An arch in an earthwall allows the loads to be transferred through the wall without the need for structural lintels.

ciated with thick masonry walls. Perfecting the formwork for building arches is virtually a prerequisite for advanced earthbuilding.

Building the Arch Form

We build arched openings in the walls using a two-piece form: a standard VDB and an arched top piece that attaches to the VDB. This way the VDB can be disassembled and removed from the finished wall in the standard fashion, after which the arch form will drop out in one piece. Construct the formwork for the arch by first marking out the shape of the arch you desire—low, semicircular, or gothic—on a piece of ¾-inch plywood. Cut two, one for each side. The dimension should be ½ inch less than the finished radius, to allow for the overlay.

Next cut a series of 2x4 blocks equal in length to the thickness of the wall minus twice the thickness of the plywood. (For an 18-inch thick wall and ¾-inch plywood, the blocks will be 16½ inches long.) Set the two arch templates opposite each other and arrange the blocks along the radius, spaced so that they are as close together as possible. Nail through the plywood into the ends of the blocks, taking care that the top edge of each block is flush with the radius edge of the plywood. Depending on the steepness of the curve, the outside two blocks may need to be bevelled to complete the radius.

Finally, measure the overall length of the radius and cut two pieces of ¼-inch masonite to fit the top of the arch. (The second piece will be a little bit longer than the first.) Bend and nail the first masonite overlay to the series of blocks, then the second overlay.

The arch top is attached to the top of the standard VDB with plywood cleats screwed to the back side of the arch template and the back side of the VDB

The form for an arched opening is composed of a top separate from the sides.

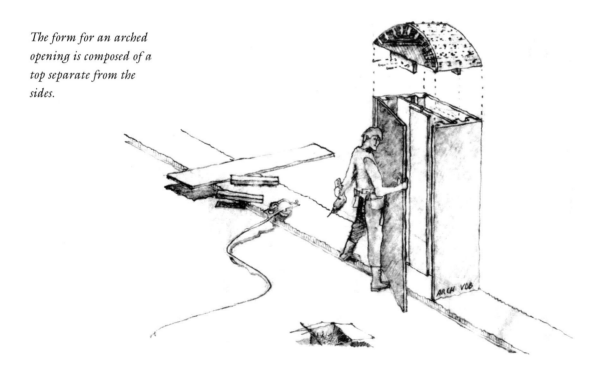

gusset. One note of caution: If you intend to remove the arch form in one piece after the wall has been rammed, be certain that the width of the arch form is a fraction of an inch less than the width of the VDB, or that the two arch templates are a fraction of an inch different from each other. Otherwise, the arch form will be locked into the wall.

Niches, Fireplaces, and Other Built-ins

Displacing volume in a solid wall is tempting. A niche for a favorite piece of art is a natural. Fireplaces tucked into a corner of the living room seem almost a part of the thick-walled language. Shelving for books, dishes, music paraphernalia, or even a recess for the kitchen stove all add to the intrigue of the mass wall.

The VDB can do it all, though its construction will vary slightly when it is not being used to completely penetrate the wall. For one thing, it must have a back piece that is supported well enough not to deflect under the forces of compaction. For another, it must be slightly tapered to allow for removal from the wall after construction. It should have no sharp edges and should be coated with form-release oil prior to use.

Fireplaces are more complex. They require a series of VDB's. The first two are used to create the firebox and to support the lintel beam. These can remain in the formwork until the wall is completed. The firebox VDB must be built large enough to accommodate a lining of firebricks. The third VDB sits on top of the firebox and is used to create the smoke shelf, throat, and transition to the flue liners (chimney). It's rectangular in plan, but tapers as it rises upwards. Because it is offset slightly behind the firebox (a necessity to allow for proper drafting of the chimney), it is difficult to remove from below. For this reason, we disassemble and remove the smoke shelf VDB as soon as the earth is compacted around it, before continuing with the chimney. To build the chimney, clay flue liners are stacked one at a time as the prepared soil mix is layered and compacted. In earthquake-prone areas, we typically terminate the rammed earth at the top of the wall and make a transition to metal flues for the rest of the chimney.

Once you've mastered constructing a fireplace in rammed earth, you can feel pretty confident. Creating spaces that draw you into them is one of the exciting aspects of building with a material that has the depth and texture of solid earth. Whatever the architectural style, the key to success is the formwork ...and mastery of the VDB.

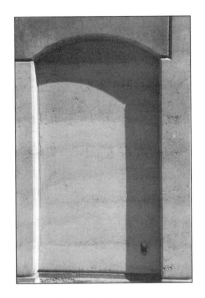

A niche for a bookcase or an alcove will accentuate the mass of the wall.

A barbecue in the backyard would be a good project on which to practice ramming and formbuilding skills.

Installing Doors and Windows

The procedure for installing doors and windows varies depending on several factors: the material surrounding the opening, the postioning of the unit within the opening, the specifications for trim, and the final wall surface treatment.

The simplest procedure combines the freestanding panel system, with the wooden formwork for the columns and bond beam left in place, and a manufactured window unit. Using this combination, the nail fins on the manufactured unit are simply attached to the exterior portion of the wooden column formwork, caulked, and covered with trim. The drawback to this installation is that the windows are right on the outside of the building, revealing nothing of the thickness and depth of the wall. They can also leak if the trim isn't thoroughly caulked.

If the door or window is to sit within the opening, a few inches from the outside face of the wall, it must be securely attached to the sides of the wall, whether the opening is framed in wooden formwork, concrete columns, or rammed earth. There are two ways to do this. One is to attach pressure-treated 2x4's to the jambs and head, then use the nail fins to secure the manufactured unit to the 2x4's. Caulk and trim as needed. The second is to order the units without the nail fins and attach the unit directly to the jambs and head. Drill a series of holes spaced roughly 18 inches apart, set the unit in place in the

A fixed window in a post-and-beam frame, as shown in this chicken house, is the easiest of all window installations.

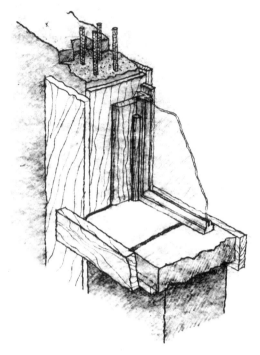

*Window unit installs
directly against column
formwork.*

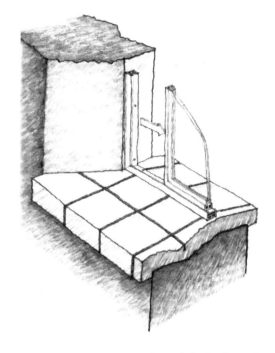

*A precisely-sized opening
is imperative.*

opening, making sure it is plumb and level, then mark the holes on the jamb, head, and sill (more on sills later) and remove the unit. Using a masonry bit if the opening is either concrete or rammed earth, drill holes as marked and insert either large plastic anchors or lead shields. Reposition the unit in the opening and screw through the frame into the anchors. Caulk and trim as needed.

When an installation with no trim has been specified by the designer or architect, it is even more critical that the VDB's be made precisely. Allowing for ¼ inch on each side, install the unit as described in the previous paragraph, then grout or caulk the gap with an appropriately colored material.

Our experience has shown that the large-sized plastic anchors are strong enough for every installation except the heaviest of doors. We've also learned that, when attaching to rammed earth, the anchors should be recessed an inch or two into the wall. (Rammed earth is never as strong at the face as it is within the wall.) As with wall forms and VDB's, my recommendation with door and window installation is to start with a relatively straightforward design detail

In the freestanding panel system of construction the electrical boxes are not set directly into the earthwall, but mounted into the formwork for the concrete posts.

and, as you gain more experience, move gradually towards increased complexity and sophistication.

Electrical Systems

Based on regulations in the Uniform Building Code, all wiring in the wall system must be in conduit, either EMT or PVC, and all outlet boxes for receptacles, switches, and fixtures must be rated for embedment in masonry. In the freestanding panel system, the boxes and conduit are typically located in the concrete columns. If the wooden formwork is to remain in place, the outlet boxes are mounted into neat holes cut in the formwork. If the formwork is to be removed, the boxes are mounted on the back side. Conduit can either come up from the foundation, installed at the time the stem wall is poured, or run up the column and through the bond beam. Running the wiring on top of the bond beam behind a trim board leaves it easily accessible.

In the panel-to-panel and the continuous-form systems, the electrical boxes must be installed directly in the rammed earth. One method for doing this is to embed one box for each receptable, switch, or fixture, coupled with conduit long enough to extend out of the bond beam. As the wall is being built, boxes with their conduit attached are set against the formwork at the

Press the electrical box against the form with your boot while embedding it in a mound of hand-tamped earth.

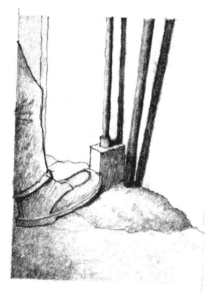

When ramming earth to encase boxes and conduits, take care to maintain the proper positioning within the wall. Conduits must be kept near the middle.

An electrician may decide to install most of the conduit and boxes before the formwork for the walls has been erected.

specified locations, held in place with a foot, and carefully compacted around with a hand tamper or the shovel handle until enough of a mound of earth protects the installation to allow for a return to mechanical compaction.

It is not unusual to forget a box or two in the excitement of building with rammed earth, and it also occasionally happens that boxes are knocked a bit out of alignment by the rammers. To avoid both of these problems, we attach small locator blocks directly to the forms for each place a box is to be installed. The blocks are cut from plywood to the inside dimension of the outlet box and back-bevelled slightly to allow for easy removal of the form panels. Once the earth has been rammed level with the bottom of each block, the box with attached conduit is slipped over the block and compacted around as described above. As the level of the wall rises, the conduit can be delicately bent away from the formwork to make room for the rammers.

Before the bond beam is poured, all of the conduits should be adjusted and fixed in place so that they emerge alongside but not through the wooden sill plate. This way, no additional holes need be drilled in the plate, and the wiring as it emerges from the conduits can all be easily hidden behind a trim board. Technically, the building codes do not allow romex wire to be run through conduits. If this requirement is enforced within your jurisdiction, then you'll need to run additional conduit on top of the bond beam, and place junction boxes at key locations to allow for the splices between romex and single-strand wiring.

Wiring in the continuous-form system is approached differently. Once all of the inside panels for any given length of wall have been set, each of the required boxes for receptacles, switches, and fixtures in that setup are attached to the formwork with bolts or tie wire fed through holes drilled in

Once the forms have been set, the boxes can be securely fastened to the plywood with tie wire.

the form. Locator blocks will help prevent twisting of the boxes. Conduits are then run horizontally within the wall, from box to box as needed for the circuitry, finally exiting the formwork through either the foundation stem wall or the bond beam. When an electrical circuit is to continue into the next setup of wall, the conduits can be fed through holes in the endboard, to be coupled onto for their continuation.

Telephone, TV cable, thermostat relays, speaker wires, and any other system which is later installed in conduit can all be dealt with in this same manner. In fact, because it is so easy to install conduits before the wall is built, and so difficult to add them afterwards, it's a good idea to provide a few extra conduits just for future contingencies.

Plumbing Systems

It is our preference to avoid placing plumbing, whether supply lines or waste lines, in the earth walls. The first reason is just the added difficulty of compacting around embedded objects. Electrical service in the wall is an unavoidable necessity, but plumbing lines can in most cases just as easily come up through the slab as through the wall.

Vent pipes, which typically run straight up and down and carry no water, present little difficulty to the rammers and can be routed into the earthwalls. Supply lines, on the other hand, run the risk of being smashed, kinked, or, worse yet, broken during the ramming. If they simply can't be brought up from

In cases where it is necessary to run plumbing supply lines inside the earthwalls, wrap them with insulation or plastic sleeves and take special care when compacting around them.

the floor, then by all means compact around them very carefully, preferably with hand tampers, until they are fully encased in and protected by a surround of rammed earth. Waste lines, like supply lines, can get broken during ramming and should be treated very cautiously. If you're not careful, the end of the waste line against the formwork can be bent downward under the force of the rammed earth, resulting in reverse fall and a line that won't drain.

Here are a few tips for those cases where plumbing is to be installed within the earth walls:

1. Wrap all lines with foam padding to protect them and to provide room for expansion within the wall.
2. Locate the lines in the center of the wall to simplify the compaction process and to decrease the chances of the lines telegraphing cracks to the outside faces of the wall.
3. Check all waste lines during compaction for correct slope.
4. Whenever possible, lay out all lines to exit walls under cabinets or behind fixtures.
5. Put all supply lines under pressure and check gauges frequently during ramming.

Miscellaneous Other Considerations

There are numerous other reasons to run holes through the walls: dryer vents, exhaust fans, range hoods, oven vents, and doggie doors, to name a few. These seemingly minor penetrations, if forgotten, can result in expensive counter-measures when the wall is 18 to 24 inches of solid earth. The cost of coring a 6-inch hole through a 2-foot-thick wall to run a drier vent, for instance, might run $200.

We have found that the simplest method of creating the necessary penetra-tions is to install chases in the walls as they are being constructed. The best material for a chase is ABS pipe. It's inexpensive, and strong enough to not collapse under the pressure of ramming. Cut lengths of ABS pipe, whatever diameter is required, to ¼ inch less than the wall thickness. Ram up to the height specified for the chase, lay the length of pipe in place, and embed it in earth with a little hand ramming, just as you would an electrical box. Once it has been sufficiently protected, return to mechanical compaction. For larger wall penetrations, such as a wood box or the pet entrance, you may need to construct a collapsible VDB.

Any niche, arch, or other detail in the wall is achievable. It's all a matter of

If possible, run the plumbing lines vertically in the wall rather than horizontally. You'll stand less chance of damaging them.

designing the right formwork, and then building it correctly. The trick to VDB's is getting them to come apart.

Creating Space Within the Wall

Aside from the superior thermal and acoustic performance that results from surrounding yourself with massive earthwalls, there is the appeal of creating spaces within the wall itself. Whether it's a small niche to house a special piece of art, or a built-in seat for a quiet place to read, the temptation to "carve" space out of the wall is a natural.

The same technique used to construct door and window openings can also be used to create niches for art, books, or seats—namely, the collapsible VDB. The difference between constructing VDB's for fenestrations and for niches is that, rather than extending the entire depth of the wall, formwork for niches is typically half the wall thickness. One face of the VDB can be open for attachment to the wall formwork, but the other face must include a well-fit plywood insert, strong enough to resist the pressure of ramming. This face will create the back wall of the niche.

VDB's used to construct niches are more difficult to disassemble than those used to construct fenestrations, because only one side is accessible once the wall has been built. To allow for extraction of the niche VDB, cut the side and top pieces on a slight angle such that the dimensions of the niche at the face of the wall will be slightly greater than those at the back. Once the wall has been completed, the plywood insert forming the back of the niche is removed first, then the sides and top.

Over the years, we've used niche forms as small as a shoebox (for a candle shelf) and as big as a closet. In the kitchen, a niche can provide a perfect recess to bring the face of the refrigerator in line with the front of the cabinets. In the library, use a niche to house bookshelves or a sound system. In the family room, use a niche to make the TV less conspicuous.

One of the more practical uses of the space within the wall is as water heater closets. This way, the noise generated by the operation of the equipment is dampened by the mass of the wall. If the water heater closet is located on the north side of the house, the waste heat absorbed by the wall will offset some of the heat loss from the building. A niche VDB as big as an opening for a double door can be set in the outside portion of the wall. Into this opening can be placed not only the domestic water heater, but also the heat source and pumps for the hydronic radiant floor. A quick comparison between the width of a standard water heater and the thickness of the typical earthwall will reveal that there is not space within the wall itself to completely house the unit. One so-lution is to add a small amount of additional framing on the outside of the building, with an abbreviated shed roof. The other approach is to construct the VDB the full width of the wall (just like a door opening) and frame out into the interior space the few inches required. If the water heaters are placed directly opposite one of the bathrooms, this solution can be particularly advantageous for the plumbing runs.

Imagination and time are your only limits to implementation of the niche VDB. Because it can take some practice (as can all aspects of building with rammed earth), a good starter project might be a backyard barbeque with a wood storage space beneath the cooking pit. The barbeque can be the simple variety, which is basically a rectangular block of earth about waist-high; or it can be a more elaborate affair complete with horizontal workspace, fireplace, and chimney.

The simple version involves one standard form with endboard cut to the width of the unit and a VDB assembly set directly on the ground. Once you have rammed to a minimum of 6 inches above the top of the VDB, set in a four-sided shallow form to define the fire pit and continue ramming to the top.

The elaborate version builds on the simple one. Set a second standard form, slightly smaller than the one below, directly on top of the base. Con-struct and install a smaller VDB to define the shape of the fireplace, then care-fully compact soil to the top of the VDB. Set a clay flue liner on top of the VDB in the center of the upper form, then carefully compact soil around the liner to the top. If you choose, set a third-stage standard form on top of the second, install another clay flue liner, then compact more soil. Stop when you have reached the desired height.

Success with a complex backyard project such as an architect-quality barbeque will help you develop your confidence. After tackling this, a niche for a bookcase or an art object will seem easy in comparison.

CHAPTER TEN

Bond Beams and Other Connections

First there is a rumble, a deep groaning sound as shock waves move outward from the epicenter. The ground begins to move, slowly at first and then often with a powerful jerk. Trees and power poles sway, rocks cascade from cutbanks, roads and fields rip apart...and poorly constructed buildings crumble into rubble.

(Facing page) In earthquake country, a concrete bond beam on top of an earth wall provides an important element of safety.

THE QUESTION MOST frequently asked of any earthbuilder in California is, "What happens to one of these earth buildings in an earthquake?" The answer should be, "Nothing."

To build with masonry in areas prone to earthquakes requires solid construction principles. Foundations must be of adequate width and depth to support the structure. The walls must be properly built, and they must be held together with adequate bond beams. Intermediate floors and roofs must be attached with strong connectors. Good engineering and careful construction together create a safe building.

There are many regions of the world where earthwalls can stand on their own, without bond beams or wall ties. Gravity alone will keep the wall and the roof in place without any supplemental stiffening, reinforcing, or connecting. Rafters for the roof are nailed directly to a wooden sill plate, which in turn is spiked or bolted to the tops of the earthwalls. Countless buildings constructed in precisely this manner have endured for centuries, in many cases with very primitive foundation systems as well. The principal reason for their survival is the geological stability of the region. In seismically active areas such as Afghanistan, Japan, Latin America, and California, though, stronger wall systems are a must.

The most common method for achieving a stronger wall system in modern construction is through the use of a bond beam. Constructed of timber, steel, or reinforced concrete, the bond beam sits on top of the earthwalls and is used to tie the system together as well as to anchor the roof. In high seismic-risk areas, the roof itself can be used to help tie the walls together by its stiffness and its strong connections to the bond beam. What both the bond beam and the roof "diaphragm" accomplish is the uniform distribution of earthquake loads onto all four walls rather than just the two which are perpendicular to the direction of the ground movement.

In a typical earthquake, the ground jerks rapidly in one direction, essentially moving out from under the walls. It's like an amateur magician trying to yank the tablecloth from beneath a setting of crystal. This causes the wall to bend, sway, and possibly break. The actual effect of this ground movement is somewhat like a truck running into the side of the building. If a wall is standing all by itself and a truck hits it, the wall might fall over. If, on the other hand, the wall is braced, as it is with a bond beam and roof diaphragm, then it can better resist collapse by sharing the impact with the other elements which support it. Every time the loaded wall tries to move, it is restrained by the perpendicular walls and by the bolts, clips, plywood, and nails on the roof.

The bond beam that we use in the vast majority of our work is made of reinforced concrete, poured in place on top of the earthwalls. The forms for this concrete beam, in both the freestanding and panel-to-panel wall systems, are wooden 2x10's or 2x12's clamped to the tops of the walls. Steel reinforcing bars, held 1½ inches above the wall, are tied around the perimeter; anchor bolts for the sill plate and any other roof mounting hardware are suspended from the formwork; and then concrete is poured to the top of the forms and vibrated.

The connection between the bond beam and the earthwalls themselves is crucial to the structure. In the freestanding panel system, where concrete columns are poured at intervals around the perimeter, the bond beam achieves a very positive connection to the walls and to the foundation. There is little room for independent movement. In the other systems of wall construction, however, where the bond beam merely "floats" on top of the earthwalls, a big earthquake could cause the walls to detach from the bond beam and roof assembly. Sometimes an adequate connection is achieved simply because the roughened wall top essentially creates a number of miniature "keyways" that, when coupled with gravity, bond the concrete and earth together. In areas where earthquake risk is particularly severe, rebar dowels can be inserted to tie the joint securely.

In some jurisdictions, especially those that fall within the most severe seismic-risk areas, present guidelines require steel reinforcing in the entire wall system, both the earth and the concrete. With vertical reinforcing extending out of the foundation and into the bond beam, connections are certain. The questions that remain, however, are: "How much steel reinforcing, concrete bond beams, and roof connections are really necessary?" and "Are we being too conservative?" Based on present test data and the design standards prescribed by the Uniform Building Code, the answers to these questions, unfortunately, are not yet known.

The bond beam, whether topping a simple rectangular building or a complex project like the one shown here, is used to tie all the walls together and anchor the roof.

Data from the Field

For 200 years, California has provided us with the opportunity to learn how earthbuildings respond to ground movement. The misconception that many people seem to have is that large earthquakes invariably result in the total collapse of earthwalled buildings. On the contrary, the oldest existing building in California is the Mission Dolores, located in downtown San Francisco. This large structure was built of mud bricks in the late 18th century, and has survived not only 200 years of wet winters, but also one of the most destructive earthquakes in recent history, the great San Francisco quake of 1906.

Not only is the Mission Dolores still standing and very much serviceable, but so are many other mud-brick buildings dating from the era of Spanish and Mexican influence. What these old structures provide for engineers is in essence full-scale laboratory testing of the responses of low-strength, unreinforced masonry walls to actual seismic activity. The only problem is that we never know where or when the tests will be conducted.

When a major earthquake does occur somewhere in California, teams of engineering specialists travel to the affected area in order to study the damage firsthand. Based on field observations and careful evaluation of the collected data, they are able to judge why certain portions of buildings may have cracked and others survived intact. In some rare cases, parts of a large structure, most frequently the bell towers on churches and very tall walls, may actually crash to the ground. More often what occurs is that gable ends or long, unsupported walls develop large cracks, necessitating repair or reconstruction.

The magnitude of the earthquake is recorded on sensitive instruments. From this data, the ground acceleration which acted on the structure can be calculated. By laboratory testing of core samples taken from the actual wall (or wall remnants), the strength of the earthen material which comprised the wall system can be determined. Finally, the shape and dimensions of the building, including the weight distribution of the roof loads, can be measured. By evaluating the combined data thus gathered, a fairly accurate hypothesis can be made of the causes of structural failure.

When the effects of several different earthquakes on dozens of earthbuildings are combined in one data base, the resulting information is invaluable. Engineers can utilize this data in designing new earthbuildings that will respond in predictable ways to future ground shaking.

Most of the old earthbuildings in California were built of adobe bricks. The adobes were made of mud, in some cases with straw as reinforcement. Of course, there was no stabilizer or binder other than the naturally occurring clay in the soil. The mortar holding the bricks together was also made of mud. The average compressive strength of a mud brick made from California clay is around 30 pounds per square inch—basically the strength of a dirt clod. When you realize that there are 200-year-old walls constructed of a material about as strong as a dirt clod scattered throughout one of the world's most seismically active regions, the safety factors imposed by modern building codes seem more than adequate. Not only were the old adobes basically a very low-strength material, but the old buildings were typically constructed without foundations and always without bond beams and roof diaphragms.

I had the opportunity to increase my personal level of confidence in the durability of historic structures when, in 1987, our firm contracted with the California Department of Historic Preservation to complete restoration work on a Gold Rush–era building in Amador County. The Chew Kee Store had been constructed in 1850 by Chinese immigrants working the goldfields of the Sierra Nevada foothills. The story of the reconstruction is included as Builders' Resource D of this book.

Bond Beams on New Buildings

Despite the lesson of Mission Dolores, the Chew Kee Store, the Vallejo Adobe, and numerous other earthbuildings, we continue to add the element of safety provided by a concrete bond beam. The methods of forming the bond beam differ, depending on the method of building the wall system. With the freestanding panel system, formwork is needed for both the vertical columns and the horizontal beam. Additionally, the door and window openings require formwork for the side and head jambs.

In the panel-to-panel system, which has no columns, only the bond beam itself need be formed. If door and window openings are not spanned with lintels, then an additional form must be set across these openings to form the underside of the beam.

In the continuous-wall system, no additional formwork whatsoever needs to be set. The bond beam is poured directly into the wall forms. The openings across the doors and windows are spanned either by dropped-in lintels or by the lid on the top of the VDB.

Forming the Concrete Frame

In the freestanding panel system, each concrete column is reinforced with vertical rebar. Typically, the reinforcing schedule is four #4 bars ($\frac{1}{2}$ inch), spliced to dowels extending out of the foundation. The vertical bars in the columns hook into the bond beam steel. The horizontal bars in the bond beam run the perimeter of the building and are spaced $1\frac{1}{2}$ inches above the earthwall. Three #4 bars are typical for an 18- or 24-inch-thick wall.

In situations where the form lumber is to remain in place after the pour as the final treatment, the wood should be selected for its appearance and

With all of the freestanding panels complete, the vertical reinforcing bars are cut, bent, and laid out ready for installation.

After the vertical bars have been tied in place, the forms for the columns can be set.

durability. Redwood and cedar are two good choices, since both have a natural resistance to decay. As you're putting together the formwork for this system, think of it as finish carpentry, not framing. Every piece should be neatly cut and fit.

You'll need two boards for every column. Eight-inch-wide boards will overlap the edges of the adjacent panels by 1 inch. If the form boards are 1-inch thick, each set of boards will require a pair of form ties every 2 feet to resist the pressure of the wet concrete as it is being poured. If the form boards are 2 inches thick, locate the ties every 3½ feet. We have found that ½-inch threaded rod makes a versatile and economical form tie. The threads allow for differential tightening against the edges of the earthwalls, which greatly simplifies the process of setting and plumbing the formwork. If the nuts on the threaded rod are recessed into the form boards, wooden plugs can be used to hide the nuts.

For installing the electrical boxes, square holes are cut in the appropriate places on the form boards. Metal boxes with the conduit attached are then fit into the holes before the forms are set in place. The conduit should be attached to the back of the form board to make sure it remains in place during the pour; conduit clamps or even bent nails will do. If the box doesn't fit tightly in the hole, tape the crack with duct tape to prevent the concrete from oozing out onto the face of the forms.

The formwork for the columns that frame each door and window opening should be set carefully to ensure that the opening is precisely square and that it matches the dimensions specified by the manufacturer. In addition to the opposing column form boards, both of the columns flanking each opening need an additional piece of forming to complete the open side of the column (the side where there is no earth). We call these pieces the liner. They are as wide as the wall is thick and as tall as the rough opening. For 18- or 24-inch-thick walls, the liner must be made up of two pieces of wood. A liner across the top to support the underside of the bond beam completes the installation. Liners are normally attached to the form boards with 10d galvanized "siding" or finish nails. Both the jambs and the head must be braced during the pour to prevent deflection.

The bond beam portion of the concrete frame is formed by clamping opposing 8-, 10-, or 12-inch-wide boards to the tops of the earthwalls, again using the threaded rod. The bottom edges of these horizontal form boards rest on the tops of the column forms. Wooden spreaders nailed to the top of the bond beam forms are used to maintain the proper width and to suspend the anchor bolts and other hardware.

Electrical boxes and conduit are installed into the formwork before it is set in place.

180

Forms for the sides and the tops of the window and door openings are set in place, plumbed, and braced. The dimensions are critical.

The formwork for all of the columns, along with the side and head liners, must be set and plumbed, then the formwork for the bond beam is clamped to the tops of the walls.

The above procedure applies to situations where the forming lumber will remain on the wall system as part of the finish treatment. In situations where the form lumber is to be removed, whether the concrete columns and beam will be exposed or plastered over, the approach differs slightly. Of primary importance visually is the quality of the seams between the edges of the earth panels and the poured-in-place concrete. The neatest way to accomplish a good seam is to install chamfer strips at all the endboards and along the top of the form panels for the rammed earth. When the forms for the bond beam are set, a second set of chamfer strips must be installed at each joint between earth and concrete. It takes time, but yields good results.

Whether or not chamfer strips are used, concrete will leak out of the formwork and onto the earthwalls during the pour, regardless of how tightly the forms are squeezed against the wall. Leaking can be minimized by sealing all of the seams with caulking before the pour, and staining can be minimized by sealing the walls before the formwork is set. In any event, have someone standing by with the hose and a scrub brush during the pour.

The quality of the lumber used for the formwork should be equal to the desired quality of the finished concrete, because the surface of the concrete will take on the appearance of the formwork, whether rough-sawn boards or smooth plywood. Snap ties rather than threaded rod should be used to hold the formwork together, since this type of tie is designed to be hidden by a concrete plug. Electrical boxes are mounted against the inside face of the formwork, not through it, so that they will end up flush with the face of the columns. The conduit must be pulled away from the form to allow for encasement in the concrete.

The procedure for forming the bond beam

(Top left) Wooden spreaders maintain the proper width of the bond beam and also serve to hold the anchor bolts in place during the pour.

portion of the frame is the same whether the forms are to be removed or remain in place. The one extra detail you may care to add is an inside chamfer to the top edge of the formwork. Depending on the finish detail between the ceiling and wall, the chamfered edge to the concrete may be preferable.

Forming the Bond Beam Only

The formwork for the bond beam on a panel-to-panel wall system is virtually the same as it is with the freestanding system. The one distinction is that there are no column form boards on which to rest the horizontal forms. The reinforcing steel remains

(Top right and above) Reinforcing steel and embedded hardware rest on small support blocks or are hung from the spreaders to guarantee proper encasement in the concrete.

182

the same: three courses of #4 bar running the perimeter of the building and held 1½ inches above the earth.

Holding the long horizontal forms in place until they are clamped firmly against the wall entails a certain awkwardness. We have three separate solutions from which you can choose. One method is to set temporary vertical support posts at every seam between panels. Cut to the same length and resting on the ledger, these posts will also establish the correct level for the bond beam forms. A second approach is to reinstall pipe clamps through the top pipe clamp holes where they appear. This also guarantees that the formwork is level. Better yet, the pipe clamps can be used to hold the formwork together, reducing or eliminating the snap ties. The third technique is to assemble the formwork on the ground (or on sawhorses), using snap ties and spacers to keep it together. The assembled section of formwork can then be lifted into place on the top of the wall, and adjusted to line up with a chalk line that was previously snapped on the wall to indicate level. Suspend the anchor bolts and other hardware, adjust the conduits as required, wet down the top of the earthwall to slow down the drying, and pour full of concrete.

The easiest of all bond beams, short of none at all, is the one poured on top of the continuous-wall system. In this case, the full-height forms set for the rammed earth portion of the wall also provide the formwork for the bond beam

Bond beam formwork on a panel-to-panel wall system can either be left in place as a band of wooden trim around the top of the earthwall, or can be removed to expose the concrete.

In this sequence of photos we see the concrete being poured and finished directly into the same formwork used to build the earthwalls. It is one of the principal advantages of the continuous-form wall system.

(Above) The floating
seam between rammed
earth and concrete
suggests the sedimentary
nature of the material.

(Right) If the language
of the architecture
demands a crisp edge
between the earthwall
and the concrete bond
beam, chamfer strips
can be used to define
every seam.

portion of the wall system. Earth is compacted to the prescribed height within the formwork, somewhere between 9 and 12 inches from the top; the loose material remaining on top of the wall is swept away; reinforcing steel is tied according to the specifications; anchor bolts and other hardware are suspended; and the concrete is poured. The seam between earth and concrete is flawless because the forms have never been loosened. As you might imagine, the seam also "floats" a bit, reflecting the layering of the earthwall. We've adopted this floating seam as a sort of signature for rammed earth construction in earthquake country.

For those situations where a floating seam is not appropriate, chamfer strips are nailed inside the wall forms to define the line between earth and concrete. The rammers complete the wall right to the center of the chamfer strip, hit the edge an extra time to ensure good compaction, then pour the concrete. The fact is, chamfered edges and details look so good in any sort of poured-in-place masonry that it's very tempting to use them to excess. Be forewarned, though; they add an incredible amount of time to what can otherwise be a pretty efficient operation.

Special Connections

The bond beam serves the function of stiffening the earthwall system to reinforce it against lateral movement in the event of an earthquake. As stated earlier, in highly active seismic regions and especially in complex house plans with large open spaces, the bond beam alone may not prove adequate. In these situations, the roof diaphragm can provide extra stiffening to the wall system.

An earthquake of a given magnitude can be expected to act against a wall with a certain force. If the roof is being asked to resist that force, it must be connected to the wall with a combination of clips, bolts, straps, and/or nails, the combined strength of which exceeds the force with which the earthquake is trying to push the wall out from under the roof. Four 16d nails toenailed through a truss into a sill plate won't provide the required strength. Neither do sheet-metal framing clips with eight teko nails per clip. For heavily loaded situations, we install steel straps or bolts for angle iron, which are used to connect key points of the roof system to the wall. Your engineer will specify which connectors to use and where to locate them. All of this special hardware must be suspended in the correct spot from the bond beam form before the concrete is poured.

More than One Story

It is both feasible and safe to consider building walls taller than one story. Numerous multistoried buildings have survived for centuries in parts of the world where building codes have never existed. The rules that govern the seismically safe construction of two- and three-story rammed earth wall systems are the same as those that govern one-story structures: anticipated loads are calculated, wall strengths are specified, and the structure is designed according to reliable engineering standards. The most important factor to take into account when considering whether or not to build a multistoried rammed earth structure is not the safety, but the expense. Setting formwork off of scaffolding and transporting soil higher than a tractor bucket can reach will more than double the cost of each square foot of wall. Additionally, concrete columns are required in nearly every multistory application in earthquake country.

For those situations where expense is not the issue and a second story is for some reason essential, we have developed three different methods of constructing walls and attaching the intermediate floors. The first method is to build the first-story wall panels, cast a bond beam around the entire perimeter at the first-floor level, scaffold the building and build the second-story wall system with a second bond beam on top. The walls for the second story are built 3 to 6 inches

One approach for two-story construction when using freestanding panels is to complete the column and bond beam system for the first-floor walls before beginning construction on the second story.

thinner than the first-floor walls, thereby providing a ledge onto which the joists for the second floor can rest. The drawback to this method is the time and awkwardness of setting formwork off of scaffolding.

Another method, which involves less form-setting, is to build the wall full-height, using endboards two stories tall and form faces that stack all the way to the top. The trick is that the endboard changes width at the line of the second floor. The outside plane of the wall remains vertical, and the inside changes thickness where the intermediate floor intersects. The point at which the endboard jogs is the shelf where the floor joists rest. Just make sure that the shelf in the earth is well-compacted before stacking the next set of form panels.

A third method, simpler yet, is to build the full-height walls of uniform thickness. Instead of a building a shelf on which to support the joists, we embed anchor bolts in the wall, protruding from the formwork, at the level of the intermediate floor. To these anchor bolts we attach a wooden 2x12 or 4x12 ledger and then hang the floor joists off the ledger using prefabricated sheet metal hangers. The size, spacing, and depth of embedment for the bolts should be checked by a structural engineer.

In all of the cases where walls are built taller than one story, the intermediate floors help to reinforce the wall system. Essentially, they work in the same way as the roof diaphragm, adding stiffness and distributing the loads of an earthquake to all of the walls. The main problem with tall walls when the earth moves

An alternate and perhaps easier approach for two-story construction using the freestanding panel system is to build the wall panels to their full height, then cast the columns and only a top bond beam. The second floor can then be engineered to provide additional stiffness.

188

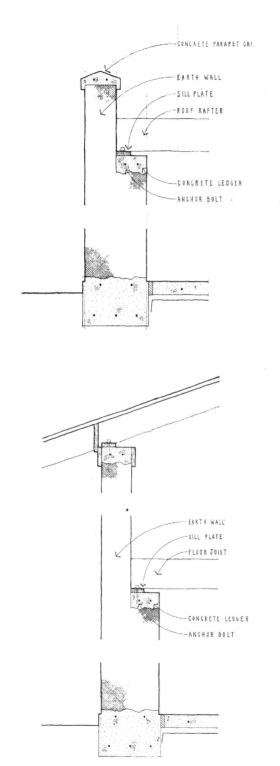

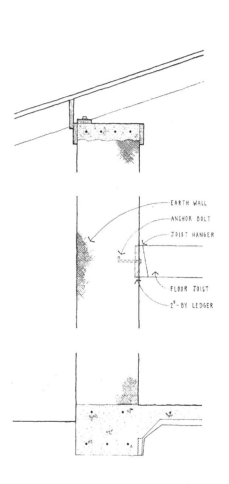

Section drawings of three different approaches to two-story construction.

Pouring a bond beam.

is that, the further they are from their connection to the ground, the more they will sway. It's like the difference between a flagpole and a fire hydrant. Both are firmly attached at their base, but the tall pole will sway when the ground shakes and the squat hydrant will not. When earthwalls are built low and stiff, they can resist the forces of an earthquake. When they are built taller than they should be, as were the bell towers on the California missions, they can fail.

Earthwalled buildings are by no means unsafe. The truth is, they've been given a bum rap over the years from far too many detractors. Rammed earth, like any other masonry building material, has quantifiable strengths and appropriate uses. Samples of the proposed wall mix can be tested and, using this information, the building can be designed within safe limits. Good design and careful construction combine to create a durable building.

CHAPTER ELEVEN

After the Wall

(Facing page) Once the walls are complete and the roof installed, a house begins to assume its identity.

W ITH THE BOND BEAM COMPLETED, the steps involved become more recognizable to conventional builders. Framed roofs mount to the top of the wall, partitions of 2x4 and sheetrock define the interior rooms, floors are finished to taste, cabinets and fixtures mount to the floor or hang on the wall, and all of the little touches are added that make a house a home. As we'll discuss later in this chapter, less can be more.

Putting on the Roof

No single construction element affects the overall appearance of a house as much as the roof. The steepness of the pitch, the length of the overhangs, the choice of roof covering, the gutters, the symmetry, and the numerous small details (or lack of them) communicate the "style" of the building. Historically, architectural style evolved in response to the climate of the region and to the resources available. The roof, most especially, has evolved to perform specific functions: holding thick blankets of snow for winter insulation, shedding rain quickly and far from the base of the walls to deal with excessive rainfall, creating copious shade, deflecting cold winds, providing platforms for sleeping, drying grain, or even fighting off invaders. For centuries, virtually all the roofs in any given region were the same.

In the past few decades, this close association between climate and the shape of the roof has broken down. Now we see the Cape Cod roof, originally designed to turn its back on cold New England winds, on houses in Las Vegas. We see flat-roofed Pueblos, designed for the dry Southwest, in wet Northern California. Please!

After the bond beam has been poured, 2x6 sill plates are bolted down in preparation for the roof framing.

The steeply pitched gable sheds rain and snow, affording needed protection to the walls in wet climates.

Timber trusses with purlins or rafters at 2-foot spacing are quickly installed on top of the sill plate.

The roof on a house with earthwalls is governed by two basic functions: It should protect the walls from heavy rain and shade the walls from hot summer sun. Where rainfall is sparse, the issue of protection is less critical, and where summers are cool, the issue of shading is not so important. The pitch of the roof can vary according to the preference of style, unless other factors such as snow, high winds, or extreme humidity are so critical as to govern the design.

How to put a roof on top of an 18- to 24-inch-thick concrete bond beam is relatively straightforward. Typically, a 2x6 pressure-treated sill is bolted to the top of the bond beam, and wood trusses or rafters are attached to the sill at the required spacing. Plywood is nailed to the rafters and the assembly covered with a manufactured waterproof roofing material such as slate, tile, shingles, or mineral paper.

There are simple roof systems and highly complex designs. The most basic of all roofs is a flat one. Beams span the width of the building, resting on opposing wall tops, and are covered with some sort of sheathing, either sticks and mud, sawn boards, or plywood. The flat roof is really only suited to extremely dry climates.

A more commonly used roof design, although still extremely simple, is a single gable, comprised of a ridge beam down the center of the building, sup-

A flat roof is typically constructed behind a raised parapet. Scuppers carry the rainwater off the roof and into the downspouts.

ported on posts, and a series of identical rafters which span from the ridge beam to the top of the wall. The gable roof facilitates runoff of rain and snow, extending the life of the roof covering and the walls which it protects. Variations on the simple gable, such as hipped ends or cut-in dormers, can be added either for function or style.

In a way, building a roof is similar to building a wall. The big areas go up fast and the details seem to take forever. But be warned: It is the details that make the roof work. At the gable-end walls, for example, the framing and siding required to close the space between the top of the walls and the underside of the roof can take a surprising amount of time. And yet how these gable ends are treated will have a big effect on the overall appearance of the building. Windows in a gable end can add quantities of daylight to the inside spaces.

The blocking between each of the rafters or trusses—important because they keep the roof straight and stiff, the birds and insects out, and the attic properly ventilated—can take almost as long to install as the rafters themselves. The metal flashing needed in the valleys and around chimneys, vent pipes, and skylights, as well as the rain gutters and downspouts, will add years to the life of the roof, and many hours to the construction schedule.

Complex roofs can seem to take forever. Changes in pitch, intersecting roof lines, clerestory windows, pyramids with glass caps, and wraparound porches all call for a reassessment of your personal sense of the cost-to-value ratio of the project. The more complicated the roof is to build, the more time you are committing to it. Remember, even after the roof is on, half the work of building the house still remains.

A complete description of the carpentry involved in constructing a wood-framed roof is beyond the scope of this text. Building a roof properly requires either a person with experience or one who is patient and is equipped with a good how-to book on the subject.

Laying Down the Floor

The options for how to finish a floor are as varied as those for how to cover a roof. Wood, tile, slate, marble, carpet, bare concrete, or bricks on sand: all offer a range of appearances, tactile sensations, and acoustic qualities. Each also comes with a different price tag.

There are two basic types of floor: the suspended wooden floor and the slab-on-grade. A wooden floor is constructed of planks laid across joists, suspended from the side of either the concrete stem wall or earthwall and supported by intermediate wooden girders resting on short posts. A minimum of

18 inches of space is required between the floor joists and the ground to prevent mold and mildew. Within this "crawl space" are located the various plumbing, electrical, and mechanical systems that service the house.

The advantages to a suspended wooden floor, besides the ease of installing the mechanicals, are that such floors can be used very effectively on sloping lots, are "springier" than a slab-on-grade, and allow for increased air circulation under the house to improve cooling in hot, humid climates. The Bungalow-style house, noted for its suspended wooden floor, originated in India in response to the need for natural ventilation in that climate.

The disadvantages to consider in choosing a wooden floor system are the expense of the wood, the increased height of the wall system required to accommodate the crawl space, the need for insulation under the floor as protection from cold winter weather, and the risk of insect- or moisture-induced decay. A wooden floor has a shorter life expectancy than a slab floor.

A slab-on-grade floor system has no crawl space; rather, the floor rests directly on the ground. The area underneath the floor is prepared before the concrete is poured, typically with a 2- to 4-inch layer of gravel, a plastic vapor barrier, and a 2-inch layer of sand. Plumbing waste lines are installed in properly sloping trenches excavated underneath the floor. Plumbing supply lines and electrical conduits are usually laid in the sand layer so that they do not cause unnecessary penetrations of the vapor barrier, and at the same time, do not weaken the concrete slab.

For heating a house with a slab floor, we recommend a system known as a "radiant slab" or "hydronic radiant floor." The floor is heated by circulating warm water through tubing embedded in the concrete itself. Water is pumped through the tubing whenever the temperature in the room drops below a preset level. The heat in the water is transferred to the mass of the concrete, which in turn transfers the heat to the living spaces. The energy to heat the water can be generated either by solar panels on the roof or by a separate water heater. The tubing, which can be either polybutylene or copper, is tied to the steel reinforcing grid to maintain the appropriate spacing until the concrete has been poured. The heat generated by this type of system is very uniform. It is quiet, clean, and dust-free.

Slab-on-grade floors have the thermal advantage of their direct connection to the earth. The temperature under the floor never drops below about 55 degrees F (13 degrees C), which means there is less heat loss than with a suspended wooden floor. Slab floors are durable and virtually indestructable. They will survive as long as your earthwalls. The disadvantages are the extra work of levelling the building pad prior to construction, the inaccessibility of the

Poured-in-place earth tiles on the floor and windowsills will absorb solar energy, keeping the comfort level high and heating costs low.

For hydronic radiant slabs, polybutylene or copper tubing is tied to the steel reinforcing grid before the floor is poured. Warm water circulating through the tubing heats the mass of the floor.

plumbing system once the floor is installed, and a sensation some people complain of that the floor is too hard.

How the structural floor is finished is not necessarily governed by the construction method. Tiles can be laid over a wooden floor just as easily as wood can be laid over a concrete slab. Methods for installing each of the floor-covering alternatives will vary depending on the product and the underlayment. Some specialty floor coverings, such as slate or glazed tile, are very expensive and can add as much as $10 per square foot to the overall cost of the house. Other manufactured floor coverings, such as linoleum, vinyl, cork, carpet, or Mexican pavers are much more affordable. Each has its own complement of positive and negative attributes from the standpoints of appearance, durability, environmental responsibility, and occupant health.

An economical flooring alternative popularized by Frank Lloyd Wright in his Usonian houses, and one that we have used on numerous occasions, is to treat the concrete slab as the finished floor. To upgrade the appearance of the standard grey concrete, pigment dyes can be added either at the batch plant or on the job, and the fresh slab can be steel-trowelled to a smooth finish. Patterns can even be created in the floor by scoring lines in the wet concrete. Once cured, the slab should be sealed, waxed, and polished. The primary complaints voiced about concrete floors, other than their simplicity, are that they can be cold and feel hard. Radiant heat will eliminate the coldness, well-placed area rugs can minimize the hardness, and simplicity should be thought of as an enhancement, not a detriment. For cost or durability, dyed concrete can't be beat.

Two final alternatives that should be mentioned are the style popular in the American Southwest, bricks laid directly on a sand bed, and a poured-in-place soil-cement floor. A brick-on-sand floor is easy to install in that there is no rush to it, unlike pouring concrete. After the walls are built, rooms can be laid with their brick flooring one at a time. Like adobe walls, a brick-on-sand floor has a forgiving quality to it. Subtle variations in the flatness add character to the floor.

Soil-cement has been one of our much-used floor systems for over two decades. Because of its clay component, soil-cement is not as hard as concrete, and the natural colors in the soil create pleasing effects in the finished floor. Best of all, especially for the owner-builder, a soil-cement floor, like bricks-on-sand, has a certain "relaxed" feeling to it. It's just not as precise a material as concrete.

A super-efficient water heater and heat exchanger can provide hot water for both domestic and hydronic systems. Solar-assisted water heaters can further reduce fuel costs.

Working with Soil-Cement

We use soil-cement not just for flooring, but also for windowsills, hearths, countertops, garden pavers, and, yes, even art. It's a fascinating material, actually: a lot like concrete, only not as hard—also not as expensive. There are many cases where soil-cement may be more desirable than concrete, even if cost weren't the issue. When used for flooring, soil-cement has a unique, handmade appearance. It can be especially attractive when the soil has a deep, rich, natural color. Another plus is that a soil-cement floor feels softer and more resilient than a concrete floor because of the clay component. The disadvantage of soil-cement is that, because it is softer than concrete, it is also less durable. Soil-cement floors will show wear over time, especially in areas where traffic patterns are heaviest.

This "softer" characteristic is a result of air pockets left inside the soil-cement matrix as the clay particles dry and shrink. This shrinkage must be anticipated and provided for. Imbued with water, the particles of clay take up extra space within the wet mix, which means the mix itself takes up a greater volume within the area defined for the slab when it is freshly poured than it will when it is dry. As the soil-cement slab dries and the clay particles return to their

A soil-cement floor can be poured in place, then cut into individual tiles as the cement begins to set.

original dry volume, the slab will shrink and crack. How much it will crack is a function of what percentage of clay was in the soil, and how expansive that clay was.

An experienced concrete finisher knows where cracks in his slab are likely to occur, and attempts to control the cracks with expansion joints and score lines. Normally, relatively small cracks will occur at regular intervals, roughly 4 to 8 feet apart. With soil-cement slabs, the cracks will be much larger and more frequent. They are harder to anticipate and harder to control.

One solution is to simply let the soil-cement slab crack without attempting to control where the cracks occur. Some people equate the look of an uncontrolled soil-cement slab with flagstone pavers. Once the soil-cement has fully cured, the cracks can be grouted and the floor sealed. Presto!

I personally have been unable to appreciate the random cracking of soil-cement, and for this reason have attempted to force the cracks where I want them. To accomplish this, we score the surface of the floor at regular intervals while it is still wet, using the same tools concrete finishers use to score sidewalks. This way, as the slab cures, most of the shrinkage will take place in the cracks we have provided. By scoring the floor in two directions, typically 24 inches each way, we can create the appearance of large paver stones. We've even given them a name: terratile. As an alternate to hand-scoring the wet slab, stamping tools can be used to cut the grid into the semi-firm slab. These stamping tools, which can be either rented or purchased, come in a variety of patterns, from 12-inch square tiles to herringbone brick. They require a certain amount of skill, so start with either the closet or the walkway out back. Give yourself plenty of time to perfect your art, and make sure you have an appreciation for the rustic look.

Other Uses for Soil-Cement

The same soil-cement material used to pour terratile floors can also be used to make countertops, windowsills, fireplace hearths, and other flat surfaces. Small slabs and individual tiles can even be poured into molds and, when cured, installed on vertical surfaces for shower walls, backsplashes, and baseboards.

For horizontal surfaces, such as counters and sills, terratile works best when poured directly in place. Use either a permanent wooden trim to define the shape, or a removable face form to allow for finishing the edge after the slab has begun to set. Large areas should be scored to control cracking. Where many pieces of the same shape and size will be used, it may be more efficient to construct a mold and pour the pieces one at a time. After they have cured, set them in place on a mortar bed.

Basically, the rules for finishing soil-cement are the same as for finishing concrete, although the clay in the mix presents a few problems. Soil-cement is stickier than concrete, which makes it harder to make perfectly flat and level. It also takes longer to setup and cure. A slow setup time may be an advantage if you need more time to work the slab and to score it, but the long cure time can be a disadvantage if your construction schedule is tight. Soil-cement is also more porous than concrete and must be sealed to prevent staining.

In summary, soil-cement is intriguing, but very tricky to work with. Soil itself is so highly variable in its composition that determining the proper ratio of cement and sand for any given soil type demands extensive trial and error. You may think you've poured a good floor, only to see it soon ripped to shreds by Rover's claws or the legs of the dining room chair. If cost is one of the driving forces in your building project, however, by all means give serious consideration to working with soil-cement.

Special tools can be used to cut through the slightly firm soil-cement, leaving the "terratiles" to cure in place.

The Final Touches—All of Them

The sad truth is, with the foundation, walls, floor, and roof complete, a great deal of work still remains to be done before the house is finished—believe it or not, roughly half. I speak from personal experience here, having fallen more than once into the psychological trap of premature celebration. The tendency is to move in, deluded by the thought that completion is merely a couple of fixtures and closet doors away, no more than a few weekends of work max.

Once you've moved in and are living in a construction zone, the days seem to drag on; sweeping wood shavings and sheetrock dust off the countertops every night can become irritating, to say the least. The mess and the frustration

Countertops in kitchen and baths are two suitable uses for terratile.

200

A terratile floor, although labor-intensive, exemplifies the beauty and appropriateness of building with earth.

of too many loose ends, of waiting for parts or professional help, can yank the rug right out from under that monumental feeling of accomplishment you were just starting to look forward to.

What are the steps remaining to completion? Of course, they vary depending on the complexity of the project, the climate, and the expectations of the occupants, but here are the basic ones:

1. Interior wall and closet framing
2. Wiring and plumbing rough-ins
3. Ceiling insulation
4. Wallboard or panelling
5. Taping and painting
6. Interior and closet doors
7. Door trim and door hardware
8. Cabinets, countertops, and tile
9. Plumbing fixtures, including water heater

10. Electrical fixtures
11. Bookcases and other built-ins
12. Mirrors, towel bars, toilet paper holders
13. Baseboards and miscellaneous trim
14. Appliances
15. Interior cleanup
16. Exterior cleanup
17. Finish grading
18. Landscaping

The list seems long. Some of the items on the checklist are relatively minor, while others are major indeed. Here's where conscientious preconstruction planning can really bear fruit. If you did your homework to begin with, and if you've been tracking your manpower allocation and your budget all along the way, then you'll be ready for the big final push.

This is your chance to decide which of the tradesmen's skills are within your capacity to master and which are not. Installing the water heater, with its gas line, water hookups, and vent stack may be a job best left for a professional; setting and grouting the tile in the shower may be a good opportunity to invest some of your own time.

"Time is money," as the saying goes. Depending on how much money you earn at your day job, and on how many bruised knuckles and smashed thumbs you're capable of enduring, you may decide to hire professionals to finish the house. On the other hand, your day job may not pay very well at all, and leave you with no other choice than to plug away on your own.

Actually, it's the finishing steps to a house that are the ones which can be accomplished with little or no experience. Mistakes can be made, of course, but they aren't of a type to threaten the structural integrity of the building. If something goes wrong, take some deep breaths, and return to the hardware store for more advice. In the worst case, swallow your pride and hire an expert.

Building a house in Nicaragua or Samoa may end with the completion of the roof and the floor. However, in the world's "developed" countries, we have been indoctrinated with a different concept of how far a house has to be taken before it's considered complete.

Living in a dozen of the houses I've built has given me a good opportunity to learn when to stop and when to keep going. All of the mistakes I've made along the way would probably fill another book. Yet here are a few parting tips I can pass along that may save you a little money, a little time, or a little of each.

1. Shop the salvage yards for usable doors, cabinets, and fixtures. A great deal of older wood products are actually better than those you can buy new today. For one, the wood itself is of a better quality, having been harvested from old-growth trees with tighter grain patterns. For another, the craftsmanship is often superior to machine-made products. Hinges and door hardware, items that can carry a high price tag if purchased new, might even be thrown in with the cost of the recycled door. Shopping for sinks, tubs, some faucets, and light fixtures at salvage yards can sometimes result in real bargains. Check that the surfaces of the porcelain are not so pitted they won't be cleanable, that the faucets have parts that are replaceable, and that the electrical fixtures can be reconditioned to meet current standards of safety. You'll undoubtedly need to refinish or recondition each of your recycled items to some degree or another. With patience and a little elbow grease, you'll be able to extend the useful life of each of these items by a few generations.

2. When it comes to buying appliances, we recommend the opposite line of approach. Durable goods such as refrigerators, stoves, and dishwashers are not the items to scrimp on. Your wisest investment is to negotiate the best deal you can on the product with the highest reputation for dependablity. Look for appliances with the lowest operating costs, the best warranty, and the longest life expectancy. By purchasing the most durable of durable goods, we can, with luck, relieve our children of the burden of replacing them. Longevity should be a consideration in all of your choices for finish materials. The longer a product can stay in service, the less hassle you will have with it, and the better off the environment will be for not having to deal with it in the waste stream.

3. Rethink your concept of finish. In the old days, details such as baseboards and cornices were not considered essential elements of a completed house. Protection from the elements, security from invaders, a warm hearth, and a place to sleep were the essence of shelter. We should be able to make do with only a slightly more elaborate version. Believe me, once you start feeling the need to trim out the interfaces between different materials, it just goes on and on. You and your chopbox will be buried in an avalanche of sawdust. For people with a limit to the time they can spend or the money they can invest, a good motto to remember might be "less is enough."

4. And, finally, be patient.

*Sketch of a simple
structure: walls, roof,
floor, and fenestrations.*

CHAPTER TWELVE

The House in the Garden

(Facing page) The ideal home is placed within a landscape, not merely on a site.

Y OU CAN'T STOP NOW. You might think a book on housebuilding would end at the point when you turn the key in the lock of the front door, but not so. I don't believe a house is finished until it's integrated into the landscape, until the usable spaces extend beyond the walls. A house needs to have some life breathed into it, to be surrounded by living things and outdoor "rooms."

From our experience, patios, porches, terraces, and gardens are nearly as essential to a home that really works as any other element in the construction. Fragrance, color, and cool natural shade: these, not baseboards and cornices, are the real finish details.

Architecture in the Landscape

With thoughtful development of the outdoor spaces, the house can effectively expand to twice its size. Not only does a house that utilizes outside areas provide more available square footage, but it makes sound economic sense as well. Here's how. Basically, a smaller house means fewer construction dollars, since inside spaces are more expensive to construct than the less formal outdoor rooms. Building permits and other fees will be less because they are based on the area of the conditioned (heated and cooled) space. Annual property taxes will be less because the assessment value is based on the size of the dwelling. Winter heating bills will be lower because of the simple fact that a smaller volume requires less energy to maintain temperatures within the comfort range. Time and money invested in cleaning and maintenance will be reduced.

Which outdoor spaces to build will be influenced by conditions on the site,

A fountain in the courtyard enhances the outdoor space by adding moisture to the air.

such as views, slope, prevailing winds, and the proximity of neighbors. The first order of outdoor spaces are those that connect directly to the house.

A veranda on the west side of a building can be very effective in hot climates. By shading the walls, temperature in the thermal mass remains low, which in turn keeps the inside spaces cool. Shade along a long, cool wall can also stimulate air movement, increasing the cross-ventilation through the house to further freshen the interior. Best of all, a wide, shady porch, filled with the smells of the garden and the light of a late afternoon, can easily become the most inviting "room" in the house.

On the east side you might consider building a greenhouse or a porch with a glass-covered roof. Located off the kitchen, this space can be a sunny morning room for those times of the year when it is not yet warm enough to be out on the patio. If positioned on the east, this room will not experience the overheating problem that south-facing greenhouses inevitably have to cope with, while still providing the opportunity to winter-over your more delicate container plants and get an early start on the spring vegetable garden.

The south side, of course, wants a profusion of winter sunlight to help the house stay warm and bright when it's cold outside. During the summer, however, in most climates the house will benefit nearly as much if the south side is amply shaded. To deal with these conflicting requirements, trellises and deciduous vines are a good solution. In the winter, when the sun is low and very much in demand, the vine is bare of leaves and the sunlight can shine in under the structure of the trellis. In the summer, the high hot sun will be shaded by the foliage. Chairs and a small table can be brought out of storage and set in the shade, creating an outdoor space that might be ideal for lunch. The one precaution to take when designing for south-side shade is to build the structure in such a way that it will not block the winter sun. Either keep the superstructure very light and open, or orient all the supports along the north-south axis.

(Right top and bottom) Covered porches along western walls create valuable shade, reducing heat gain and providing outdoor rooms for sunset watching.

A wall of glass can turn winter sunlight into a valuable source of free heat.

Roof overhangs on the south-side walls provide important shading in warm climates. Size them to keep out only the summer sun.

The north side of the house will be in the shade all winter long. In some climates, piles of snow may pose a problem. In others, wet, slippery paving will prevail and could even become a hazard. If the entry is on the north and the climate is cold, a covered front porch will make a big improvement. In a hot climate, the north side may be the most pleasant of all summer spaces, and won't require any shading other than the building itself. Here, a brick patio and plants in containers may be all that's needed to create a much-used outdoor space.

The challenge and enjoyment in creating outdoor rooms involves the way they change depending on the time of the day and the season. The western veranda that was so pleasant in August might be cold and windy in November. The eastern greenhouse, perfect for breakfast in April, might be too hot and bright in July. Throughout the course of construction, study the weather patterns on your site and the way the sunlight falls on the building. The more you know about the microclimate of the site, the better the chances are that you will make the right choices for how to design the outdoor architecture once the inside spaces are finished.

Beyond the Built-space

The outdoor rooms that attach directly to the building are the transition spaces between the house and the gardens. They represent the first-order spaces outside the core of the house itself. The second-order spaces are the pergolas, patios, courtyards, fountains, and garden walls. More remote from the house, these are occupied less frequently and for shorter periods of time than the first-order spaces, but their importance should not be overlooked. Their style and configuration will

(Top) Arbors on the south, planted with deciduous vines, can create summer shade while still allowing for the penetration of winter sunlight.
(Bottom left) A covered entry on the north side provides a place for leaving boots and umbrellas. In cold climates, the entry should be covered and enclosed.

(Bottom right) This expansive terrace on the west side, near the Pacific Ocean where summers are relatively cool, has no arbor but rather an unimpeded view of the sunset over the water.

210

Closed-in porches represent the "first order" of outdoor spaces.

Outbuildings scattered through the garden can be used for tool storage, potting sheds, or private retreats. They also make good starter projects for the first-time builder.

An earthwall along the property line can provide a backdrop for ornamental plantings as well as privacy.

As a surprise bonus to gardeners, solid earthwalls store heat, extending the outdoor growing season.

vary from region to region and from site to site. The challenge is to make the house and the gardens work in harmony, to create a small biosphere. The interior rooms represent the heart of this "organism," but the exterior spaces contribute to its healthy functioning. Fountains add moisture to the air. Blossoms add fragrance, trellises and vines filter the harsh sunlight. In combination, the elements of the garden help establish a symbiotic relationship between you and the other life forms with which you share your building site.

The transition from built space to natural space is constructed in such a way that things gradually become less formal, less controlled, as the distance from the core of the house increases. A patio of gravel or paving stones, with a part of the garden spilling into it, is less defined than the nearby veranda. A small pool or fountain in the patio can draw the natural world a little closer to the house, with a quietly bubbling water source luring birds to bathe.

Garden walls of rammed earth can be used to further enhance the transition. Build them high enough to define a space as separate from its surroundings, but still low enough to climb and sit on. Their ability to store heat make them ideal for the north side of a vegetable garden. Tomatoes, for instance, will ripen earlier in the summer and stay productive longer in the fall when they are planted against an earthwall. The southeast corner of a walled garden might even be warm and sheltered enough to allow a citrus tree to survive a cold winter and bear fruit in the spring.

As much as possible, try to create a variety of spaces throughout the second order. Each place you create will have its own season of use. It may be that a corner of the patio receives perfect sunlight for a morning cup of coffee for only two months out of the year, one in the fall and one in the spring. After a few years, you may find yourself marking the shortening of the sun's shadow in anticipation of the reopening of your favorite café.

On smaller building sites, an earthwall may be used to define the limits of your "estate." Whether to discourage the neighbors from trampling your gardens or to keep Rover in the yard, a property wall of rammed earth provides a natural backdrop for the perimeter landscaping. Bushes and low trees along a wall will soften the visual boundary between your private world and what lies outside. And, when you're really finished building, plant a fruit tree near the wall at the end of a gravel path and set a bench under the tree with its back to the wall. From this place, looking back through the garden, across the patio, and under the veranda into the house, you can meditate for a moment on the magnitude of your undertaking. Was it worth the effort?

Two walls meet in the garden, with a rose to enjoy and a bench to sit upon and think.

Completing the Circle

Throughout the course of construction our giant compost pile has been brewing somewhere out back. For months (or was it years?) this mountain of scraped topsoil, laden with roots and grasses, has been slowly fermenting, breaking down the tough fibers into loose, rich humus. It is now time to put it back where it belongs. The worm population by this time should be healthy and well-fed, the soil teeming with microbial life.

Clean up all the construction debris, from scraps of paper and sheetrock to bits of broken concrete and Terratile. Rake the surface clean and scarify the bare ground slightly. Fill all the planter beds with 6 to 12 inches of the fresh compost, and spread 2 to 4 inches over the areas designated for lawn or groundcover. Loose and fertile, this reinvigorated soil will provide the best possible growing medium for seed stock and young plant material. It will hold water more efficiently than the heavily compacted soil surrounding the construction zone, and it will stimulate fast and vigorous root growth.

There should be enough of this "super soil" to fill all the beds and still have

Here a low wall is used to screen the parking area from the entry path and the walk down the rammed earth colonnade.

some left over as a starter for a continuing compost and soil-enrichment program. Periodic garden maintenance will yield ingredients to add to the pile, as will daily food scraps from the kitchen. Compost is easy to make and essential to maintaining the vigor of all the planting beds. Every spring an application of a few inches of fresh compost to each of the beds will add vital nutrients.

Much has been written about the different ways to make compost. There are dozens of theories about the right ingredients and the correct proportions,

214

Planting beds that surround the building encourage the healthful practice of gardening.

about how often to turn the pile, and how quickly it can be made usable. Experimenting with compost and gauging its effects on your vegetables, may in fact, become a lifelong hobby. To one who dwells in a house with earthwalls, surrounded by gardens growing profusely in lush soil, working with compost just comes naturally.

One enhancement to the home composting program, ideally suited to thick-wall construction, is the use of what we call "the kitchen food scrap shredder." It's practical, efficient, and, in a way, educational. Basically it involves nothing more than diverting the standard kitchen-sink garbage disposal from the municipal sewer line or household septic system into a 5-gallon bucket. At the time the walls are being constructed, use a VDB to create a space in the wall directly behind the kitchen sink. Either create the space in the lower portion of a solid section of wall or else build it under a window opening in much the same way as a door opening. When it's time to install the sink drains, run a separate 1½-inch ABS line from the outfall of the garbage disposal, through the back of the cabinet, into a large plastic bucket. This way, rather than clogging your septic tank or wasting tax dollars at the municipal sewage plant with otherwise usable organic material, you can actually speed up the composting process. Assign one of the children the task of hauling the bucket to the compost pile once a day, and you may raise some organic consciousness as well as better vegetables. A few words of advise, however: The bucket will need a lid with a hole cut in the top for the outfall pipe in order to eliminate fruit flies; also, the floor of the bucket space should be sloped outward to allow for hosing down the area when the bucket inadvertently overflows. At our houses, we always locate the kitchen sink under a window, and combine the compost-bucket space with the recycling bins. This way, with a trap door in the counter behind the sink, we can dump the cans and bottles directly into their bins, check on how full the compost bucket is, and have access to both of them from the same set of outside doors.

Water in the Garden

Preparation of the planting areas should include a strategy for watering the gardens as well as for soil improvement. Over the course of many years, a well-planned and properly installed irrigation system will not only save countless hours spent dragging hoses from one area to another, but it will conserve water and actually improve the health of the gardens.

For most landscaping situations, drip irrigation is a far more efficient method of distributing the necessary water to a plant's root system than over-head sprinkling or flood irrigation. Sprinklers waste water by exposing the droplets to both rapid evaporation and wind dispersal. Flood irrigation compacts the surface of the soil, leaches nutrients out of the ground, and can subject the roots to the stress of super-saturation followed by total dehydration. A drip system, on the other hand, slowly disperses a uniform volume of water directly to the root mass. Evaporation and wind dispersal are eliminated because of the proximity of the water source to the point of demand. Installed on timers and electric valves, the system can be adjusted accurately to deliver the desired amount of water over the required course of time. Moisture in the soil can be maintained at ideal levels for the growth of each specific plant. Supremely loose and fertile soil, coupled with correctly applied drip irrigation, can result in a veritable miracle of horticulture.

Water—how it is stored, purified, and distributed around the site—is actually a very important component to a well-designed and properly functioning household. Just as we have attempted to design and build a house which has the ability to fully utilize the free sun and wind on the site, we can create a plan that can take maximum advantage of the available water.

The household recycling center. An access door through the kitchen counter allows for the easy disposal of cans and bottles. The "food scrap shredder" connected to a bucket grinds up vegetable wastes for the compost pile.

If your landscape plans are grand, take the time to design a well-organized and thorough irrigation system.

There are typically three sources of water in a household: the rain that falls on the land during the wet season, the fresh water delivered to the residence either by the municipality or a bored well, and the waste water that flows from the building's sewers. Since the fresh water is the most expensive of the sources, its use should be restricted to those cases where purity is essential to health. Rainwater is of course pure when it falls from the sky (in most regions of the world), but it can collect contaminants from the roof or ground it pours over and from the containers it is stored in. Water from the sewer system is the least clean of the three sources, but with carefully supervised treatment, portions of this waste water can be reused in selected locations throughout the gardens.

Harvesting rainwater from rooftops or paved areas can make a big difference to a garden's lushness in many situations. Even in drought-prone climates, one season's rainfall, captured from the roof and stored in cisterns, can be rationed to a garden that might otherwise be impossible to grow. How effective a cistern-based irrigation system can be is a factor of the climate itself. In some parts of the world, rainwater and cisterns are the only sources of water for both irrigation and domestic use. Wells and other sources of fresh water are simply not available for many people.

In situations where rainfall is low, there may not be enough total volume of collectible water to make the cost of constructing the cisterns practical, especially if the rainy season is short. However, in climates where storms, even mild ones, are likely to occur over a greater period of time, a cistern can prove very effective, especially when used in an integrated system of graywater treatment and drip irrigation.

Constructing a rainwater storage system is relatively simple. Roof gutters and downspouts are connected to a storage tank. The tank can be made of metal, fiberglass, or concrete, located above ground or buried. Simplest of all systems is a wooden barrel or 50-gallon drum installed directly under the downspout of each gutter. A complex system might involve underground piping connecting all of the downspouts and terminating at a large underground tank. A below-ground storage system will require a pump in order to distribute the water to the gardens.

Another valuable source of "free" water is the lavatories, showers, baths, and washing machines in the house. Water from these sources can very easily be made pure enough for use in irrigation systems, especially if a little thought goes into what goes down the drain. Known as "graywater," it can be used to irrigate nonedible plant material so long as it is kept free of detergent, bleach,

In some climates cisterns are a must. In almost all climates they can provide a much appreciated supplement to the irrigation system.

218

Graywater systems contribute to water conservation. When designed properly, they can add an attractive visual element as well.

(Facing page, top) The sound of gently splashing water adds a measure of calmness to the outdoor patio.

(Facing page, bottom) A swimming pool offers far more than mere recreation. Evening breezes blow across the water, bringing cool relief to the western patio.

and other chemicals. A typical graywater system is comprised of a screen to trap unwanted material such as lint or hair, some sort of filter such as sand or gravel, a storage tank, and a distribution system. If the house is at a higher elevation than the gardens, the entire graywater system can be powered by gravity.

An unfortunate circumstance is that graywater systems, although safe and irrefutably logical, are not currently approved by most county and municipal governments. The problem is that, in order to install a graywater system, the waste lines from the kitchen sink and the toilets must be separated from the other, cleaner, waste sources. When the building inspector comes to the job site to sign off on the undergrounds, he may require that the systems be tied together, in which case you will have to comply and then provide a means of separating the systems after the appropriate inspections have been made.

Cisterns and graywater systems are a means of utilizing sources of water for irrigation that otherwise might be wasted, thus helping to conserve a valuable resource. Another important way in which water can enhance the relationship between a building and its site is as architectural water elements such as pools, ponds, and fountains. Water has a naturally soothing capacity. The sound of a gently splashing fountain and the added moisture a body of water, even a small one, contributes to the spaces surrounding it can create a very inviting private courtyard. A larger body of water, such as a pond or swimming pool, with a wind blowing across its surface, can significantly reduce the air temperature in and around the building.

To the truly adventuresome, a pond or marsh, built a considerable distance from the house, can even be used to treat blackwater (kitchen sink and toilet waste water). Retain the solids in a buried concrete septic tank, allow the leachate to fill a shallow concrete or plastic-lined basin, and plant the basin full of water hyacinth, duckweed, papyrus, and other aquatic plants. Water thus treated can be captured from the low end of the basin and used to irrigate ornamental plants or the woodlot.

The Right Plants and Where to Put Them

The continuous strand I've tried to weave throughout this text is the importance of understanding the site. We've designed the building with an orientation that would take the best possible advantage of sun, shade, and wind. We've considered the changing of the seasons and how the weather would vary throughout the year. We've planned and built our outdoor spaces only after thoroughly studying the sunlight and weather patterns on the site.

Now that we've come to the end, it's time to choose and install the plant

material. The accumulated lessons point to the importance of selecting the type of plant that is right for the job, whether it be to provide shade, fragrance, color, or food.

The most logical of all schemes is edible landscaping, plants that produce either flowers, fruits, leaves, or roots that are good to eat. This way you can enjoy the visual and environmental benefits of plant material while at the same time providing food for the table. Include fruit and nut trees and an herb garden in your edible landscape plans, and you'll add shade and fragrance as well. The best place for a small herb and salad garden is right outside the kitchen door. Not only can you snatch a handful of parsley, arugula, and radicchio for a last-minute garnish to a meal, but every time you walk through the door you'll appreciate the complex aroma.

Growing food can in fact be one of the most rewarding of all hobbies. Not only will the fruits, herbs, and vegetables themselves make a big contribution to the food budget, but the taste and nutritional value of the foods grown in your own organic gardens will be far superior to anything you can purchase in the store. Best of all, working in the garden is good for the body and the soul. Fresh air, sunshine, a little hard work, and connection with the earth can work miracles on a psyche that's out of sync.

Next to growing plants to eat, the next most logical choice of which plants

Plan it right and the vegetable gardens can practically cascade into the kitchen door.

Raised beds allow for easy gardening and deep, loose soil.

Choosing plants that are native or appropriate to the region means that they will require less water and less maintenance.

Blue oaks and black mission figs line the walkway from the parking area to the front door.

to use are those varieties that are native to the area. These are species that have evolved over time to survive and prosper under the temperature and water patterns normal for the region. By selecting native varieties, your gardens will require less maintenance and less irrigation. The plants will survive the winter cold or the summer heat with less worry on your part. Planting a Monterey pine in Tucson, Arizona, or a saguaro cactus in coastal Northern California is just as illogical as building a Cape Cod saltbox in Biscayne Bay, Florida. The pine tree will be stunted and forever thirsty in Tucson, the cactus will die on the coast, and the saltbox will be like a bread oven in Biscayne Bay.

Within the limitations of selecting regionally appropriate landscape materials, we choose plants for their function. Shade is extremely effective in maintaining comfortable temperatures inside the building during the summer without excessive dependence on mechanical systems. Shade trees and vines on arbors should be positioned in such a way as to throw shade onto the western wall of the building and into all of the outdoor spaces where you anticipate spending summer afternoons. The south side of a building can also benefit from summer shade, as long as the trees and vines chosen are deciduous and allow plenty of winter sun to penetrate through their branches.

Trees can also be used for numerous tasks other than shade. They are very effective as privacy screens and windbreaks. Plant a hedge of cypress or bamboo along the property wall to screen out an unwanted view of the neighbor's backyard, or his view into yours. If the winter wind howls against your house out of the northeast, plant a row of cedar or redwood trees in its path. Your winter heating budget will be the beneficiary. It may be that a tree-lined drive, a magnificent specimen in the front yard, or a small orchard of walnuts will

(Above) Profusely blooming Mexican evening primrose line the pathway that parallels the garden wall.

(Top right) Consider planting a deciduous tree on the south side to shade the space near the base of the wall.

(Bottom right) An old specimen tree can be incorporated into the landscape plan to provide a special outdoor place.

Late in the winter, while the sun is still low in the sky, the narcissus begin to bloom, sure signs that spring is on the way.

add the final touch needed to capture the sense of place you've worked so hard to create.

In the patios and the flower beds, along the paths, and against the back wall, choose plants that grow well in your region and ones that will accomplish your design goals. Carefully consider each plant's shape, height, color, and flowering time, as well as how each plant complements its neighbors. Close to the house, especially near the verandas and operable windows, select plants for their pleasing fragrances.

Just as weather patterns and our lifestyles change with the seasons, the color and smells in our gardens also change. Build your house in tune with the planet, surround it with livable outdoor spaces and a profusion of living things. Soon you will find yourself, as I do, eagerly awaiting the first bloom on the flowering crabapple, the first scent of the night-blooming jasmine, and the first sounds of the finches returned to the garden in the spring.

A Photographic Step-by-Step

The following step-by-step sequence of photographs is a greatly abbreviated representation of the processes and methods described in the preceding chapters. Although the building featured in these photographs is quite complex, and required a team of very experienced wall builders and a skilled general contractor, the basic stages shown on these pages are characteristic of any rammed earth project.

1. Services are roughed in through gravel sub-grade. The concrete stem wall with reinforcing dowels is ready for earthwall formwork.

3. The backside of continuous-wall formwork, with 2x4 verticals and 2x12 walers at 24 inches on-center vertically. Note the additional components: one backfill tamper with hoses, and one VDB jamb.

2. VDB (volume displacement box) components ready to install in the completed earthwall formwork. Note the electrical conduits and vent pipe.

4. (Above) Continuous formwork with all components in place. The section in the foreground has been filled and compacted to bond-beam level.

5. (Right) A shoveller moves soil from a hopper into the formwork. Meanwhile, a rammer works his way towards the top of the forms.

6. *Filling the earthwall formwork. Sections in the foreground have been completed to the tops of window VDB's while workers fill the remaining wall forms.*

7. *Once the rammed earth has been completed to the prescribed height, the concrete bond beam is poured directly into the continuous formwork on top of the earthwalls.*

8. *Conduits and anchor bolts extend from the finished bond beam as part of the complete system.*

9. As soon as the concrete for the bond beam has cured, the earthwall forms can be disassembled for reuse in another part of the building.

10. Form panels are removed as quickly as they were set up.

11. The finished wall, if compacted properly using good soil, needs no additional treatment.

12. (Above) Sill plates and roof trusses can be set as soon as the bond beam has been poured.

13. With earthwalls complete, conventional roof framing techniques apply.

230

14. Manufactured trusses span the living room. The rammed earth fireplace transitions to metal flue-pipe at the plate line.

15. Finished earthwalls, brown coated gable ends, entry columns of rammed earth, and plywood roof sheathing ready for cover.

16. (Above left) A finished gable end in earth-colored stucco finish complements the natural earth finish.

17. (Above) Finished window openings, created with a re-useable VDB, with bond-beam head and cast-in-place terratile sill.

18. (Above) Manufactured door and window units install neatly into precisely cast openings.

232

19. Trellises mounted on top of rammed earth columns, shading entryways and western walls.

20. Natural earthwalls and simple detailing combine to a create timeless appeal.

A Sample Home Design Program

Overview

This project is a single-family home for a professional couple planning for a family of four or five (two or three children). The couple is planning this home as their last dwelling, so adaptability to different phases of life (small family → larger family → children maturing → empty nest → active retirement) should be used as design criterion. There is the possibility for one set of parents eventually living with the family for an extended period. The family is active with frequent entertaining (usually 4–20 guests for parties; visiting groups of family/friends of 2–6 people for 4–10 days) and numerous outdoor activities (windsurfing, skiing, hiking, mountain biking).

General Design Goals

The house should be a single-story structure of approximately 4,000 square feet with high energy efficiency and maximum utilization of natural light and heat. The building site is gently sloped with a southern exposure which lends itself well to passive solar heating. Multiple levels would be desirable for interest and to follow the land contour; beautiful views should be complemented by house design and initial entry into home should emphasize expansive southerly view through house. Easy access to the outdoors for projects, living, and entertaining should be emphasized in all areas possible. The home will be planned for three or four bedrooms (including master suite) with a detached guest cottage combined with garage. The design should include an integrated area for outside living (pool, spa, and outdoor entertaining "ramada" with barbecue and fireplace or pellet stove). Varying high ceilings should be planned (9–14 feet) since owners are tall; open-beam ceilings should be the rule in common areas and master suite. Work counters, desks, and clothing storage should be built into place whenever possible.

Specific Room Design Goals

Entry: Guests will be greeted here; should give preview of southerly view which expands as guest moves into main living space.

1. Will be north end of house
2. Should be open and airy with expansive view through house to the south
3. Possible one- or two-step step-down into main living area
4. Adjacent coat closet
5. Adjacent guest bathroom

Living Room: Living room will be for entertaining small groups of people and as possible music room.

1. Should be somewhat smaller than traditional "living room," i.e., should be more like a visitors' "parlor"
2. Should be adjacent to main entry
3. Should be well-lighted with natural light; possibly as a solarium
4. Should fit a baby grand piano
5. Woodstove or fireplace insert

Dining Room: Should facilitate frequent entertaining of 6–8 people but should be able to accommodate up to 12 comfortably.

1. Should be adjacent to kitchen
2. Subdued afternoon and evening light—no direct westerly sun
3. At least two entrances for traffic flow
4. Rectangular design

Kitchen: Large country kitchen will be a gathering place for guests and family and will be a center for entertaining; needs morning light.

1. Equilateral triangle workspace between sink, refrigerator, and gas stovetop
2. Double oven separate from stove
3. Center island with food-preparation sink

4. Elevated modular refrigerator
5. Countertop bar for kids' lunches
6. Built-in desk with adjacent workspace for telephone; hanging files
7. Generous walk-in pantry
8. Rectangular breakfast/casual dinner nook with southerly views and access to outside porch or deck; should be large enough for 7-foot country table
9. Sink should have window; multiple windows elsewhere
10. Built-in nook for microwave oven
11. Room for dishwasher and trash compactor
12. Emphasize storage area and counter space!
13. Should be near main living space and may be slightly elevated to hide clutter
14. Kitchen should be close to entry from garage (or porte-cochère)

Mudroom: Will connect kitchen area from garage/porte-cochère entry.

1. Should have ¾ bath
2. Cabinets for storage
3. Coat hooks
4. May double as laundry room if able to be placed in close proximity to master suite

Laundry Room: Used for laundry, ironing; may also be sewing room if enough space.

1. Built-in ironing board
2. Large, deep sink
3. Storage cabinets
4. Built-in desk for sewing machine

Family Room: The main living area of the house, entered from front entry; used for entertaining, reading, unwinding, and as possible media room.

1. Should have large glass area for view and solar heating
2. Needs multiple entrances for traffic flow
3. Masonry fireplace
4. Built-in bookshelves
5. Pre-wired for audio/video system (components concealed)
6. Multiple French door access to outdoor porch or deck
7. Should accommodate seating for up to 12 people

Media Room (Optional): This is a separate room designed specifically for large-screen TV viewing and music listening; may also be a place to read when family room is occupied.

1. Should be able to seat up to 8 people for TV
2. Built-ins for electronic components with pre-wiring in walls

Master Bedroom: Should be large enough for king-sized bed on one end with south wall primarily glass for views and morning sun.

1. Exposed beam ceiling
2. Skylight with electric opener
3. Ceiling fan for air circulation in summer
4. Walls should be pre-wired for stereo speakers
5. Alarm console in wall by head of bed
6. Built-in reading lamps
7. French doors to outside into entertainment area
8. Small built-in cabinet with sink and room for small refrigerator and coffee maker

Office/Nursery: This room should have entrance into master bedroom and separate entrance into master bath; will be used for infant's room initially, but main use will be office and exercise room.

1. Should have outside entrance to porch or deck
2. Built-in desk area for computer/printer/modem
3. Large enough for Stairmaster and weight machine

Master Bath: Not overly large, but should have room for dressing and relaxing for two people.

1. Morning light with southerly view and lots of windows
2. Separate walk-in closets with lots of built-ins; should be enough storage so that freestanding furniture for clothes storage in bedroom not necessary
3. Separate sinks in communal bathroom area
4. Commode, Jacuzzi, and shower should be adjacent to sink area but should have door
5. Shower and tub should be open to each other
6. Shower should be designed so that curtain is not necessary to prevent water splashing

7. Shower, tub, and sink areas should all have outside views and morning sun
8. Continuous window above sink counter to ceiling with integral round mirror over each sink at chest/face height
9. Two showerheads on different walls of shower
10. Skylight in shower/sink areas

Children's Wing: Should be an area where kids can play, do homework, and entertain friends.

1. Outside entrance if possible to play yard
2. Two sleeping rooms share bath with two sinks, tub, and shower
3. Separate room for watching TV, listening to stereo, playing computers
4. Large closets in each room with large built-in cabinet for stereo and TV
5. Cross ventilation in each sleeping room
6. North side okay

Outdoor Living Areas:

1. Directly accessible from kitchen (either through doors or pass-through)
2. Separate outdoor eating areas, one with morning light and one afternoon
3. Herb garden within range of kitchen door
4. Water element within view of living room (and entry if possible), but placed to preserve views
5. Some covered area for shade adjacent to barbecue
6. Garden area with fruit trees near entertainment area—needs pathway for access

How to Identify Soils

From Handbook for Building Homes of Earth *by Lyle Wolfskill,*
Wayne Dunlap, and Bob Gallaway

Here are some simple tests that will tell you what kind of soil you have. Do *all* of them on all your samples. Be sure that the samples that you test accurately represent the soils you will use in building.

If you are testing sands or gravels, first dry the soil by heating or spreading a sample in the sun. Make it into a cone-shaped pile, and carefully divide it into four equal samples (by breaking down the cone into four quadrants). Combine two opposite portions into one sample and set aside the other two. You should end up with about a shoveful of soil. If there is too much soil after one such separation, repeat the process of dividing and discarding until an adequately-sized soil sample remains.

Visual Tests

The appearance of a soil can tell you some important things about it. First spread the dried soil out in a thin layer on a flat surface. Then roughly separate the sand and gravel sizes by hand.

Do this by putting all of the particles from the largest down to the smallest that you can see with the unaided eye in one pile. This will be the sands and gravels. What is left (normally this will be very fine powder-like materials) will be the silts and clays. If the silt and clay pile is larger than the sand-gravel pile, call the soil silt-clay for now and remember this. Other tests, described later, will distinguish between silt and clay.

If the sand and gravel piles together are bigger, you have a sand or a gravel. Decide which it is by putting all of the particles larger than ¼ inch (gravels) in one pile and all of the smaller particles (sands) in another pile. The soil is gravelly if the gravel pile is biggest and sandy if the sand pile is biggest. Remember which it is.

Here is what you do if you have a sandy or gravelly soil:

Take a small handful of the entire sample (not just the sand and gravel), get it moist but not soupy, squeeze it into a ball, and let it dry in the sun. If it falls apart as it dries, call it "clean." Clean sands and gravels are not suitable for earth houses unless they are mixed with other materials.

Here is what you do if you have a silt-clay soil or a sand or gravel that is not clean:

Take the *entire* sample and collect all of the soil that is smaller than medium sand (⅟₆₄ inch) by sifting through a very fine screen or a piece of coarse cloth. The tests described below should be made with this fine material.

Wet Shaking Test

Take enough of the soil to form a ball the size of a small hen's egg and moisten it with water. The ball should have just enough water in it so that it will hold together but not stick to your fingers. Flatten the ball slightly in your palm and shake the ball vigorously. This is done by jarring the hand against some firm object or against the other hand until the shaking brings water to the surface of the sample. The soil may have a smooth, shiny, or "livery" appearance when this happens. (What you are looking for is to see how fast the water comes to the surface and gives the livery appearance.) Then squeeze the sample between your thumb and forefinger to see whether or not the water disappears.

The following are terms used in describing the speed of the above reaction:

1. *Rapid Reaction.* When it takes only five to ten taps to bring water to the surface, this is called a rapid reaction. Squeezing the sample should cause the water to disappear immediately so the surface looks dull. Opening the hand quickly should accomplish the same result. Continued pressure causes the sample to crack and finally crumble. This type of reaction is typical of very fine sands and coarse silts. Even a little bit of clay will keep the reaction from being rapid.
2. *Sluggish (or Slow) Reaction.* When it takes 20 to 30 taps to bring the water to the surface, you have a sluggish reaction. Squeezing the

sample after it has been shaken will not cause it to crack and crumble. Instead, it will flatten out like a ball of putty. This shows that the soil has some clay in it.

3. *Very Slow or No Reaction.* Some soils will not show any reaction to the shaking test, no matter how long you shake them. The longer it takes to show a reaction, the more clay the soil contains. These soils will require the other tests described below before you can proceed.

Thread Test

With a lump of soil about the size of an olive, mix just enough water so the lump can be easily molded in your hands, but is not sticky. Next, on a flat, clean surface roll out the soil into a thread. Use the palm of your hand or fingers and exert just enough pressure to make the soil thread get continually smaller. If it breaks before you roll it out to a ⅛-inch diameter thread, it is too dry and you need to add some more water to it. When the soil is at the right moisture content, the thread will begin to crumble into several small pieces just when you get it to a diameter of ⅛ inch. If the thread does not crumble and break at ⅛ inch, lump it together again, knead it into one lump, and repeat the rolling process until the thread crumbles at ⅛-inch diameter. (The thread will eventually crumble because it dries as you keep rolling it out.)

As soon as the thread crumbles, remold the sample into a ball and see how much pressure it takes to squeeze the ball between your thumb and forefinger.

This test gives an idea of how much clay is in a soil and also what type of clay it is. If the soil crumbles easily and you cannot roll the soil into a thread at any moisture content, it means that the soil does not have any clay in it. Here are some of the other reactions you can expect:

1. *Tough Thread.* If the remolded ball can be deformed only with a lot of effort and it does not crack or crumble when you do it, your soil has a lot of clay in it. It probably will not be good for earth walls unless you use a stabilizer.
2. *Medium-Strength Thread.* This kind of soil can be remolded into a ball, but when the ball is squeezed, it will crack and easily crumble. This soil may be good but may require some stabilization for certain areas. Check the table on pages 244–47 to be sure.
3. *Weak Thread.* When the soil has a lot of silt or sand and very little clay, you will find that the threads cannot be lumped together in a ball without completely breaking up or crumbling. This soil may be good for earth walls. Check the table below to be sure.

4. *Soft, Spongy Thread.* Sometimes you will find that the threads and the ball that you make with them will be spongy and soft. You can squeeze the ball between your fingers, but it acts like a sponge and bounces back. When this happens, the soil is organic and is not suitable for building earth houses.

Ribbon Test

This test gives about the same kind of information that the thread test gives. It helps to do both tests. One checks out the other.

Take enough soil to form a roll about the size of a cigar. The roll should not be sticky, but wet enough to permit being rolled into a $\frac{1}{8}$-inch diameter thread without crumbling, as in the thread test. Put the roll in the palm of your hand and, starting at one end, flatten the roll by squeezing it between the thumb and forefinger to form a ribbon between $\frac{1}{8}$ and $\frac{1}{4}$ inch thick. Handle the soil very carefully to form the maximum length of ribbon that the soil will support. See how long the ribbon will hold together without breaking. The reactions you can expect are described below.

1. *Long Ribbons.* With some soils the ribbon will hold together for a length of 8 to 10 inches without breaking. This means that the soil has a lot of clay in it. Soils of this type will make long-lasting earth walls only if they are stabilized.
2. *Short Ribbons.* If you can—with some difficulty—ribbon the soil into short lengths of about 2 to 4 inches, the soil has a medium to small amount of clay in it. It will be about the same as the soils that give a medium or weak thread in the thread test. This soil will make good walls in many cases, but check the table on pages 244–47 to be sure.
3. *Will Not Ribbon.* Some soils cannot be formed into ribbons at all. This means that they contain either a very small amount of clay or none at all. Such soils with a little clay may make good rammed earth walls. If the soil is all sand, it is not suitable unless stabilized heavily with Portland cement; to be sure, check the table on pages 244–47.

Dry Strength Test

This is another simple test that will help you determine how much clay you have in the soil. Prepare two or three wet pats of the soil about $\frac{1}{2}$ inch thick and 1 to 2 inches wide. Use enough water to make the soil quite soft but still strong enough to hold its shape when you form it into pats. Then allow the pats to dry in the sun or in an oven until they are dry all the way through. Break the soil pat and then try to powder it between your thumb and forefinger. Here is what you are looking for:

1. *High Dry Strength.* If the sample has high dry strength it will be very difficult to break. When it does break it will snap sharply, like a crisp cookie. You will not be able to powder the soil between your thumb and forefinger. You may be able to crumble it a bit with your fingers, but don't confuse this with powdering the soil. Soils with this reaction have a lot of clay in them and they will be satisfactory only if stabilized.
2. *Medium Dry Strength.* When a soil has a medium dry strength, it will not be too hard to break the soil pat. With a little effort you will be able to powder the soil down to its separate grain sizes between your thumb and forefinger. This soil is good but may require a stabilizer to reduce shrinkage; check the table below.
3. *Low Dry Strength.* A pat with very little clay will break without any trouble. It will powder easily. Pats of very sandy soils will crumble in your hand before you have a chance to powder them. Before a final decision on the use of this soil, check the table below.

The four tests described above are the most important ones, and it will pay you to use them all in finding out about your soil. There are some other simple tests that will also aid you. Use them if you need to. They are given below.

Odor Test

Organic soils have a musty odor, especially when freshly dug. You get the same odor for dry organic soils by wetting and then heating them. Don't use these soils for earth walls.

Bite Test

This is a quick and useful way of identifying sand, silt, or clay. Take a small pinch of the soil and grind it lightly between your teeth. Identify the soils as follows:

1. *Sandy Soils.* The sharp, hard particles of sand will grate between the teeth and will create an objectionable feeling. Even very fine sands will do this.

2. *Silty Soils.* Silt grains are much smaller than sand particles and, although they will still grate between the teeth, they are not particularly objectionable. They feel a lot smoother than sands.

3. *Clayey Soils.* The clay grains are not gritty at all. Instead, they feel smooth and powdery like flour between the teeth. You will find that a dry pat of soil with a lot of clay in it will tend to stick when lightly touched to your tongue.

Shine Test

Take a pat of either dry or moist soil and rub it with your fingernail or the flat side of a knife blade. If the soil contains silt or sand—even with the remainder being clay—the surface will remain dull. A soil that has a lot of clay in it will become quite shiny.

Additional Tests

You can tell a lot about a soil in the way it washes off of your hands. Wet clayey soils feel soapy or slick, and they are hard to wash off. Silty soils feel powdery like flour, but they are not too difficult to wash off. Sandy soils rinse off easily.

Color is important in classifying soils. Olive-green and light brown to black colors may mean organic soils. Red and dark brown colors may come from iron in the soil. Soils with a lot of coral, limerock, gypsum, and caliche may be white or some shade of gray.

After you have done all of the tests given above and have decided what the reactions to them are, you are ready to use the table. It will tell you exactly what kind of soil you have and what kind of house you can build with your soil.

Here is the way to use the table: Suppose you found that your soil was a gravelly soil. This means that the sand and gravel piles together were larger than the silt-clay pile, and the gravel pile was larger than the sand pile. Use the gravel chart in the table. Suppose the tests you did on the portion that passed the fly screen showed your soil reacted rapidly to the shaking test, had weak soil threads, and very low dry strength. Then your soil would be a silty gravel. It would not be suitable for earth houses without stabilization.

Silt-Clay Soils

If the silt-clay pile was larger than the sand and gravel piles together, then use the table below to determine what kind of soil it is.

Names of Soil	Reaction to Wet Shaking Test	Dry Strength Test	Thread Test	Ribbon Test
Very fine sands, silty fine sands, clayey fine sands, clayey silts	May be rapid to sluggish, but never very slow	Low to none; usually none	Weak thread to no strength in thread	Short ribbons; may not ribbon at all
Silts, very silty sands, very silty clays	May be anything from sluggish to none	May be low to medium	Weak to medium strength thread	Short ribbons
Gravelly clay, sandy clay, silty clay	May be very slow to none	May be medium to high	Medium strength thread	Short to long ribbons
Clays, fat clays	None	High to very high	Tough thread	Long ribbons
Organic silts, organic silty clays	Sluggish	Low to medium	Weak thread and feels spongy	Short ribbons or may not ribbon at all; spongy feel
Organic silts, organic clays	May be very slow to none	Medium to high	Weak to medium; threads feel spongy	Short ribbons, spongy feel

Gravel Soils

If the gravel pile was larger than the sand pile, then use the table below to decide what kind of gravel it is.

Silty gravels, sand-silt-gravel mixtures	Rapid	Low to none; usually none	No strength of thread	Will not ribbon
Clayey gravels, gravel-sand-clay mixtures	Sluggish to very slow	Medium	Medium strength thread	Short ribbons, may be long
Clean gravel	Not necessary to run these tests on clean gravels			

Additional Tests	Suitability for Earth Homes	Stabilizers	Comments
Washes off hands easily; will not stain hands	Usually suitable for all types, particularly adobe if stabilized	Portland cement most suitable; asphalt emulsions also work as do most waterproofers	May be affected by frost
	Should not be used if possible; stabilize heavily if necessary to use	Portland cement, asphalt emulsions if soil is not too sticky	Will usually require surface coatings in addition to stabilizers
	Will usually require stabilizers; most suitable for rammed earth and pressed blocks	Lime, Sand, Gravel	Can be very good if amount of sand or gravel is high
Very sticky when wet, difficult to wash off of hands	Should never be used for earth houses		
A pat of moist soil has a musty odor when heated	Should never be used for earth houses		
A pat of moist soil has a musty odor when heated	Should never be used for earth houses		
Fine material washes off easily. Will not stain hands	Usually suitable if it is first stabilized; if almost a "clean" gravel it may be necessary to first add more fines	Portland cement most suitable; asphalt emulsions may also work	May be affected by frost
Finer material not easily washed off of hands	May be very suitable for all types of earth houses; if almost clean, it may be necessary to add some fines	Lime most suitable; Portland cement may work if soil mixes easily	
	Not suitable for earth houses; can be mixed with fines (silt or clay) to make suitable soils for earth houses		If well graded, will be very good for aggregate in concrete for foundations

Sand Soils

If the sand pile was larger than the gravel pile, then use the table below to decide what kind of sand it is.

Names of Soil	Reaction to Wet Shaking Test	Dry Strength Test	Thread Test	Ribbon Test
Silty-sands	Rapid	Low to none; usually none	No strength of thread	Will not ribbon
Clayey sands	Sluggish to very slow	Medium	Medium	Short ribbons but may be long
Clean sands		Not necessary to run these tests on clean sands		

Additional Tests	Suitability for Earth Homes	Stabilizers	Comments
Fine material washes off easily; will not stain hands	Usually suitable if stabilized; if almost a "clean" sand it may be necessary to add more fines	Portland cement is best; asphalt emulsions may work. Clayey fines	May be affected by frost
Fine material not easily washed off of hands	Usually very suitable for all types of earth houses; if almost clean, may add some clayey fines	Lime is best; Portland cement will work if soil mixes easily	
	Not suitable for earth houses unless mixed with fines	Clayey fines	If well-graded, will be good for aggregate in concrete for foundations

Restoring the
Chew Kee Store

In 1986, our firm, REW Associates, was hired by the California Department of Historic Preservation to undertake the restoration of a Gold Rush-era rammed earth building near Sacramento. Built in 1850 by Chinese immigrants working the goldfields around Fiddletown, the Chew Kee Store is the best surviving example of rammed earth in the state. It's logical that the Chinese would build in rammed earth, since the technique has historically been widely used throughout the provinces of China.

We were chosen over other firms who specialize in historic preservation because of our unique experience with rammed earth. The work specified by the structural engineer hired by the state was comprised of four separate tasks: (1) excavate and reinforce the perimeter foundation; (2) expose the wall tops and cast a perimeter concrete bond beam; (3) remove the existing composition roof and replace it with a replica of the original roof; and (4) repair all cracks and replaster the exterior walls.

Working on this old, unstabilized rammed earth building was enormously enlightening. I had the chance to dig, pound, scratch, and drill holes in raw earthwalls that had been built by hand over 130 years ago. These walls had endured rain, sleet, hail, snow, fire, earth tremors, and vandals; yet here they were, still housing the herb jars, incense, and other sundries guarded by Jimmy Chow, the last of the store's caretakers, before he died in the early 1960s. My experience at the Chew Kee Store resulted in what I like to call "the great credibility leap."

It started when we began the hand excavation of the building's perimeter. Our instructions were to dig a trench 2 feet wide around the base of the wall, as deep as needed to expose the foundation stones. Imagine our surprise when all we could find below grade was raw rammed earth! There was no foundation. The 20-inch thick earth walls merely started about 2 feet below grade. There were no foundation stones, no thickened footing—just raw earth rammed on top of raw earth.

Upon careful inspection, we discovered that the parts of the wall which had been below grade for all this time were still hard and dense. Little if any deterioration of the surface had occurred underground. Where the walls had eroded was from a point beginning at the soil line extending upward approximately 1 foot. Here, where snow and weeds were allowed to pile up against the base, the seasonal wetting and drying of the wall had caused the raw earth to become soft and flaky. In the worst places, the wall integrity had failed as much as 6 inches in from the face. As part of our repair, we removed all the loose material and recompacted with fresh, moistened earth.

Our reinforcement of the "foundation" took the shape of a buttress wall of stabilized rammed earth. In the trench we had dug, we set a wooden form at a slight angle to the existing wall, approximately 18 inches from the wall at the base, braced back against the sides of the trench. Into the space between the wall and the form, we layered and compacted our typical soil-cement mixture until we reached the level of the existing ground. We packed this same mixture into the eroded areas along the base of the wall that had deteriorated over the years, then shaved the repaired areas flat and straight. After removing the formwork, we installed a perforated PVC drain line and drain rock into the remaining portion of the excavated trench, completing the foundation-repair portion of our assignment.

The second portion of the work was to expose the wall tops and pour a concrete bond beam. This procedure proved every bit as enlightening as our work on the foundation. The engineering specifications called for $5/8$-inch steel dowels to be set into holes drilled in the top of the existing earthwalls, to tie the old walls to the new bond beam. To work on the tops of the walls, we had to remove the existing roof, built during the 1930s after the original roof had burned off in a fire. Since phase three of our contract was to reconstruct an historically accurate roof, this dismantling was completely in order. In fact, it allowed us easy access to the work area and the opportunity to study the original method of construction.

The walls varied in height from approximately 12 feet on the street side to 16 feet on the back side by the creek. The roof rafters rested directly on a roughsawn 2x6 plate spiked to the wall tops with 6-inch-long hand-forged nails spaced roughly 4 feet apart. The plate we undercovered appeared to be not from the original roof, but from the replacement. Above the entire inside area

The Chew Kee Store before and after restoration.

of the store was a flat board ceiling, located approximately 9 feet off the floor. The roughsawn, wide-plank ceiling boards were nailed to timber joists that spanned the narrow direction of the building, a distance of approximately 16 feet. The joists were resting in pockets that had been carved out of the raw earth. No connection between the joists and the earthwalls existed other than those imposed by gravity. To insulate the living space below, the attic was covered with several inches of loose earth. Silk fabric had been laid on top of the ceiling boards to prevent the earth from sifting through the cracks in the boards.

There were two large cracks in the earthwalls at the back corners, where the short crosswall had broken from the long sidewalls and was leaning approximately 3 inches out of plumb. We observed that the replacement wooden sill plate, installed in the 1930s, spanned these 3-inch cracks, yet met up correctly with the rafters in line with the endwalls. This led us to the conclusion that all of the movement of the endwall had taken place before 1930, whether it had occurred gradually over the first few decades of the structure's existence or had taken place in one cataclysmic shift, perhaps during the San Francisco Earthquake of 1906.

To proceed with the bond-beam phase of the reconstruction, we drilled 1-inch diameter by 12-inch-deep holes, spaced 24 inches apart and centered in the top of the 20-inch-thick wall. The rammed earth was so solid that we needed a heavy roto-hammer to drill the holes—a standard rotary drill was not powerful enough. During the few hours that I was drilling these fifty or so holes in the top of this 130-year-old raw earth wall, I had plenty of time to reflect on the strength and durability of the material. It was clear beyond doubt that when the right type of soil is compacted under the right conditions, and when the finished product is kept dry, the result is a perfectly suitable structural wall system.

After setting the rebar dowels into the holes with epoxy, we tied three rows of perimeter horizontal-reinforcing steel, set wooden forms much like those used for our standard bond beam, suspended anchor bolts for connecting the new roof, and pumped the formwork full with six-sack concrete.

Phase three of the work involved constructing a new wooden roof, complete with full dimension lumber and hand-split 36-inch long shingles of sugar pine. This we accomplished using current methods of carpentry, including power saws and machine-made nails.

Phase four of the work was repairing the cracks and replastering the entire exterior wall surface. Portions of the original plaster were still intact on the walls, especially near the top, where the roof overhangs had provided good protection. From these original pieces of plaster, we were able to match the color and take a good guess at the formula. We hand-packed the cracks full of stabilized rammed earth, wrapped the building in stucco wire, applied a first coat of sand, soil, and cement, and let the plaster cure for two weeks. The final coat of plaster, which we had selected from our test samples to match the original, was a blend of red clay soil, fine sand, and lime. We trowelled it imperfectly smooth to approximate the finish texture of the original.

Today, thanks to the generosity of the Chinese Cultural Society and the taxpayers of California, the Chew Kee Store is open to the public. It affords a remarkable glimpse into the past. Our work on the restoration of the Chew Kee Store gave us a fascinating opportunity to appreciate the beauty, simplicity, and durability of raw earth walls, and to gain an enormous measure of confidence in the strength of the system.

Structural Engineering Design

by Bruce King, PE

Rammed earth construction is not new; in fact, some of the oldest buildings extant today are of stone and/or earthwall construction. Rammed earth buildings can be found on every continent, some having been occupied for dozens, hundreds, or even thousands of years. We therefore know that earthwall buildings can be made and maintained to last, and to provide safe shelter.

It is also true that many earthbuildings do not last very long, due to limitations of knowledge, resources, or both. In modern times, newspapers periodically contain reports of earthquakes that occur in undeveloped parts of the world, causing multiple deaths due to the structural failure and collapse of masonry, earth, or concrete buildings. Even without earthquakes, the effects of wind, ice, and rain can fairly quickly damage an improperly built earth structure.

By carefully studying the available case histories, and, where available, results of modern testing programs, we can now begin to define a rational basis for the structural design of earthwall buildings. (The umbrella term "earth construction" includes rammed earth, adobe brick, cobb, gunite-applied material, and dozens of variations and hybrids. This section will limit itself to *rammed earth* as described in David Easton's text, but it will also refer to rammed earth as *earthwall construction*.)

Understanding the Material

Structural analysis begins with a thorough understanding of the material, its constituent parts, and how it behaves (or interacts with other materials) under load. Physical and chemical properties have already been discussed in the main text of this book. What, then, are the structural properties of rammed earth?

Fully cured rammed earth, like concrete, is macroscopically homogeneous and microscopically inhomogeneous—an irregular blend of aggregate, sand, and admixtures, contained and attached in a matrix of binder, be it clay, cement, fly ash, asphalt emulsion, or some combination. As such, its strength will vary, and cylinder compression tests of the same batch of material yield results that can differ (as with concrete) by 30 percent or more. Experience to date suggests that rammed earth cures more slowly than concrete; the typical twenty-eight-day strength test may not be representative, or less so than with concrete.

As a material, rammed earth is also similar to adobe. In physical composition it may be identical, but structurally it will always prove stronger because: 1) there are no mortar joints, and 2) the material is compacted in place. The finish material is nevertheless similar to masonry in that there are a series of semicold joints between lifts, and within each lift the density varies from highly compacted at the top (directly under the ramming head) to increasingly less densely packed below the top of the lift. (Both of these aspects will generally have little effect on the large-scale wall strength, unless lifts are thicker than 5 or 6 inches.)

Strength will vary widely with the quality of the mix design. Some earth mixes can attain compressive strengths greater than 800 psi without added binder, while others can barely manage 300 psi with two sacks of cement per cubic yard added (often because of too high a proportion of silt fines "soaking up" the available binder). Generally, increasing the amount of binder will increase strength. However, the limited amount of water in the optimal mix (generally 10 to 13 percent) can only hydrate (activate) a certain amount of Portland cement; further added cement becomes simply more fines, which can actually decrease material strength. Further variables, only slightly less important, include: the strength of the parent material for the earth and sand; the on-site control of mixing and wetting; and the degree of care that is taken in placing and compacting the material inside the forms.

The stabilizing addition of Portland cement to a sand/earth/water blend makes what is called *soil cement* in the parlance of the construction industry. Soil cement has been used extensively to date for paving, pond liners, and slope stabilization, and as such has been extensively studied as an engineering material. Much has been learned about the interaction and blending of the various soil types with cement, but that research has focused on slab-on-grade construction, not load-bearing walls. Where structural properties are a concern, the design of a mix to create a desired compressive strength (and, by inference, other types of strength) should be based on actual tests; theoretical prediction is not yet adequately reliable. The earthwall designer must generate a tentative design using accepted soil-classification and investigative methods, then cure and test sample mixes for confirmation of desired properties. Also, site inspections are perhaps more important with rammed earth construction than with any other material. Quality control of on-site mixing, wetting, and compacting is essential to achieve design structural strength.

Design

In seismically active areas, earthquakes are usually the dominant consideration in earthwall analysis. Therefore, this discussion will start with design in non-seismic areas, and then expand to consider earthquake forces.

As a general rule, wall dimensions should be constrained by height-to-thickness ratios such as those published in the Uniform Code for Building Conservation (UCBC) for masonry walls:

1994 Uniform Building Code for Building Conservation Table.

Allowable value of height-to-thickness ratio of unreinforced masonry walls

Wall Types	Seismic Zone 2B Buildings	Seismic Zone 3 Buildings	Seismic Zone 4 Buildings with Crosswalls	Seismic Zone 4 All Other Buildings
Walls of one-story buildings	20	16	16	13
First-story wall of multistory building	20	18	16	15
Walls in top story of multistory building	14	14	14	9
All other walls	20	16	16	13

These values will usually provide ample latitude to the designer. Earthwalls are by their nature massive: wall widths are often governed by the design of formwork and the ability of workers to place and compact the mix. Although a 9-foot-high wall could theoretically be as narrow as 8 or 9 inches, a 12-inch width may be the practical minimum to allow access to the bottom of the form, even with an extended pneumatic tamper. Furthermore, if there are to be any rebar, conduit, plumbing, or other inserts in the formwork, the minimum width needs to be even greater, both for access and to insure a thick enough material cover for embedments to avoid cracking. Wall widths of 16, 18, and 24 inches are common, and wider or battered walls are also possible.

With such massive walls, the design is governed by gravity loads: dead loads (predominantly the wall itself—generally about 120 pounds per cubic foot—and the permanent weight of supported roofs and floors), and live loads (varying loads, as defined in the building codes, of workers, construction materials, occupants, furniture, etc.).

Foundations

The foundation design must provide support for the gravity loads, a stable base for the walls, and a moisture or capillary break between the ground and the earthwalls. It must also be stiff, as the earthwalls can be sensitive to uneven settling, which could cause cracking. Many historic earthwall buildings have been founded directly on the ground, or on gravel-filled trenches, and have lasted for decades or even centuries. Still, modern building codes, as well as common sense, generally dictate a stout, reinforced concrete foundation, reinforced to span soft spots in the ground and tied to the earth construction with vertical rebar dowels. As in all construction, good foundation design depends chiefly on understanding the supporting ground pad, local climate, and appropriate foundation systems.

Gravity loads

The weight of the roof, and sometimes the floors, must be born at the top of the earthwall. Standard practice is to provide some sort of *bond* (or *cap* or *tie*) *beam* along the top of the wall. The bond beam serves both to evenly distribute the weight of the supported structure, and to tie together the tops of walls in a manner analogous to the strapping around packing crates. The bond beam can be wood: various lapped, nailed, screwed, or strapped combinations of lumber, plywood, and/or steel plates. A more effective bond beam, however, is made of reinforced concrete by laying rebar along the top of the last lift, and pouring concrete into the tops of the forms. To keep finish wall colors similar, the bond beam might be made of the same mix as the wall, with more cement and water for strength and pourability. At a minimum, the bond beam should be at least 6 inches thick, and have a sill plate to receive roof and/or floor structures.

Door and window openings can often be spanned by the earthwall itself without the need of lintels, but the opening formwork must be stout enough to take the load of ramming. Even so, it is generally wise to provide a wood, steel, or concrete lintel designed for the weight above, or at least lay horizontal reinforcing into the lift above the opening.

Lateral Loads

Wind and earthquake loads (by which we mean, roughly, the wind forces produced by a 100-year storm or the seismic forces generated by an 8.0 Richter magnitude earthquake in the nearest credible location) fall into the general category of *lateral loads* on structures. Common sense, as well as experience, tells us that even very high winds are rarely a problem to a massive earthwall structure of one or two stories. (For higher buildings, such as the multistory structures being built in Western Australia, wind design becomes a factor but is beyond the scope of this discussion.) By contrast, even in seismically active areas such as coastal California, wind loads on relatively light, small, wood-framed structures will often be higher than the forces generated by earthquakes.

Earthquake Loads

Earthquake forces are of particular concern to the earthwall designer for two reasons. First, they are dynamic: that is, they reverse, repeat, and come from any and all directions, including up and down. Then, after ceasing, these forces often occur again a few minutes or hours or days later (when they are known as aftershocks). Second, the size of the force is in direct proportion to the mass, or dead load, of the building. Ride a bus on a busy, potholed urban street for a few blocks, and you have a pretty good slow-motion earthquake simulation. Thus, the same stout, massive walls that make rammed earth buildings relatively impervious to wind make them more susceptible to earthquake damage.

In designing earthwalls, as with any structural walls, consideration must be given to in-plane forces and out-of-plane forces. *In-plane* means parallel to the face of the wall—loads that tend to rack the wall from side to side (see Figures 1 and 2). *Out-of-plane* means perpendicular to the face of the wall—loads that tend to bow the wall inward or outward (see Figure 3). During an earthquake or windstorm, both types of forces will be acting simultaneously in some combination. But it is common practice to analyze each separately, and then review the entire, three-dimensional structure for locations of stress concentration, connections, and coherence.

In-plane forces

Initially, in-plane shearing loads are rarely excessive for earthwalls. What are often called shear cracks are in fact tension cracks (see Figure 1), which develop when the wall racks and points 2 and 3 move farther apart, creating a line of tension. Rammed earth, like concrete and masonry, is relatively weak in tension, and will readily crack. If the direction of the loads reverse, as in an earthquake, matching diagonal cracks will open in the opposite direction (Figure 1). In this case, the fractured wall has lost some or all ability to resist tension or shear; any subsequent shearing loads now *are* excessive, and can cause complete failure or collapse.

By extension, portions of a wall with openings, called *piers*, will behave in the same way, and are likewise susceptible to tension cracking and failure. Openings in a wall will also create stress (tension) concentrations as the wall tries to change shape under lateral loading (see Figure 2). Thus, the size and location of openings (or, more exactly, piers) in a wall are crucial to its structural stability.

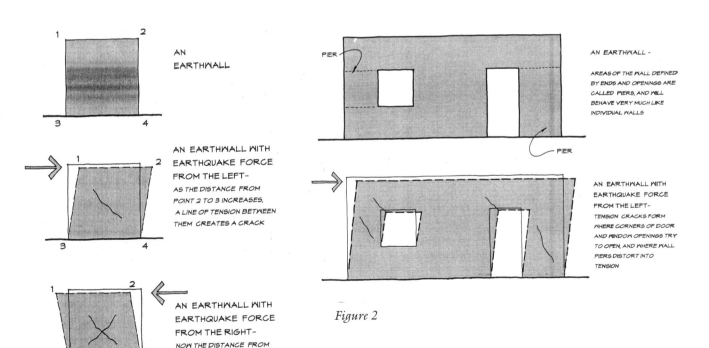

AN EARTHWALL

AN EARTHWALL WITH EARTHQUAKE FORCE FROM THE LEFT–
AS THE DISTANCE FROM POINT 2 TO 3 INCREASES, A LINE OF TENSION BETWEEN THEM CREATES A CRACK

AN EARTHWALL WITH EARTHQUAKE FORCE FROM THE RIGHT–
NOW THE DISTANCE FROM POINT 1 TO 4 INCREASES, CREATING ANOTHER TENSION CRACK

Figure 1

PIER

AN EARTHWALL –
AREAS OF THE WALL DEFINED BY ENDS AND OPENINGS ARE CALLED PIERS, AND WILL BEHAVE VERY MUCH LIKE INDIVIDUAL WALLS

PIER

AN EARTHWALL WITH EARTHQUAKE FORCE FROM THE LEFT–
TENSION CRACKS FORM WHERE CORNERS OF DOOR AND WINDOW OPENINGS TRY TO OPEN, AND WHERE WALL PIERS DISTORT INTO TENSION

Figure 2

In designing an earthwall for in-plane forces, the following factors are important for avoiding cracking, and can be adjusted in relation to each other:

1. The strength of the cured rammed earth material.
2. The thickness of the wall: the seismic stresses decrease with increasing thickness. As an example, put graphically, an 8-foot-high wall only 6 inches thick might be suspect, but the same wall built 10 feet thick would cause no concern.
3. The size, number, and proportions of wall openings. Here, rules of thumb can be borrowed from unreinforced masonry construction:
   a. limit the total length of openings along the wall to one-third of the total wall length (or more, if the wall is reinforced);
   b. provide horizontal reinforcing, or lintels, over openings, that extend at least 24 inches past the sides of the openings;
   c. limit the proportions of piers; they should not be made too tall and narrow. In particular, the corner piers at the ends of the wall should have a height (h) no more than four times their width (t) (h/t < 4), and should be at least 4 feet wide.
4. The presence (or lack) of steel reinforcing. As with poured concrete, a grid of horizontal and vertical bars can be placed by wiring vertical bars to matching dowels from the foundation, and laying horizontal bars between lifts. By keeping the bar spacing tight, usually no more than 12 or 16 inches each way, there will always be several bars spanning across any potential tension crack in the wall.

Design of this steel reinforcing must be conservative, for here the similarity between rammed earth and poured concrete construction is uncertain. Of particular concern is the *bond strength*—the amount of "grab" between the surface of the reinforcing bar and the surrounding rammed earth. Without firm bond, the rebar is not an integral part of the earthwall, and cannot fully provide the intended reinforcing, particularly across a tension crack.

A recent laboratory pullout test of a horizontal rebar in a rammed earth wall gave a bond strength of 380 psi, which is higher than a working stress analysis or code might predict or allow. This may not be so surprising, as the process of ramming will mechanically pack material against and around the bar. However, the vertical bars have less of this advantage, and may in fact have diminished bond strength because of being inadvertently jostled during the ramming process of each lift. Finally, the aesthetic nature of earthwalls is such that the desired look is, often, one of sloping, irregular, and/or curving strata (lifts), not even, horizontal bands. In such a case, the layout, placement, and bond of horizontal bars requires special scrutiny.

Out-of-Plane Forces

How an earthwall will respond (bend) under load against its face will somewhat depend on how it is secured at the foundation and roof (or floors; see Figure 3). If the wall is restrained at the top, it can be considered to be *pinned* (free to rotate) top and bottom. Design of the top restraint for an earthwall in a seismically active area is both important and, assuming a wood-framed restraining floor or roof, somewhat difficult. The connection plates, bolts, and straps must be carefully designed, and the floor/roof itself designed to be able to act as a stiff diaphragm capable of transmitting the reaction (which can be on the order of 800 pounds per foot) to the supporting crosswalls. Though feasible, this approach may add unnecessary cost to the job, and undesirable structure to the ceiling.

An alternative, then, is to consider that the wall is *fixed* at the foundation and *free* at the top. (Even though the attached structure will always provide some restraint, that restraint can then be considered redundant, or backup, strength.) In this system, the footing is made wide enough to provide the wall stability against overturning. The supported roof or floor is then considered to "float" on the walls, which will be self-supporting in an earthquake.

Figure 3

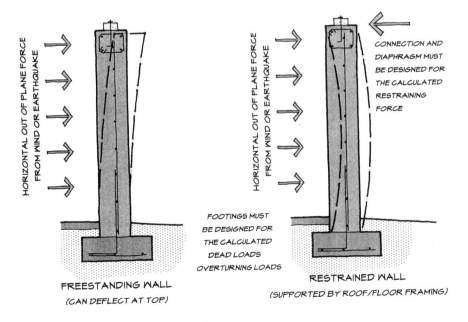

HORIZONTAL OUT OF PLANE FORCE FROM WIND OR EARTHQUAKE

CONNECTION AND DIAPHRAGM MUST BE DESIGNED FOR THE CALCULATED RESTRAINING FORCE

HORIZONTAL OUT OF PLANE FORCE FROM WIND OR EARTHQUAKE

FOOTINGS MUST BE DESIGNED FOR THE CALCULATED DEAD LOADS OVERTURNING LOADS

FREESTANDING WALL
(CAN DEFLECT AT TOP)

RESTRAINED WALL
(SUPPORTED BY ROOF/FLOOR FRAMING)

In either case, the absence or presence of crosswalls also comes into play. If corner and crosswalls are of the same construction (or something else of comparable strength and stiffness; wood studwalls cannot be used), and are properly tied to the supported wall, then they comprise vertical lines of support which should be considered in the design.

Analysis

To date, engineers in California have been adapting the Working Stress method of design for masonry walls as defined in the Uniform Building Code. Allowable stresses in the earthwall are defined as a function of the material compressive strength f'_c (in masonry f'_m) as follows:

allowable shear stress in wall	$F_v = 1.0 \sqrt{f'_c}$
allowable flexural compressive stress in wall	$F_b = 0.33 f'_c$
allowable bearing stress in wall	$F_{br} = 0.26 f'_c$
Modulus of Elasticity	$E = 750 f'_c$
allowable tensile stress in deformed bars	$F_s = 0.5 f_y$
allowable bond stress in deformed bars	$u = 100$ psi

Because, as with concrete, most calculations will key off of f'_c, it is essential to establish as clearly as possible the real compressive strength. Again, given the wide variety of soil types, theoretical prediction is difficult. Where strength considerations are really important, as in seismically active areas, the designer should generate trial mixes specific to the job, to be sampled, cured, and tested before final analysis. Test specimens can be rammed into standard 4-inch concrete-testing cylinders, or taken as cores from a small section of test wall (ramming a section of test wall also affords an opportunity to test construction methods, train workers, and provide color samples to the owner). Having established the strength of the mix, most designers will then use one-half of the established f'_c (akin to assuming uninspected masonry) to generate other working stresses. If there will be little site control, or if there has been no testing program, substantially lower values should be assumed, such as $\frac{1}{4} f'_c$ or $\frac{1}{8} f'_c$, depending on the occupancy importance (potential hazard) and the designer's judgment. Under lateral loads of wind and earthquake, a 33 percent allowable stress increase can be used.

Following are three sample calculations for the same wall in three different conditions. Though presented as simply as possible, some of this will inevitably be comprehensible only to structural engineers, and is intended for their reference in generating their own earthwall analyses.

Examples

Design a 16-inch-thick wall, 9 feet high from foundation to plate. Tests have shown f'_c to be at least 800 psi. Total imposed loads from the supported roof are 300 pounds per linear foot applied at the wall centerline.

Case 1: Seismic Zone 1 (essentially a non–earthquake-prone area)

check h/t ratio: 9x12 / 16 = 6.75 < 20 allowed   *OK*

compressive stress at top of footing:

f_{br} = (roof weight of 300 pounds divided by the wall width of 1.33') + (weight of a 1' x 1' x 9' column of earthwall @ 120 pounds per cubic foot) divided by 144 (square inches in one square foot)

= (300 / 1.33 + (9x120 pcf)) / 144 = 9 psi

allowable compressive stress = ½ (800) = 400 psi   *OK*

If wall openings are constrained as described, and have lintels, the wall is okay, with no reinforcing, by empirical analysis.

Case 2: Seismic Zone 4 (earthquake-prone area., wall freestanding

h/t ratio = 6.75 < 13 allowed   *OK*

Horizontal earthquake load F_p = ⅔ ZIC_pW_p

⅔ modifier for wall freestanding at base is allowed by UBC

Z = 0.4 = the coefficient assigned depending on the seismic risk area (0.4 is highest, as for coastal California)

I = 1.0 = the coefficient assigned depending on the occupancy importance; it is higher for hospitals, schools, fire stations, etc.

C_p = 0.75 = a structure coefficient reflecting the type of load-resisting system (in this case, a massive, rigid "concrete" shearwall system)

W_p = the structure dead load = 1' x 1.33' x 120 pcf = 160 pounds per foot (for simplicity's sake, we will neglect in this example the dead load of the roof, which would be an additional horizontal force at the top of the wall)

Horizontal earthquake load F_p = ⅔ ZIC_pW_p = 0.2W_p = *32 lbs/vertical foot*

Design moment M = 32 lbs/ft x 9' x 9' / 2 = 1,296 ft-lbs = 15,552 in-lbs.

(A "moment," in engineering parlance, is the arithmetic product of a force acting at a distance. Hold a brick out at arm's length. The weight of the brick times the length of your arm is the moment at your shoulder. In the example, we are measuring the moment at the base of the wall.)

Design shear V = 32 lbs/ft x 9' = 288 lbs.

try #4 grade 40 bars @ 12" oc each way in wall centerline (A_s = 0.20)

design f'$_c$ = 800/2 = 400 psi n = modular ratio = 29000000/(750x800) = 48
d = depth of reinforcing from compression face = ½ wall t = 8"
p = ratio of reinforcing steel area to compression area = 0.20/(12x8) = .0021
np = .101   k = .3597   j = .8801   (k and j are values derived from np)
compressive bending stress = 2M / kjbdd = 101 psi
Allowable bending stress F$_b$ = 0.33 f'$_m$ = 0.33(400) x 1.33 = 176 psi   *OK*
shear stress = V / bjd = 4 psi
Allowable shear stress F$_v$ = 1.0 √f'm x 1.33 = 1.0(√400) x 1.33 = 27 psi   *OK*
tensile bending stress in reinforcing = M / A$_s$jd = 12,135 psi
Allowable tensile stress F$_s$ = 0.5 fy = 0.5(40,000) = 20,000 psi   *OK*

Case 3: Seismic Zone 4 (earthquake-prone area), wall restrained at top
Horizontal earthquake load F$_p$ = 32 lbs/vertical foot
Design moment M = 32 x 9 x 9 / 8 = 324 ft-lbs = 3,888 in-lbs.
Design shear V = 32 x 9 / 2 = 144 lbs. = min. reaction to be carried by roof
try #4 grade 40 bars @ 16" oc each way in wall centerline (A$_s$ = 0.20 / 1.33 = .15)

design f'$_c$ = 400 psi   n = 48   d = 8"
p = 0.15/(12x8) = .0016   np = .075   k = .3194   j = .8935
compressive bending stress = 2M / kjbdd = 35 psi < 176 psi allowable *OK*
shear stress = V / bjd = 2 psi < 27 psi allowable   *OK*
tensile bending stress in reinforcing = M / A$_s$jd = 3,626 psi < 20,000 psi   *OK*
Design wall connection at top for 144 pounds per foot—*use code minimum of 200 pounds per foot for masonry wall anchorage in Zone 4.*

Conclusion

The abundance of historic and modern earthwall structures around the world gives us some empirical basis for the design of new buildings. Though not yet specifically defined or acknowledged in the major building codes, rammed earth construction can now be described, specified, and also analyzed in a rational way as allowed in the alternative materials provisions of the major codes (section 105 of the Uniform Building Code). Where large seismic forces are probable, the analysis must be cautious, and strength assumptions must be based on a verifiable testing program, but earthwalls can certainly be designed to meet code requirements for life safety. As is the case with every other building material, we in the building and engineering community will continue refining our understanding as more and more rammed earth projects are completed, and more testing is done. Hopefully, the day will soon come when the modern building codes will recognize earthwall construction, and provide chapters to define and guide safe practice.

Bibliography

Alexander, Christopher, et al. *A Pattern Language: Towns, Buildings, Construction*. New York: Oxford University Press, 1977.

Berglund, Magnus. *Stone, Log and Earth Houses*. Newtown, CT: Taunton Press, 1986.

Bourgeois, Jean-Louis. *Spectacular Vernacular*. New York: Aperture, 1983.

Bunting, Bainbridge. *Of the Earth and Timbers Made*. Albuquerque: University of New Mexico Press, 1974.

Commoner, Barry. *Making Peace with the Planet*. New York: Pantheon, 1990.

Dethier, Jean. *Down to Earth*. New York: Facts on File, 1983.

Easton, David. *The Rammed Earth Experience*. Wilseyville, CA: Blue Mountain Press, 1982.

Fathy, Hassan. *Architecture for the Poor*. Chicago: University of Chicago Press, 1973.

Gore, Al. *Earth in the Balance*. Boston: Houghton Mifflin, 1992.

Hawken, Paul. *The Ecology of Commerce*. Boston: Houghton Mifflin, 1993.

Hoffman, Eric. *Renegade Houses*. Philadelphia: Running Press, 1982.

Houben, Hugo, and Hubert Guilland. *Earth Construction: A Comprehensive Guide*. Villefontaine Cedex, France: Intermediate Technology, 1994.

Howard, Ted. *Mud and Man: A History of Earth Building in Australia*. Melbourne, Australia: Earthbuild Publishers (In Tin Press), 1992.

Iowa, Jerome. *Ageless Adobe: History and Preservation in Southwestern Architecture*. Santa Fe: Sunstone Press, 1985.

Marinelli, Janet. *The Naturally Elegant Home*. Boston: Little, Brown, 1992.

Mazria, Edward. *The Passive Solar Energy Book*. Emmaus, PA: Rodale Press, 1979.

McClintock, Mike. *Alternative House Building*. New York: Popular Science, 1984.

McHenry, Paul Graham, Jr. *Adobe and Rammed Earth Buildings: Design and Construction*. New York: John Wiley and Sons, 1984.

Meadows, Donella, Dennis L. Meadows, and Jørgen Randers. *Beyond the Limits*. Post Mills, VT: Chelsea Green Publishing, 1992.

Merrill, Anthony. *The Rammed Earth House*. New York: Harper & Bros., 1947.

Metz, Don (ed.). *New Compact House Designs*. Pownal, VT: Storey Publishing, 1991.

Middleton, G. F. *Build Your House of Earth*. Revised edition. Melbourne, Vict.: Compendium; Katoomba, NSW, Australia: Second Row Back Press, 1979.

Pearson, David. *The Natural House Book*. New York: Simon and Schuster, 1989.

Rossbach, Sarah. *Feng Shui: The Chinese Art of Placement*. New York: E.P. Dutton, 1982.

————. *Interior Design with Feng Shui*. New York: Penguin, 1987.

Vale, Robert, and Brenda Vale. *Green Architecture*. Boston: Little, Brown, 1991.

Venolia, Carol. *Healing Environments*. Berkeley, CA: Celestial Arts, 1988.

Wright, David. *Natural Solar Architecture*. New York: Van Nostrand Reinhold, 1978.

Index

CHELSEA GREEN

Sustainable living has many facets. Chelsea Green's celebration of the sustainable arts has led us to publish trend-setting books about organic gardening, solar electricity and renewable energy, innovative building techniques, regenerative forestry, local and bioregional democracy, and whole foods. The company's published works, while intensely practical, are also entertaining and inspirational, demonstrating that an ecological approach to life is consistent with producing beautiful, eloquent, and useful books, videos, and audio cassettes.

For more information about Chelsea Green, or to request a free catalog, call toll-free (800) 639–4099, or write to us at P.O. Box 428, White River Junction, Vermont 05001.

Chelsea Green's titles include:

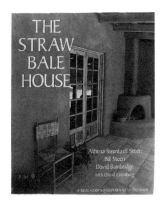  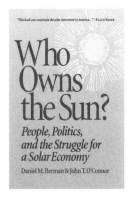

The Straw Bale House
The Independent Home:
  Living Well with Power from
  the Sun, Wind, and Water
Independent Builder:
  Designing & Building a
  House Your Own Way
The Rammed Earth House
The Passive Solar House
The Sauna
Wind Power for Home &
  Business
The Solar Living Sourcebook
A Shelter Sketchbook
Mortgage-Free!
Hammer. Nail. Wood.

The Flower Farmer
Passport to Gardening:
  A Sourcebook for the
  21st-Century Gardener
The New Organic Grower
Four-Season Harvest
Solar Gardening
The Contrary Farmer
The Contrary Farmer's Invitation
  to Gardening
Forest Gardening
Whole Foods Companion

Who Owns the Sun?
Gaviotas: A Village to Reinvent
  the World
Global Spin: The Corporate
  Assault on Environmentalism
Hemp Horizons
A Patch of Eden
A Place in the Sun
Renewables are Ready
Beyond the Limits
Loving and Leaving the Good Life
The Man Who Planted Trees
The Northern Forest